**Kate Figes** is the author of five works of non-fiction and two novels. She is a family mediator, a journalist and Books Editor of *You* magazine. She lives in London and is married with two daughters.

Visit Kate's website at www.katefiges.co.uk or her blog at http://spotsandcellulite.wordpress.com

*By Kate Figes*

NON-FICTION

Because of Her Sex: The Myth of Equality
for Women in Britain

Life After Birth

The Terrible Teens

The Big Fat Bitch Book

Couples

Our Cheating Hearts

FICTION

*Available as ebooks from www.katefiges.co.uk*

What About Me?

What About Me Too?

# Our Cheating Hearts

## Love and Loyalty, Lust and Lies

### KATE FIGES

virago

VIRAGO

First published in Great Britain in 2013 by Virago Press
This paperback edition published in 2014 by Virago Press

A CIP catalogue record for this book
is available from the British Library.

ISBN 978-1-84408-729-7

Typeset in Plantin by M Rules
Printed and bound in Great Britain by
Clays Ltd, St Ives plc

Papers used by Virago are from well-managed forests
and other responsible sources.

For
Fridge Bag

# ACKNOWLEDGEMENTS

I am deeply grateful to a number of dear people for enlightening conversations, helpful guidance and reading drafts. Huge thanks in particular go to Susanna Abse, Evelyn Cooney, Jean Duncombe, Liza Glenn, Brett Kahr, Julie Powell, Jenny Riddell and David Williams. I also wish to thank a number of experts for taking the time to talk to me anonymously, especially three top divorce lawyers and 'Verity' the infidelity detective. I could not have written this book without their help.

I spent many hours in the company of forty courageous, honest men and women, whose testimonies form the backbone of this book. Infidelity is still such a tortured, taboo subject that I felt hugely privileged to have been trusted with their stories. Thank you all. Every effort has been made to disguise the true identity of those I have interviewed. Sometimes people recognise themselves; that doesn't mean that others will too. You have all made a valuable contribution to a book which I hope will provide a more sophisticated understanding of the complex nature of affairs.

Huge thanks go to everyone at Virago – especially the wonderful Lennie Goodings, Zoe Gullen, Judith Greenberg and Andy Hine. My agent Felicity Rubinstein is a constant source of support. Thank you Christoph for being my rock, my best friend and such a loving husband. And of course Eleanor and Grace – I hope you know how much I adore and admire you both.

# CONTENTS

# 1

# IS MONOGAMY POSSIBLE?

M ost of us manage, most of the time, to be monogamous.

Monogamy is synonymous with commitment in modern
relationships. We no longer need to marry to enjoy sexual
pleasure, to have children or increasingly for economic security, so it is fidelity in sexual love which now above all stands
as the primary symbol of commitment to that love. The statistics, however, as well as anecdotal evidence from couples
counsellors and divorce lawyers, indicate that absolute fidelity
is rarer than we care to think. The reality is far from the symbolic ideal.

Accurate figures are hard to come by but a range of surveys
in the UK and the US suggest that between 25 and 70 per cent
of women and 40 and 80 per cent of men have engaged in at
least one extramarital sexual activity.[1] Most estimates of cuck-
oldry rates – where children are fathered by men other than the
mother's partner – range from 10 to 15 per cent.[2] A quarter of
all couples present for therapy because of an affair. In a further

30 per cent an affair will be disclosed during counselling. The therapists I have spoken to estimate that approximately three quarters of men and one quarter of the women they see individually in their consulting rooms are living through marital difficulties because of an affair. Divorce lawyers say that infidelity is still one of the leading causes of separation, and often the result is the most acrimonious of partings.

The statistics do not tell us how many instances of infidelity were the briefest of flirtations, never discovered or destabilising. People often play with the idea of sexual adventure but reject it once the most casual encounter becomes a reality. We don't know how many sexless marriages are happy and sustained by a weekly discreet encounter. We don't know how many couples survive an affair without telling anyone what they have been through. And we don't know how many divorces are triggered by the betrayal of an affair or how many of these relationships died long before the affair began. There is still so much that we don't know about extramarital dabbling – and when I use the words 'marital' or 'marriage' I am referring to all committed relationships, gay or straight, married, cohabiting or living apart.

Infidelity appears to be so common that it is likely to happen at some point in a long relationship. Yet when it comes to understanding why people stray sexually, and how to limit the likelihood or recover from it, we are still living in the dark ages of ignorance, blame and shame. We just hope, even assume, that it won't happen to us. The modern ethos is that any infidelity is always wrong, that it ruins the special sanctity of trust within coupledom and consequently can rarely be recovered from, when in fact, for many, affairs are like epiphanies. The adventure of a love affair enables them to understand more about intimacy, their own unrealistic expectations of relationship and what they really might want from life, either with this new person or within their existing, revived relationship. However painful it may be, infidelity can help couples to accept that it is foolish to think of a relationship in terms of ownership or to take each other for granted. An affair can be devastating emotionally, not just for the spouse who has discovered that he or she has been betrayed but also for the tortured soul who is doing the straying. It can feel like a grenade lobbed into the heart of a couple's life precisely because it is such a seismic event that it has to provoke change. Many then go on to form far stronger partnerships because of what they have learned about themselves and each other, alert to the fact that they could lose each other for ever.

There are perhaps as many different reasons for affairs as there are people, for as Anthony Burgess once said, 'Adultery is the most creative of sins.' While every affair and relationship is unique there do seem to be common triggers. Affairs are often provoked by boredom, loneliness, depression, marital unhappiness and the need to spice up the ordered predictability of life with the exhilarating edge of danger. Infidelity can be motivated by childhood insecurity, anger, hate or revenge for some other marital crime. An affair can be a powerful weapon of abuse or an effective means of injecting distance into a relationship when we feel trapped, failed or unable to meet each other's every need. We can find it so hard dealing with one person that we decide to complicate things still further by getting involved with two.

Circumstance can play a part, as does too much to drink. Sometimes we are merely flattered by the fact that anybody outside our relationship might want us at all, particularly at key transitional moments: after the birth of a baby, when children leave home, a partner gets seriously ill or a parent dies. 'Any

close relationship or marriage is such an entangled web that the
timing of an affair can tell you a great deal,' says couples counsellor Liza Glenn. 'Is it when she has got pregnant or in the
months after the baby is born? Has she withdrawn from him or
has he failed to reclaim her as a woman because he has in fact
married his mother. Many men do!'

Affairs sit on a wide spectrum ranging from the casual one-
night stand which is never discovered or threatens the stability
of a committed partnership to a prolonged means of ending a
relationship by finding a way out. Affairs are often about the
drama of transgression, for every emotion, including guilt,
unhappiness and fear of the devastation of loss, is pushed to
the point where we feel truly alive. Affairs can give people a
sense of achievement, omnipotence even, for they have to dare
to do things they might never have done before. Extramarital
liaisons can take place in thrilling places: hotels, snatched
moments, weekends away, 'car seats, rugs, tree undersides seen
through windshields', as John Updike writes in *Rabbit Redux*,
'the beige-grey carpeting in the narrow space between the three
green steel desks and the safe'.

There is the emotional roller-coaster of seduction and conquest, the scary ride full of secrets and sleuth-like deceptions
to cover give-away signs. In the triumph of securing the attention of a third party many believe, usually foolishly, that with
this new sense of potency they will be able to maintain the
duplicity of a double life. The most passionate love requires
people to overcome huge obstacles. 'It's the buzz of the
pulling,' says Oliver, an unhappily married man who has been
having an affair with a married woman for the past six months.
'She is cheating too and she says that if we were together she
wouldn't cheat on me but I don't believe her for a minute
because I loved all that too as a young man. I wasn't even

bothered about the sex at the end of the evening. It was all about the cloak and dagger, the secrecy of intimacy, the chase.'

Affairs can offer the illusion of improving a relationship by taking the pressure off it, for less is expected of a partner when some of your needs are being met elsewhere. Affairs offer many people the opportunity to enjoy a very different sort of sex outside the familiarity of home, whether that is paying to be spanked or exploring homosexual or heterosexual tendencies. Affairs offer the ultimate halcyon, drug-like escape from the realities of daily life. 'Sex, wine, food, sleep. I am a physical being,' writes Dani Shapiro in her account of being a mistress, 'living on the other side of a clear, thin membrane that separates me from anything to do with the world.'[3]

In this carefree world people can engage with fantasy by having affairs with the sort of person they would like to be – younger, more successful, beautiful, richer, freer. In this magical land people foolishly believe that no one has noticed what they are up to and that they enjoy a special protection from pregnancy and sexually transmitted diseases, for sex is often sudden and without contraception. Infidelity allows people to live in a romance where all of one's dreams can come true for a few hours. 'She was entering something marvellous where everything would be passion, ecstasy, delirium,' writes Flaubert of his famous adulterer Emma Bovary. 'The great summits of sentiment glittered in her mind's eye, ordinary existence appeared far below in the distance, in shadow, in the gaps between these peaks.'

People often turn to a lover outside their relationship for a sense of validation, to be told they are beautiful, desirable, the best fuck on God's earth. We turn to others for all that maternal soothing and stroking without questions or judgement when we feel we lack such support from our partner, or daren't ask for it. The craving for a perfect love, the romantic notion that one can lose oneself in an ecstatic passionate union with another human being, is understandable. We all long at particularly difficult moments in life or in our relationship to be able to dive into a parallel world where someone might be strong enough to take all of us, where we do not need to explain ourselves or compromise, where we feel cosseted and scooped up into the arms of an adoring and unconditional love. Affairs allow people to wallow in the safety of play with a wide range of possible reinventions: 'Mother, father, sibling, angel or devil – with very little risk because, unlike marriage, adultery does not, at the outset, include permanence. Truth need never be revealed; the inadequacies of the reality of the self need never be demonstrated to the other,' writes Annette Lawson in her major study *Adultery*, published in 1988. 'So long as the adultery is brief, the fantasy can endure. In this sense adultery is far from dangerous; it is safe. Partners can switch gender roles, play with sex and fantasy, satisfy particular desires, *be* all the things for which marriage has no room.'

No wonder then that affairs are so common. Is there anybody who has picked up this book who has not felt some or all of the above at some point in their established relationship? How close do we all come to sexual and emotional betrayal at difficult times or in moments of weakness and immaturity? We live in an 'I want therefore I can have' culture where we are greedier, fatter and consume more than ever before. We seem to need dozens of handbags and shoes, even several houses, to feel whole or be seen to be living the good life. 'Good' sex is increasingly regarded as a commodity too. When you consider the amount of new sexual pressures on marital commitment, for regular, satisfying sex is now a sign of a healthy relationship (and its absence a sign of one on the rocks), as well as the ease of access to a variety of sexual temptations from pornography to chatroom flirtations, it's a miracle that anybody remains entirely faithful to their partner at all. 'Adultery is both ordinary and forgivable,' writes Siri Hustvedt in her novel *The Summer Without Men*, 'as is the rage of the betrayed spouse.'

So what does being unfaithful mean within the new relationship ethos of total togetherness? Do thought crimes count? Does a text flirtation or an affair in 'third life' matter? And what about that regular lunch date with an ex-lover or a friend from work whom we would never want to sleep with but actually quite like? Is that an emotional betrayal and just as bad if we do not confess to it? Does paying for it count? Many men don't seem to think so. And what about masturbating or looking at pornography alone? What does infidelity mean within the new soul mate philosophy of being each other's everything – sexually compatible lover, intellectual equal, co-parent and best friend?

The couple relationship has for centuries sat uncomfortably at the apex between private and public life, yet subject to controls by religion and state. The contract of 'marriage' in its widest definition forms the foundation of society, both for the raising of children and social care for each other. Infidelity or adultery therefore threatens more than just a marriage: it destabilises the roots of a contract between two people where trust and loyalty matter, and undermines the whole institution of society. Newspapers, magazines and websites disclose the private sexual misdemeanours of sexually straying politicians and celebrities as if they were betraying not just their partner but everyone else as well. Television shows such as those of Jerry Springer and Jeremy Kyle put adulterers on trial in front of an audience that mocks and cheers, echoing the punishment of shame meted out to adulterers in the Middle Ages. The subtle complexities and everyday difficulties of relationship are rarely acknowledged. The whole focus is on the idea that if you could lie or cheat on your partner, you cannot be trusted with anything, even though there is no evidence to suggest that those who engage in extramarital sexual activity are any more criminal or corrupt than the rest of the population. There is perhaps a sense that if this contract made between two people privately and publicly cannot be upheld, then nothing else, no other bond or contract, can be trusted either. The centre of our social structure as a society cannot hold. And yet – and here is the rub – we also know that unlike with other sins such as murder or theft, adultery is the 'crime' we could all, at difficult times, imagine ourselves committing.

The sanctimony surrounding total fidelity as the most important emblem of commitment in sexual love is now so absolute that many find it hard to talk about their attractions to others and their sexual pasts with complete honesty. But that can also feel like a kind of betrayal because there are supposed to be no secrets within a happy relationship. Total loathing of any form of 'cheating' means that the emotional and psychological complexities of sexual betrayal are never considered or discussed. It is just always wrong. The new ethos is: one strike and you are out. When couples then find themselves living through the reality life gets confusing. Should they leave or kick the other one out? What if they don't want to? Who do they turn to for help? 'Couples often don't know whether they can stay together, whether they want to stay together or whether they should stay together,' says psychoanalyst and couples counsellor Brett Kahr. 'And then they don't know whether taking their partner back is an act of generosity, self-preserving behaviour or sado-masochism.'

Absolute monogamy has become an individual achievement in itself, a near-spiritual act of sacrifice and tolerance of disillusionment as well as a very public display of morality and commitment. When absolute monogamy fails for whatever reason, as it often does, our entire sense of place both within our relationship and in the wider world is threatened. The one who strays is considered weak or flawed. The one who is 'betrayed' feels they were not loved or good enough to keep their partner 'true'. It's threatening practically and financially too, given the likelihood of separation and divorce. So rising numbers maintain the fiction of a monogamous marriage by not asking the other or turning a blind eye. As this book will reveal, there is a very complex dance of deceit and denial by both partners, particularly when sexual betrayal is used as a form of abuse.

Monogamy is an admirable ideal. It is still what most people aspire to in their relationship. We all share a primal urge for an exclusive bond with another person, to feel special. We need consistency and continuity in our most important relationships, not just as children when we are entirely dependent, but throughout life. Sexual novelty and continual ecstasy might be sold to us now as key to our health and happiness, as if we had a right to perpetual sexual arousal and satisfaction, but restraint is good for us too. Being faithful to our spouse means we show care for someone, we value their needs above our own by refusing to hurt them. It means we place others above our own selfish need for vicarious sexual gratification when there are plenty of people out there with whom we could have a very good time. As Winston Churchill once said about democracy, monogamy seems to be the worst possible system until you consider the alternatives.

The essence of trust in a good relationship is feeling safe enough to love, safe enough to reveal our true selves and know that we will not lose love as a result and find ourselves rejected for someone who is seemingly 'better'. Monogamy is possible and many couples manage it either throughout their relationship or for long periods of time. But for the countless others who fall from this paradigm of virtue either briefly or repeatedly, a more honest and humane public debate around the subject of infidelity is essential if we also want as a society to underpin the stability of committed relationships and family life.

The essays in this book are as much about our yearning for fidelity as they are about the numerous myths surrounding the experience of infidelity. The testimony of experts and those who have lived through the ordeal, as well as psychology, history and literature, throw light on the love knots that we tie ourselves into today, when sexual infidelity has emerged as the Great Betrayal of modern relationship, when paradoxically it has never been easier to find opportunities to be seduced. New expectations of perfection and total togetherness in a relationship have increased the allure of affairs. The new ethos of complete, confessional honesty increases the need for deceit and denial over the slightest flirtation and exacerbates the wounds of betrayal, the guilt and the idea that only the person who strays bears the blame. This heady cocktail inevitably destroys many relationships with otherwise good foundations, such as a shared history and interests, genuine love and affection for one another, as well as the all-important welfare of children and their family life.

Many of those who separate because of an affair come to regret that decision later. There were so many other threads that united them as a couple that they wonder, with hindsight, whether they could have worked things out. Instead we seem to need to preserve the mythology and the hope that it is possible to have a perfect and therefore permanently sexually exclusive relationship by trying again – but with someone new.

There is such a disconnection between expectations of absolute fidelity and the messy reality of how we live and love that people cannot help but feel they have failed shamefully when they fall, or are pushed, off the pedestal. Trust cannot last if it is based on an ideal which is assumed but never discussed. The monogamous ideal hangs by a thread, and is held together by social and cultural condemnation of infidelity rather than internally by two people who are grown-up enough to be able to talk about their attractions to others, their problems within the relationship and how they could build a better future together.

Relationships are undergoing radical change as a result of new pressures and demands on couples over gendered expectations, work-life balance and the modern ethos where individual happiness and continual sexual excitement seem to be paramount. We may well have become more accepting of separation than we are of sexual betrayal within marriage. Yet we are all human and we make mistakes. A close, loving relationship ought to be the one place where we can be flawed and still feel loved. In some respects we are like pioneers, in search of a new way of loving. A more truthful understanding of monogamy has to be central to a new dialogue, if we also want to enjoy the many other benefits that a long and lasting loving relationship can provide.

There is no one right way to be together as a couple. We are all learning through trial and error how to forge a lifelong partnership where we might be able to match compromise and togetherness with enough of a sense of autonomy not to feel swallowed whole. Nowadays commitment is being hammered at the very time when we lack a philosophy of love and relationship that has tolerance and forgiveness of each other's frailties at its heart. It is interesting that it is when an adulterous woman is brought before Jesus in the Gospels that he utters the words that have come to symbolise man's inability to be perfect: 'He that is without sin among you, let him first cast a stone.' For the line of restraint that we draw around us with absolute monogamy is a particularly tenuous and difficult one when it comes to our natural attraction to the allure of others. 'The monogamous ideal is just that – an ideal,' writes marital psychotherapist Warren Coleman.[4] 'There is always a gap between ideals and the possibility of their realisation in the world, but ideals are nevertheless necessary to give life meaning and value. They act as beacons pointing out the way, something to strive towards but never to reach. There is loss involved in recognising this, but it is far preferable to the futile and doomed attempt to deny the gap by omnipotent fantasy à la Madame Bovary.'

# 2

# THE ANATOMY OF MODERN LOVE

It is not a coincidence that mutual fidelity has emerged as the most significant marker of love and commitment at a time when it has ironically never been harder to achieve. In the past fifty years we have lived through a seismic revolution in attitudes to relationships. Women have become more empowered through having both the financial means to support themselves and control over their fertility with contraception. Society has become much more open about sexual pleasures and the expectation now is that people stay together for as long as love lasts, not until death parts.

Monogamy is a central tenet of many religions yet religious values no longer keep us in check. We don't need to get married to have children, for economic survival or just to experience the thrill of another naked body beside us. We commit to each other because we want to, because we love, sexually as well as emotionally, and so it is fidelity, absolute sexual fidelity, which now adds the lifeblood to that love, barring access to the sexual playground of the past, and of the future. But what is to hold us to our vows other than will when things move to the humdrum ordinary togetherness of commitment? Aren't we also 'owed' a happy, fulfilled, sexy life?

The affair calls like a siren whenever we feel lonely, unhappy or trapped, and we are likely to feel more trapped than ever before by the intense togetherness inherent in modern relationship, as well as lonelier and unhappier when things go wrong. When our dreams hit reality, the choice seems to be whether to leave in the hope of finding someone else who might fit our needs hand in glove or to stay and be unhappy. Few of us seemingly have the tools to improve what we already have. We concentrate instead on the growing tension between the monogamous romantic ideal and sexual temptation. We feel we have to give up more in the way of individual pleasure once we commit, and that makes the act of commitment harder. And we have to work harder to say no to extramarital seductions once the first passionate paroxysms of ecstasy in a relationship have waned.

Fidelity is trust made flesh, a new spiritual and moral achievement of sacrifice and renunciation. Trust is key, yet harder to achieve. We try to trust each other at a time when entirely new concepts have evolved around what being in a 'good' relationship means. It is love, good communication, honesty, shared interests, mutual investment in the home and family, as well as regular great sex, which are now all considered to be the crucial ingredients of a long and happy marriage. Less important are the more traditional, pre-scribed roles, integrity and promises of 'for better or for worse'. We are rewriting the rules of relationship and that's not easy. 'The perfect couple now must be everything to one another,' writes historian John Gillis in his book *A World of Their Making*, '– good providers, super sexual partners, best friends, stimulating companions – roles that earlier generations turned to others to fulfill.'

Fidelity has emerged as key to a happy marriage and some surveys indicate that many of us now consider this to be more important than tolerance, mutual understanding, good communication and a happy sex life. We have seen huge changes in social attitudes, with increasing acceptance of homosexuality, cohabitation and divorce. Yet when it comes to sexual straying we are more censorious than ever. Several surveys in western Europe have shown that we became less tolerant of extramarital sexual relationships from the mid-1980s onwards.[1] The young appear to be even more moralistic. A YouGov poll in the UK in 2011 found that 91 per cent of those aged between eighteen and twenty-four believe that infidelity is 'mostly or always wrong' and that half of men under forty believed that a couple should separate if a woman has had an affair, whereas in men over forty the figure was 31 per cent. Other research suggests that young people are more faithful to each other while they are together, but that their relationships tend to be shorter.[2] The rise in sexually transmitted diseases and experience of their own parents' dalliances and divorces inevitably play a large part. As does the new romanticism and the idea that there is a higher level where true love and therefore absolute fidelity prevails.

What does being unfaithful mean now that we are supposed to be each other's everything? Infidelity is no longer solely defined as sexual; it can be emotional too. It used to be the humiliation of bringing up a child who wasn't yours that mattered most, hence the heavier penalties for adulteresses, explored in the next chapter. Now there are many other betrayals on top of the preservation of genetic inheritance. 'I see more and more emotional affairs where one of the pair has got closer to someone outside the relationship and the other feels a real sense of betrayal even though nothing physical has happened,' says Evelyn Cooney, relationship counsellor and psychosexual therapist. Men and women mingle more as equals at work and can spend a great deal of time with each other, often more than they do with their partners at home. They have to talk to each other as they work on projects together, and often share similar interests because of their choice of job. Shirley P. Glass, author of *Not 'Just Friends'*, estimates that 46 per cent of women and 62 per cent of men who have had an affair met through work. These friendships slide easily into love affairs and consequently become far more threatening to an established relationship than any quick and purely physical shag.

Perhaps the definition of what it is to be unfaithful has widened because there are so many new potential threats. We've become so fixated on the idea that true love requires a soul mate fit that anything which could divert a spouse's attention, from too much time at the football or in internet chatrooms to an intense friendship with someone outside that relationship, could challenge the notion of togetherness. 'I think I made a mistake in assuming that in a good relationship you should want to do everything together and that this is the sign of a strong couple,' says Sharon, whose fourteen-year marriage ended recently when her husband had an affair. 'Actually it's not healthy because you end up with nothing to talk about. Our lives were so intertwined and that has made the separation very painful and difficult. We miss each other a lot, he was my best friend. But that also meant he didn't have anyone else to talk to about what was going on, which compounded his sense of isolation and pushed him closer towards her.'

It could be that the more togetherness we expect of each other, the greater the temptation to go out and have sex as a way to differentiate oneself as an individual and gain some erotic distance. In a romanticised, sexualised culture, the necessary secrecy and escapist drama of an affair and the search for a truer, better love become highly attractive. If infidelity is the one transgression that is likely to destroy a relationship, then it becomes all the more alluring as a way of fuelling passion and spicing up with a little danger the dull sense of safety that can accompany commitment. Affairs are often a form of escapist fantasy, a longing for intensity and a sense of destiny. People choose to provoke a crisis in their relationship – to scream, 'I am bored/ignored/unfulfilled.' When you try to impose the reality of day-to-day life on the notion that someone else, some other greater passion, can make you happier, it is rarely strong enough to take the full load. 'It's also trying to base the foundation of a new life on someone else's unhappiness, someone you cared for, and that is never a good basis,' says psychoanalytic psychotherapist Jenny Riddell, 'whereas the person who might come after that affair partner is very different.'

'A greater emphasis upon emotional companionship and sexual intimacy in marriage brought risks,' writes Claire Langhamer in 'Adultery in Post-War Europe'. 'It made marital infidelity more, rather than less likely as well as increasingly capable of dealing a fatal blow to the marriage itself.' If we expect to get everything we need from one person for a 'happy marriage' we are more likely to feel as if our partner is failing us when we do not get what we want. A man whose partner puts on weight after the birth of their children and loses much of her 'go' and vigour for life feels justified in satisfying his needs elsewhere. A woman whose husband works long hours,

provides well for his family but has little time for them feels a
sense of entitlement in seeking emotional solace from someone
else. Yet each is a double betrayal, because they kick their partner squarely in the gut when they are vulnerable, for not being
everything to them all of the time.

The trouble with the intense togetherness of modern love is
that should a sexual betrayal happen, it devastates in ways
which would have been unlikely in the past, when romantic
love was less important, marriages resembled business contracts and were for life. Now, with the soul mate notion of
romantic love, when a relationship begins to go wrong, we
must have chosen the wrong person. It wasn't True Love. With
the right person all of our dreams will come true and their
fidelity is never questioned. We do not need to explain ourselves or work to understand each other. We trust that love will
be enough to see us through rather than taking responsibility
for making it do so. The more we define marital partnerships
by the quality of the intimacy that we fashion, the more likely
it is that the betrayal of infidelity will tear at the very fabric of
those emotional ties and our entire sense of self-worth, for s/he
would not have done this if we were truly loved. We feel more
vulnerable because we could lose everything, our best friend,
provider and protector as well as the mother or father to our
children. 'Infidelity takes away all your dreams of togetherness,'
says Carol, whose husband had a nine-month affair when their
first child was a baby.

Romantic love allows people to make excuses for their moral
choices, avoiding responsibility for their actions if they stray
sexually – 'I fell madly in love with him/her and couldn't help
myself.' The subsequent emotional chaos can also be avoided
with a sudden switching of emotional allegiance – 'I am not in
love with you any more,' which is rarely true, for the emotions

associated with a committed relationship can never be this cut and dried. The idea that an infidelity spoils something special and pure between two people is now so strong that many would rather issue ultimatums, cleaving their partner to them with threats of 'I will leave/kick you out if you ever have an affair.' For others the suspicion or discovery of an infidelity is such a devastating admission of shame and personal failure – 'I could not keep him/her "true"' – that it is easier to turn a blind eye than deal with the consequences.

If everything has to be shared in a truly loving, companionate marriage, then a secret sexual encounter becomes yours alone and a particularly sweet memory as a result. The prevailing view that infidelity is always morally wrong means that any sexual thought or encounter has to be kept more secret, for the consequences of exposure will be more explosive. The risks accrue and so does the aphrodisiac nature of such a temptation, of feeling overtaken by emotion, a yearning for something one is denied. If a person feels trapped or insignificant, there is nothing like transgressing and challenging the social order to make them feel more powerful and alive. Like the dangerous dares of children, we want to know what it would really feel like, and how we would cope. As Tim Parks writes in his essay on adultery in *Adultery and Other Diversions*, 'In this finely managed, career structured world we've worked so hard to build, with its automatic gates and hissing lawns, its comprehensive insurance policies, divorce remains one of the few catastrophes we can reasonably expect to provoke, offering a truly spectacular shipwreck. Oh to do some serious damage at last!'

So trust is our bond but an increasingly tenuous one. Not so very long ago people hired private investigators to gather proof of adultery in order to sue for divorce. Now infidelity detection services are a lucrative industry for the large numbers of people who cannot trust their own instincts or that their partner is entirely loyal. I have spent hours drinking coffee with the delightfully named Verity, who has worked as an infidelity detective for twelve years. We met on several occasions in a small hotel bar to talk about the themes of this book, her work and the clients she meets. With their permission her company can install monitoring software in computers and tracking equipment in cars and conduct visual surveillance, so that suspicious spouses can build up a picture of what their partner might be up to when they are not together. We cannot necessarily trust what we see.

Verity estimates that they receive about a hundred calls a week and says that the volume of calls has increased steadily year on year. She believes it's because 'Women are more independent and they don't see it as their duty any more to be the loyal wife.' But the more shocking element of our conversation revolved around the fact that she wasn't at all surprised by the fact that between 70 and 80 per cent of the people they are monitoring are *not* having an affair at all. They really *are* working late at the office. It really *is* just a friendship. 'That can be a bitter pill to swallow too, accepting that your partner might be happier talking to someone else than to you. That's the most difficult thing for people, when there isn't something going on,' she says. 'All the signs were there that a husband was playing away but it turns out to be totally innocent and then there is no one else to blame for whatever has been going wrong between you.'

It's harder still to trust that our partner could be entirely loyal when sexual opportunity is rife. Men and women work together, share flats and friendships. They can easily disappear for a few hours in crowded, anonymous cities or travel quickly

to other places. Contraception, the morning-after pill and legalised abortion limit the possibility of complications. Facebook,
Friends Reunited and Skype allow people to reconnect with old
friends and lovers who seem more attractive through the misty
eyes of hindsight. The internet offers people unlimited opportunities to connect with strangers and it is often easier to confess
to difficulties, failings or transgressions with an anonymous username than it is with one's own partner, and this contact then
builds into an online intimacy. An extramarital liaison can
mature quickly. Consequently growing numbers of people regularly check up on their partner's movements covertly. A major
research study conducted by the Internet Institute at Oxford
University for the report 'Me, My Spouse and the Internet'
found that in 44 per cent of couples, at least one of the pair
monitors the other's behaviour, reading their emails or texts, or
checking their browser history. They also found that there was
a 65 per cent chance that when a husband is being monitored
by his wife, he is also tracking her.[3]

An infidelity detective like Verity is often the first person a
worried caller gets to talk to about their relationship difficulties.
'They come to us because the trust has gone but they feel dis-
loyal just picking up the phone, they feel they shouldn't be
talking to anyone about it,' she says. Verity acts as both counsellor and business associate, and it isn't difficult to sell them
her services because, she says, so many people are looking for
peace of mind. 'People tell me that they want concrete proof
for their own sanity because each time they question their partner they feel they are being lied to or are told that they are
paranoid and imagining things. A lot of them haven't begun
to think through what they might do with the information once
they get it because it takes such a lot of courage just to call
me in the first place. They don't realise that once you get to the

stage that you are even thinking about having to check up on your partner, the trust has gone. Infidelity is not just about sex: it's not telling your partner something, whether that's an affair or another secret part of your life.'

With so much temptation around us we have had to endorse complete sexual fidelity as the most important symbol of our commitment to each other, for that is the most testing of trials when it comes to loyalty. But we also subscribe to a new ethos within a committed relationship where every secret has to be shared, which means we have to lie more about every single encounter outside that relationship, from the most minor attraction and flirtation at the school gate to a full-blown nine-year affair. Deceit always costs less than disclosure which could cause upset, argument, the loss of their marriage, children, home and friends. Greater secrecy increases the pressure on an individual who is cheating to confide in someone else if that liaison is conjuring up new and difficult emotions such as guilt, shame and indecision which could be construed as another betrayal of intimacy. The new confessional culture of tell-all fusion with your partner, who is also your best friend, can make even the smallest lie of omission seem like a threat and a betrayal if it is then discovered by someone feeling insecure about their spouse's commitment.

New sexual expectations also compromise our ability to find peace in love. Narrow cultural depictions of 'good' sex as youthful, vigorous, passionate and orgasmic exacerbate yearnings for something better than what we have. It must be out there somewhere and we simply have to find it. We are owed it for happiness. Sexual boredom is now considered unacceptable, the sign of a failing relationship. Rising numbers of men and women visit their doctors complaining of lack of sexual desire.[4] A comparative study in Finland found that couples were less satisfied with their sex life and the frequency of intercourse at the end of the 1990s than they were in the early 1990s. It wasn't that their sex lives had deteriorated: expectations had risen.[5]

So the lure of an affair, of another body, takes hold as the answer. 'Infidelity has always happened,' says David Williams, founder of lovinglinks.com, a website which specialises in facilitating discreet extramarital liaisons. 'But there has been a huge explosion in the numbers and the media has a lot to do with it, with top ten tips to excite your lover, written by people who have probably never experienced these joys in their lives; they are just making it up as they go along. Thirty years ago people thought they were entitled to a comfortable marriage and having someone around. Now that sense of entitlement has changed to incredible amounts of sex and a huge variety of sexual content, like having a new Louis Vuitton handbag, because I am worth it. You think OK, who with? Not him indoors after eight years.'

David told me that when he set up his business nearly twenty years ago the *Daily Mail* called him a threat to every house in Britain and he was condemned by the Synod of the Church of England. 'It was really pushing the limits to say that there was a place for people to have some fun outside a long-term celibate relationship. There was no internet so we used the postal system and people were incredibly vulnerable to being discovered. I would stagger to the post office with six hundred envelopes and say a little prayer, hoping no one else would see them. Now the media demystifies the notion of "playing away", it normalises it with countless stories implying that every celebrity is at it and ordinary people have their noses pressed up against the window looking through to a shop of sexual expectations which just doesn't exist. No one normal looks down the aisle and thinks, I can commit adultery. They think, finally I have found someone I can share things with and my friends are all here to witness my pledge to be faithful. But then when something happens in life or it doesn't work out for one reason or another, monogamy is just something you make the furniture out of.'

I met David Williams in the bar of a swish London hotel. Halfway through the interview I discovered that this was a regular rendezvous spot for richer clients who want a personalised service and that the waiters hovering around our table presumed I was there for the very same thing. David explained, 'I have sat in this bar with men who don't have time for an affair but think they can just slot someone else into their lives, like an unpaid prostitute. Or they say things like, "I don't do intimacy," so you can understand why their wives won't have sex with them. They want no-strings sex but they don't want to pay for it. I tell them to get a grip because the moment sex is not a commercial transaction there are strings. I have had women turn up here with their babies in buggies, sat here with someone's favourite daughter-in-law or someone's trophy wife and found it hard to believe they could be doing this. "English Rose" types with innocent eyes have told me too much information about what they want in bed. One even said, "At the risk of sounding a slut, the blacker the better."' The waiter chose this moment to put down another expensive cappuccino in front of me. David went on, 'They do it because they are bored, because they are disillusioned with marriage, because they have read about some sexual act that they would like to try out with a stranger, because they love new lingerie. I am in a monogamous relationship and I think I know my partner inside out but I think I would find it hard to trust anybody now because of what I have heard in this room.'

The fact that David Williams, a man who makes a considerable amount of money out of the infidelity business, is concerned about the way our sexual expectations have changed should be sending out alarm bells. He understands the numerous ways in which people can be duped and seduced and the effect that can have on relationships, particularly for those growing up in this new sexual landscape. 'I worry terribly for the younger generation and the young men I know who have inevitably been exposed to pornography. How can that not affect their views of what is expected of them in terms of sexual proficiency? My feeling is that one loses track of what sex is really about and what it can achieve, and that's very sad. But I don't think there is anything that you or I can do to put that back on track when these people are continually presented with images of fluffed-up guys achieving these prodigious acts with women who seem happy to be penetrated every which way and that's presented as sex, but that's not part of a loving or an adulterous relationship. It's just triple-X activity. I also think young people are more susceptible to the idea of casual sex, "friends with benefits", and there is this new laddish culture with lap-dancing clubs and the Spearmint Rhino culture where you can just get a blow job for some instant gratification. The internet too creates this notion that relationships and casual sex can be downloaded like iTunes.'

He is right to be concerned for all of the evidence suggests that people are being adversely affected by an overtly romanticised, sexualised culture, and the very male pornographic interpretation of how 'good' sex should be. Confidence in our bodies, in our ability to please others or experience pleasure during real sex with a real person gets reduced. It appears to be informing sexual behaviour and what young men and women think each should be doing. And it affects the nature of marital sex and our perceptions of its quality, a subject which is explored in Chapter 4.

Sex with the same body tends to be the same sex. The passionate, can't-leave-each-other-alone sex of the first few months, even years, mutates into something far more intimate with time, greater knowledge of each other and commitment. But that isn't the instant 'good' sex we see in romantic films on television or in the ubiquitous, pervasive presence of pornography. Research conducted at Heriot-Watt University between 1995 and 2005 found that avid consumers of romcoms such as *Notting Hill* or *Sleepless in Seattle* were more likely to believe that sex should be perfect and that a loving partner should know what they need in every respect without having to communicate their sexual desires.[6] When that fails to materialise, extramarital excitement, whether that is sex-texting, chatroom flirting, use of pornography or an affair, surfaces as the Answer.

The message that we are entitled to seek sexual satisfaction almost as if it were an individual human right is so relentless that the age range of those 'cheating' appears to have widened. Research conducted by Dr David Atkins of the University of Washington between 1991 and 2006 on nineteen thousand people found a rise in the number of under-thirty-fives having affairs and these appeared to be internet-led. David Williams concurs. 'When I started in this business it was people in their middle years, now it's people in their thirties and lots in their late twenties. I tend to think if you are twenty-eight and not happy, why the hell do you stay? You have a lifetime ahead where you can be unfaithful but if you have no kids, why not go?'

David Atkins also found a jump in the number of men and women over sixty dabbling in extramarital liaisons.[7] Many older people enjoy better physical health than those of previous generations at the same age. Those over sixty discovered sex with great abandon in the 1960s and are more likely to exhibit the urge to keep on going sexually if they possibly can. They also have the added bonus of Viagra, often the third party in relationship breakdown as older men leave for younger women, for Viagra prolongs the time during which a man *can* be unfaithful. While few things confirm a man's masculinity more than the ability to 'get it up', women now have access to HRT, Botox and cosmetic surgery, prolonging their own sense of self through their sex appeal. Both men and women are ironically rendered more vulnerable sexually because of these props, for there are always others out there too who could be even more virile or attractive, able to steal your partner away.

The boundaries of transgression become hazy too as we lie to ourselves about what it really means to be unfaithful to our spouse. A growing number of people have found new ways to dabble off-piste without actually touching another human being in inappropriate places, consequently maintaining the illusion of complete 'fidelity' to their spouse. People play with the idea of an extramarital encounter while salsa dancing on a Tuesday night, for example. We relish the dangerous liaisons of countless plays, fiction and films or wallow in the vicarious detail of the scandalous affairs of those in the limelight. It's easy to begin an email flirtation, or wander into a chatroom protected by username anonymity, in the safety of your own home. The frisson of an ongoing text flirtation, the sexual chemistry fuelled by an exchange of pictures and pornographic suggestion, can be more exciting than physical sex itself. With very little effort we can relish instant gratification, the exhilaration of cheating, as if we've done nothing more than escape into a romantic novel, or *Fifty Shades of Grey*, for an hour, and delude ourselves that we have done nothing wrong.

New technology offers people all of the advantages of an affair without perceiving it as such. In an in-depth study of eighty-six married people recruited in Yahoo and MSN chatrooms, 83 per cent did not consider their online behaviour as cheating because there was no physical contact, or they justified it as adding a certain spice to their marriage.[8] All of the benefits of infidelity can be enjoyed – except the most obvious sexual one. These include flirtation with desire and being desired; dabbling in 'what if' fantasies while projecting your wildest imaginings and alternative personas on to the screen; the secrecy and deceit necessary to find time to 'chat'; the freedom to express yourself and experiment without losing face; enjoying the instant soother, like having a drink or a cigarette; and all with the safety of being in complete control. You can shut down a laptop in an instant.

It's never been so easy to enjoy both the 'safety' of marriage and the thrills of illicit encounters online at the same time. So it's hardly surprising that 'chatting' has quickly become the most common form of 'infidelity'. Without this technology, many of those who stray virtually would perhaps never have dared cross the line into a full physical liaison outside their relationship. Chatrooms, emotional affairs at work or the school gate and telephone sex offer the illusion of individual freedom and autonomy at a time when the emphasis on total togetherness and fusion in modern relationship has intensified. We can say things online we couldn't say face to face with our partner. We can talk dirty to someone anonymous and separate sex from intimacy, in much the same way as a man pays for a prostitute to perform acts he cannot ask for or doesn't want from his wife, and still not see this as a betrayal. 'We know that today's young men and women are far more likely to masturbate than earlier generations were when living with a steady partner, apparently because it is a refuge for self-determined, freely available, autonomous, secret and refreshing sex,' writes Gunter Schmidt in his essay 'Sexuality and Late Modernity'. 'For them masturbating is not a poor substitute for too little sex à deux, but another easier variant, to be enjoyed in its own right.' Masturbation, going 'Downtown' as Petula Clark sang so memorably in her hit song, allows people an essential private space without worrying about the sexual or emotional needs of a partner.

It's never been easier to stretch the definitions of what constitutes loyalty. 'I've been married eleven years and all that time I've never been unfaithful to my wife ... in the same city,' George Segal says as he bumps into Glenda Jackson in the pouring rain in the film *A Touch of Class*. 'She's out of town just now.' Delusions include the belief that it is not infidelity if you keep a mistress in a separate flat, for she entered the arrangement voluntarily and gains materially. Some religious people have been known to argue that it isn't infidelity if you sleep with someone from a different faith, or that if you bury your used condom in the garden after a visit to the massage parlour, you haven't engaged in a wasteful spilling of seed. Paying for sex as a business transaction doesn't count either. One man, when confronted by his wife on his regular use of prostitutes, replied, 'It was just a hole I stuck it into.' It is also said that up to 70 per cent of Americans believe that blow jobs don't count. So far as I know the same criterion is not applied to cunnilingus. 'Americans are such poor cheaters that we're even prone to suffer during the act of extramarital sex,' writes Pamela Druckerman in *Lust in Translation*, her book about cultural differences around infidelity. 'I didn't find any other country whose citizens get naked with their lovers but specifically don't have intercourse, so that they can semi-truthfully tell themselves and their spouses that they didn't have sex.'

For some, sex-texting and internet affairs are a form of salvation. Karen is married with four children under the age of ten. She met an old friend on Facebook, someone she had always fancied but had never had a relationship with. He too is unhappily married and they are now actively engaged in an emotional affair. 'This is my one guilty pleasure,' she told me. 'He lives in Canada now, so there is no way we could ever meet. But it makes it easier for me to get through each day.'

For others, touch-less infidelity is played with simply because it is there, in the delusion that it can be controlled, boxed off as separate to our real relationship. While this may not feel like real 'infidelity', the danger is that it can quickly become addictive, diversionary and therefore undermine a relationship. Maintaining such a secret life sucks energy away from our partner. It can and often does slide into something physical and more serious. Skype, email, Facebook and texts leave trails which, according to Verity the infidelity detective, are easily uncovered. The risks accrue, as does the aphrodisiac of danger.

For some it is an exciting game. The snatched moments 'And stolen glances, sweeter for the theft,' as the serial seducer Lord Byron writes in his poem *Don Juan*, 'Tremblings when met, and restlessness when left; All these are little preludes to possession, Of which young passion cannot be bereft.' The more something is forbidden, the more desirable it tends to become. The threat of pain, the agony of potential discovery, adds fuel to passion for 'the longing of what sears us and annihilates us', as Denis de Rougement writes in *Love in the Western World*. 'To love love more than the object of love, to love passion for its own sake has been to love to suffer and to court suffering all the way from Augustine's "Amabam Amare" to modern romanticism.' The longer the secret continues, prolonged by the social stigma attached to sexual infidelity, the more sexual tension there is to this 'insider' knowledge. Secret lovers have a special, unspecified hold over the one who is left out.

For others the illicitness of the affair isn't dangerous enough, they want to risk even more by being seen to do normal things in public. David Williams organises regular nights out at jazz clubs and burlesque bars for up to ten couples, where each person has left their regular partner at home. 'It never ceases to amaze me. If you came along (needless to say, he wouldn't let me when I asked if I could) you would see these hugely nice professional, middle-class people going out for dinner together as if they were normal couples, yet each of them has someone else at home. Sometimes they have group photos taken. How bizarre is that? They could be seen by someone. It's how they cope with their own guilt, I suppose: it normalises things for them. I help them validate what they are doing too, and give philosophical reasons and reassurance that they are not alone in needing sex outside their marriage. I live in this strange world where most of the people I meet in my daily life help to reinforce that what I do for a living is normal and healthy. But I tend to avoid telling other people outside that world because they freak out. It's too threatening.'

It is worth repeating that sexual infidelity has become the Great Betrayal of modern relationship. Consequently the taboos surrounding what it means to be unfaithful have hardened. If, because of the social stigma attached to infidelity, we cannot discuss the tortured landscape of our emotional lives with anyone outside the relationship, we exclude balanced judgement and constructive criticism. We risk falling into stereotypical beliefs about marriage and affairs which compound the denial about our own responsibility for the betrayal as the 'victim'. For the 'cheater', concealing such a large secret can corrode and corrupt from within. They can become obsessive, for the effort involved in suppressing or hiding certain feelings means that they think about those or the 'secret' more than they would otherwise. It is this pernicious deception which destroys so much of the stability in committed relationships, as well as two sets of families, rather than the mere physical act of sex with another body. 'The most threatening aspect is not the affair itself,' writes Emily Brown in her textbook for marital therapists *Patterns of Infidelity and Their Treatment*, 'but the dishonesty that casts doubt on the entire relationship.'

The longer a secret, diverting passion goes on unrevealed because to do so could provoke explosive consequences, the more likely it is to become entrenched and provoke the inevitable explosive consequences. The impact will be greater in terms of the sense of betrayal, the social humiliation if they separate and the personal self-doubt which ensues for both partners. Research on the impact of various marital problems such as drink or drug abuse and aggressive, controlling behaviour has found that extramarital sex is the biggest predictor of subsequent divorce, that it is likely to hurt the most, with an impact twice as large as any other problem, and that any subsequent separation is likely to be messier and more vengeful as a result.[9]

Many would rather their partner died than betrayed them in this way. Grief feels like it must be easier, for we are then able to reach out unequivocally to others for support. 'I had just been widowed and had taken the children on their first summer holiday without their father and I couldn't believe the heart-lessness of another single mother I met there whose husband had been caught in flagrante with his dental hygienist,' says Alice. 'She had the nerve to tell me that I was "lucky" and that she wished her husband had died instead!'

The pain of betrayal is often exacerbated by the fact that the infidelity has taken place with a person you know, or someone even closer such as a good friend or a family friend. People tend not to choose total strangers from countries on the other side of the world to engage in illicit sex with; they form an attraction and an attachment to someone they see regularly and get to know. If the betrayed spouse discovers that others outside their relationship knew of the affair before they did the double betrayal means double humiliation too. 'Who else knew and how could I have been so stupid not to have noticed?'

Verity the infidelity detective tells me that affairs tend to flourish with brothers- and sisters-in-law because there is regular contact. It is easy for that goodbye kiss to turn into a more meaningful hug, ripe with sexual frisson. She tells me chilling stories of double betrayals: women refusing to believe that their partner is having an affair with their best friend, even though there is photographic evidence, until they have gone round to the house and seen the evidence for themselves, through cracks in the curtains or by ringing the doorbell. 'They need to know that there is someone anonymous they can talk to,' she says, 'but they also need to understand that it could be really dangerous to talk to anyone else about it. She could tell her best friend but it is actually that friend her husband is having an affair with and my tracker ends up at the bottom of a ravine. People are much too trusting and an awful lot of people just put their head into the sand in the hope that it will all go away.'

Verity tells me jaw-dropping stories about groups of inter-
locking friends, where the mothers meet regularly after school
with their children and while the kids are playing one asks the
other if she can mind hers for a while so that she can pop out
on an errand. In fact she has prearranged to meet the other
woman's husband nearby for a quick bit of nookie. 'With
dumbfounded disgust I realised that I must have provided
child care for Amy after school while Steve was at work and
Cathy and Henry fucked on her couch,' writes Julie Metz in her
memoir *Perfection*, as she goes to confront a close friend after
discovering their affair seven months after her husband's death.
She wanted to smack Cathy's face, 'But the thought of touching her skin felt toxic. I never wanted to touch her again.'
Instead she gives her a week to tell her own husband and punishes their daughters, who were good friends, by banning them
from ever being in the same room again.

The social humiliation and damage to one's reputation can
be so great after an infidelity that only a very public show of
retribution will avenge the slight. Women tend to make the
headlines when they cut up suits, chop off penises or superglue
them to their husband's stomach because these acts of violence
are actually rare. Cars are a soft and symbolic target when they
are not being used to repeatedly run a husband over, as Clara
Harris, a Texan dentist, did in 2003 in a motel car park after
she had found him with a mistress. Cars epitomise machismo
and greater freedom. It feels deliciously just to be able to slash
the tyres, hurl their precious golf clubs through the windscreen
or scratch the words 'cheater' or 'hope she was worth it' into
the paintwork, when men seem to care so much more about
their wheels than anything else.

I have heard of women who pinned details of their husband's
shameful acts on public notice boards. And of others who

distributed their husband's most expensive and precious wine collection to the neighbourhood. Then there were those who packed all of their husband's belongings into large crates and had them delivered to their office with the word 'adulterer' scrawled across the top. 'I wanted to tell everybody, even the dry cleaners,' Clare told me when she first discovered that her husband of more than twenty years had been having an affair with a much younger woman. 'I wanted to hold him up and say, "This man is a liar, he is not who you think he is" and I don't know whether that is revenge or just a need to give yourself some acknowledgement because you feel so invalidated by the betrayal.'

While women may be painted as the more vengeful sex – 'hell hath no fury like a woman scorned' – both genders are equally capable of extreme jealousy and retribution. The knee-jerk, defensive reaction of retaliation is deeply ingrained into biological, psychological and cultural aspects of human nature. It appears to exist in most species and across cultures. But it is men who are more likely to use violence and rape as a means of control and a deterrence against imagined infidelities. They are also more likely to stalk and kill their partners when they feel a strong need to restore 'honour' to their family. It is men who are more likely to inject acrimony into divorce proceedings, pressing claims to the limit, happy to lose the house if they can't have it, or to give a great many of their assets to lawyers rather than to their children, just to avenge a sexual betrayal. And it is men who will post naked pictures of their ex-partner on the internet, knowing full well that other men will masturbate over them. The meanest then post photographs of cocks spouting sperm over the faces of their exes and then post those back on the internet. Revenge may feel sweet at the time, but the messages all this sends are deeply ugly.

Verity tells me lots of stories of public revenge but there is one that surpasses any I have ever heard for sheer brilliance and meanness, planned and executed by a man. Her client was in his sixties and he asked Verity to accumulate months of photographic evidence of his wife's affair, which cost him a small fortune. He was planning a special wedding anniversary party with the screening of a film. 'All of their family and friends were there,' Verity told me. 'The film started off nicely with photos and videos of them when they first got married and then there were photographs of her with her lover, who was at the party. The room fell silent and his wife started screaming like a banshee. He told me it was the best money he had ever spent because now he could look his kids in the eye and know that no one would ever back her side of the story.'

While the accepted truth is that sexual betrayal and infidelity should end a relationship, the statistics on remarriage after an affair has ended a marriage are not good. Roughly 90 per cent of those studied do not marry their lover and 70 per cent of the remaining 10 per cent who do commit will separate eventually, a higher figure than the average of 40 to 50 per cent. Too many marriages and relationships come to a swift end because of the taboos, the shock and the righteous indignation, or because an undisclosed affair has been allowed to continue for too long, or because the 'betrayer' feels they have no choice but to flee into the arms of their lover rather than confront the problems in their relationship.

Sarah's husband told her that he had never loved her when she became pregnant with their second child. 'It was like a knife going into my heart because it invalidated everything we had done together over the years, even having the children.'

It took Sarah years to recover and to recognise that this was not true, just a way for her husband to justify his switched loyalties to a younger lover in France, with whom he now lives. 'I remember taking the children skiing out there one year and my ex-husband rented a chalet for us and we all went together, including his new wife, who doesn't ski, so she stayed by the fire with a book. We had the most amazing fun time, the four of us together. I remember sitting next to him on a chairlift and thinking, what went wrong? We could have had such a good time as a family. It was just like the old times with him laughing and joking and then when we got back to the chalet at night he just stopped talking to me – it was bizarre.'

I have heard many sad stories around infidelity and separation but Sarah's situation is one of the saddest simply because both she and her husband found it so hard to accept what had happened, which exacerbated the pain for both them and their children. They had met and married young and there had never been a divorce in either family. His affair with the woman to whom he is now married began early on in his marriage to Sarah and he kept schlepping between the two, clearly very unhappy. Sarah knew something was wrong. 'I just kept thinking that things would sort themselves out. What else could I do with two small children? He denied there was anybody else whenever I asked and so I just thought naively that it must be something else. But I now think that he kept up with this charade because he had the pressure of his own family to deal with, where adultery and divorce was completely unacceptable. His mother still can't cope with the fact that her son could have behaved in that way and it isn't talked about, twenty-five years later.'

When the affair was finally uncovered Sarah filed for divorce but her husband refused to accept responsibility for child support and maintenance and she had to take him to court twice. 'At one point he rang me up and said, "I am going to tear you limb from limb," which was just horrible. He couldn't admit to being in love with someone else because that meant he was failing his family, but then he went on to do just that, because he couldn't cope with the guilt, I suppose. I think I could have coped if he had been honest and not put me through years of self-doubt because of course I thought all that time that there must be something wrong with me and it has taken me a long time to get over that. I kept thinking, what have I done? when I had done my best to be a good wife, mother and friend. I could have forgiven him so much more easily if he had just come clean about the affair but I think it went on for so long with him not confiding in me that it became entrenched. What I couldn't forgive was the way he not only betrayed me and the children, but then went on to say he didn't owe me anything. I had to fight him tooth and nail and it was war for years.'

Had the taboos around infidelity been less strict, Sarah and her husband might have been able to talk about his affair earlier and either salvaged their marriage or separated more amicably with less guilt. Sarah might have been spared years of uncertainty and self-doubt, enabling her to find happiness again with someone else. They would also have saved a fortune in lawyers' fees.

So how can we trust each other to be 'true'? It isn't easy to preserve commitment and loyalty in relationships when they are being battered by so many threats. The new ethos of for as long as it's good, not 'till death us do part', means that the onus of responsibility rests with us to keep it together. The answer does not lie in tightening the clamp around couples and showing greater hostility to those who 'cheat', in threats and ultimatums to try and keep people 'true' to each other or in very public acts of revenge for the slight to reputation. We cannot bind ourselves together around the promise of complete fidelity, when people are merely human beings and make mistakes, when they dig themselves into deep psychological holes from which they cannot extricate themselves without sending up the flare of an affair, when change and the messiness of life get in the way. But we can do a great deal to stop a good relationship from ending prematurely if we bust through the bigotry, the myths and the taboos surrounding infidelity with some hard truths, *before* the secrecy, shame and blame of sexual 'betrayal' turn a brief interlude into an entrenched and troublesome tangle. 'I wonder now, years later, if we should have paid closer attention to that odd confluence of crushes,' writes Ellen Sussman in *Invite the Bitch to Dinner*. 'We were already looking for someone else, someone who understood us, someone who shared our passion. We would never have said to each other: I need more. I need something else. We wouldn't even say it to ourselves.'[10]

If we want all of the other rewards from a long, loving relationship, and they are worth fighting for, we are going to have to get real about infidelity. It cannot help but be a constant threat with so much erotic opportunity around us unless we find new ways to make relationship stronger from the inside. That means genuine honesty about our darker feelings such as jealousy and insecurity, as well as the loving ones. That means talking to each other about what we lack and need from the relationship and an acceptance that nobody can be another's everything. In a good relationship each respects the other's autonomy within their togetherness and understands that they are bound to find others alluring. Talking about that fact shouldn't be undermining if there is enough trust in all of the other threads that unite us.

Trust lies at the heart of any committed relationship, but the notion of what trust actually is gets distorted by the romantic notion that with true love you can automatically trust. In the world of work and community, trust has to be earned through the give and take of relationship. We choose to trust: it isn't foisted upon us by Cupid or the institution of marriage. Trust lies in the spaces between us. That means talking about where the borders of fidelity might lie, what upsets us and why, without feeling that your trust in the other has been undermined by talking about the subject at all. 'Of course I am not having an affair, don't you trust me?' is not an embracing or positive way of helping someone feel safer within the relationship. Talking about why they might be feeling so insecure is. Trust is not a constant: it fluctuates according to our past and how vulnerable we feel generally. There are times in every relationship when people trust less, doubt themselves and their value more and need reassurance, for example after childbirth, or during difficulties at work, ill-health or unemployment. Many find that they need each other more as they age and grow more vulnerable. They have more to lose and also have the wisdom of hindsight. 'I have changed my mind about infidelity as I have got older,' says Isabel. 'When I was younger I didn't care really, I would sleep with people and there weren't the same consequences. But when your lives are knitted together, infidelity complicates things to such an extent that life becomes untenable because it creates such havoc and you don't want havoc. You want to have a clear head and feel safe.'

The more secure we are made to feel, the less likely we are to sense that we are being 'left out' from our partner's other relationships with work, family, children, friends or football. That sense of security can only be built by a constant, honest dialogue between two people. How much reassurance does each need to allow the other time to pursue their individual interests? How long a lead can we give each other? Too short and we are choked; too long and we are liable to wrap ourselves around several lampposts. 'Trust is built by sharing one's emotional self, by accepting the reality of who the other person is, by making and following through on commitments, by positive interactions, by working together to resolve differences and by having fun together,' writes Emily Brown in her textbook on affairs for marital therapists. Only then can a strong enough sense of self develop within a relationship which will in turn strengthen that relationship enough to increase the chances that it will last.

# 3

# HEIRS AND SPARES

The sexual double standard, the idea that a man can engage in sexual pleasures while single and has natural urges to 'play away' when married, pervades the history of marriage, sexual desire and divorce. But when a woman indulges similar urges, the whole fabric of society is undermined. That double standard is with us still. It is only by studying the historical development of this double standard that we can begin to understand why mutual fidelity in both men and women became so important for the health and longevity of a committed relationship. Interestingly, it was only once women became more empowered as individuals in the 1960s and 1970s, through contraception and having their own income, as well as through feminist concepts of equality, that infidelity in either sex became completely unacceptable. Once a woman could divorce an unfaithful spouse just as easily as a man, the accepted norm changed to one where any betrayal could end a relationship.

History is peppered with famous infidelities, from Homer's

seizure of Helen by Paris, through generations of kings and aristocrats and their mistresses, to the more recent open marriages of artists and intellectuals such as the Bloomsbury group. Until the late nineteenth century most marriages were arranged and often loveless, and it was widely accepted that men were likely to have lovers. It was understood that the main purpose of marriage was childbearing and the production of an heir as well as a 'spare' should something happen to the first-born son. Sexual incompatibility or lack of fulfilment was not something which could break a marriage and men could freely indulge their sexual passions with as many available women as they had the time for.

When it came to the fairer sex, 'It was perfectly permissible for a married woman in society to have an affair, preferably after she had produced the heir and spare and as long as she was discreet,' writes Maureen Waller in her history *The English Marriage*. However, should a woman reveal her husband's shame by being discovered publicly, she suffered hugely, for as the historian Lawrence Stone describes in his book *The Family, Sex and Marriage in England 1500–1800*, honour had a very different meaning in the sixteenth, seventeenth and eighteenth centuries from today. The worst slur for a man was that he was a liar and for a woman that she was unchaste. 'The world in this is somewhat unequal and our sex seemeth to play the tyrant,' comments the first Marquess of Halifax in a letter to his daughter at the end of the seventeenth century. 'The root and excuse of this injustice is the preservation of families from any mixture which may bring blemish to them: and whilst the point of honour continues to be so plac'd, it seems unavoidable to give your sex the greater share of the penalty ... Remember, that next to the danger of committing the fault yourself, the greatest is that of seeing it in your husband.'[1]

The double standards surrounding sexual betrayal are inextricably linked to the history of divorce and the difficulties people faced trying to leave unhappy marriages. For those rich enough, adultery was the only means of separation and many of the most sensational divorce trials of the eighteenth and nineteenth centuries involved couples who had barely met before they married and did not much like, let alone love, each other. If a man could prove adultery he was not liable for any maintenance, although he could not subsequently remarry without an expensive petition through the House of Lords until the Matrimonial Causes Act of 1857. However, a separated woman faced severe penalties and stood to lose everything: all her savings, future legacies or the wages she might earn after her separation, all her possessions and property were liable to seizure by her ex-husband. She was not permitted to play any part in her own defence, to testify or call witnesses. Her children were entirely controlled by their father, their legal guardian, and he could deprive their mother of ever seeing them again. Few wives and only those with independent property rights would take advantage of their right to gain a separation from a husband on the grounds of his adultery.

For much of our history there has been more to the sexual double standard surrounding chastity and a woman's sexual fidelity than ensuring that bastards did not infect the family line. A woman, whatever her age, was not free to do as she pleased. She was unable to enter into a legal contract, to use credit to borrow money, or to buy or sell property. Her chastity was her parents' asset, their bargaining chip when it came to forging alliances through matrimony. With marriage a woman became a man's property, her legal position was absorbed into that of her husband in every way and adultery with another man's wife was theft or trespass. The church service used the words 'Whom God hath joined together let no man put asunder' and should that happen a husband could avenge the loss of his sexual property with spontaneous violence against his wife or her seducer, by challenging the seducer to a duel, or by demanding money from him as compensation. A wife was of such little value that it was only in the late seventeenth century that duellists began to be prosecuted for manslaughter if they killed their opponent.

From 1670 onwards a cuckolded husband could restore his honour by suing his wife's lover for 'criminal conversation'. Damages, often ruinously high amounts, were awarded arbitrarily, and by 1800 the ports of Calais and Boulogne were said to be full of fugitives from 'crim. con' actions. The law now placed a financial value on a woman's fidelity, endorsing her status as property. A woman could not use the same principle to challenge her husband's sexual behaviour, so he was free to enter into as many extramarital liaisons as he liked, without impunity. The upper hand was transferred in adultery cases from the wife's seducer to the injured husband, and retribution passed from being an individual matter to one determined by a common law judge and a jury of specially selected gentlemen. The sexual double standard, as well as the concept of a woman as property, was consequently brought right into the heart of the English legal system. In no other country in Europe were women so ill protected by the law. ''Tis the established custom for every Lady to have 2 husbands, one that bears the name and another that performs the Dutys', writes the adventuress Lady Wortley Montagu to Lady Rich in 1716 in reporting on her travels to Vienna. 'These engagements are so well known, that it would be a downright affront and publickly resented if you invited a

Woman of Quality to dinner without at the same time invite-
ing her 2 attendants of Lover and Husband.'[2]

The idea that a man could earn substantial damages from
his wife's adultery and then, because of her sin, divorce her
without the need to pay alimony was an attractive option for
any man keen to trade in his spouse for a new model. Some
were devastated by the discovery of their wife's infidelity and
keen to avenge their honour. 'In 1769 Mr Heatley went into
convulsions when informed that his wife had infected him with
venereal disease. William Middleton of Stockfield Park was
so broken in spirit by the proofs of his wife's infidelity that he
was never the same man again,' writes Lawrence Stone in
*Road to Divorce*. 'By and large, however, what is so striking is
the contrast between the relative calm and sometimes even
calculating greed with which many a husband greeted the news
of his wife's infidelity, and the ferocious passion sometimes
unleashed by the news of similar behaviour on the part of a
mistress.'

From the 1770s onwards there was a marked rise in the
number of crim. con cases. Public interest mushroomed as the
growing newspaper industry and collections of pamphlets on
the more sensational trials publicised details of the betrayals
of the elite. For some, anxious to avoid the public humiliation,
reparations were settled privately. But the increased publicity
also had the rather more perverse effect of making these cases
more acceptable. In addition, at this time the damages awarded
to cuckolded husbands were raised sharply in an attempt to
dissuade people from committing adultery, for there was a
general fear that sexual immorality was on the increase and
that it was the wives, those siren temptresses, who were mostly
to blame. But this too only had the reverse effect as greedy
husbands tried to raise their fortunes either by conspiring with

an alleged lover in order to obtain a divorce and remarry, or sending out their wives in a form of amateur prostitution to entrap someone.

The notoriety of these cases began to generate a general repugnance at the idea that honour could be traded for cash in this way. There was also mounting criticism of the unequal legal treatment of women, championed by early feminists such as Mary Wollstonecraft and Harriet Martineau. A wife could be falsely charged by a husband eager to get rid of her and was unable to testify in her defence against the lies of bribed servants or raise evidence of her husband's infidelities or cruelties. It took the horrific experience of Caroline Norton, as well as her tenacity, her writing skills and her political contacts, to help bring about a change in those laws.

George Norton, Caroline's husband, was a violent bully and mean with money, and their marriage was not a happy one. Even so, Caroline bore him three sons and sought political advancement for her husband by lobbying friends of her grandfather, the playwright Richard Sheridan. This brought her into contact with Lord Melbourne, the Home Secretary, in 1831 and they became friends. Both protested that their relationship was entirely platonic until their dying days. As her marriage deteriorated, Caroline considered fleeing back to her family with her children, but George kicked her out before she could do so and secreted her children away so that she could not see them. Then, in 1836, he sued Lord Melbourne, who had meanwhile become Prime Minister, for the alienation of his wife's affections. The trial generated unprecedented amounts of publicity and speculation about the fate of the government. Norton lost his case and was therefore unable to divorce Caroline, who became a separated wife, grieving the loss of her children.

Caroline began to campaign tirelessly for changes to the law, writing pamphlets and lobbying parliament for an Infant Custody Bill, which was finally passed in 1839, the first alteration to the marriage laws in relation to women since the Middle Ages. A mother now had the right to petition the Lord Chancellor for a hearing with regard to access to her children, and while this helped other women and their children, Caroline's husband had moved her sons to Scotland, beyond the reach of English law.

In 1853, George Norton went back to court in a further attempt to end his financial responsibilities to Caroline by maintaining she could earn her own living through her pamphlets. He revealed in court that he had stopped her allowance because he had discovered that she was receiving money from another man in the form of an annuity of £200 left to her by Lord Melbourne. Norton won his case on a technicality but he subpoenaed Caroline in the hope that she would incriminate herself. Instead her eloquence won her huge public support. Again she protested her innocence, but if her husband wanted to defraud her there was nothing she could do about it, for 'I have no rights: I have only wrongs'. Caroline Norton then went on to campaign for greater rights for women after divorce.

During the 1850s there was a sea change in public sensibilities towards adultery and the double standard. In early modern England the death rate was so high that over a third of all marriages were second marriages for at least one of the partners (much like today). However, from the early nineteenth century longevity began to rise, marriages lasted longer and consequently divorce became more popular. Increasing cultural value was placed on the importance of romantic love, family life and the welfare of the child through the circulation of the new and highly popular novel form. There was a growing unease about the sexual licentiousness of men and the vulnerability of women, who could be seduced or raped and become 'fallen', 'harlots' or prosecuted for bastardy.

In crim. con cases the emphasis began to shift so that adultery, formerly regarded as theft or sexual trespass, was now increasingly seen as the loss of 'the comforts of matrimony'. In assessing damages judges began to take into account other factors such as how many children the couple had, how happy the marriage had been before the adultery took place and how much blame lay with the husband for pushing his wife into the arms of a lover. In addition there was increasing political concern over the failing sexual morality of the nation, as evidenced by a rise in the more overt nature of extramarital sexual activity, as well as over the spiralling costs of poor relief given to support abandoned mothers. Several attempts were made in parliament to turn adultery into a criminal offence. After a flurry of pamphlets, articles and speeches denouncing the unfairness to women of criminal conversation, it was abolished in 1855. Even so, discussion about how to compensate a poor husband for the costs of divorce and the loss of his wife to a lover continued through the months of debate surrounding the Matrimonial Causes Act of 1857.

It is no coincidence that around this time were published two of the most important and widely read novels about adultery ever written, *Anna Karenina* and *Madame Bovary*: the story of Flaubert's Emma in 1857 and that of Tolstoy's great tragic heroine just twenty years later. Fontaine's *Effie Briest* appeared in 1895 and the shocking theme of a married woman seduced by an unmarried man of the same class was adopted by several less well-known novels, among them Jacobsen's *Marie Grubbe* (1876) and Pérez Galdós's *Fortunata and Jacinta* (1876). Earlier novels such as Laclos's *Dangerous Liaisons* (1782), Stendhal's *The Charterhouse of Parma* (1839) and Balzac's *Cousin Bette* (1847) positively groaned with themes of lust, jealousy and infidelity, but these were not considered 'novels of adultery' where the importance of marriage was being threatened by female sexual passion.

In the censorship trial of *Madame Bovary* in 1856, Flaubert was charged with posing an 'outrage to public morals and religion' for Emma's flagrant enjoyment of adulterous sexuality and the threat this could pose to the rest of society if other married women decided to do the same. Flaubert won the case, citing that Emma had paid for her sin with her death and that he was therefore setting a moral example. Both Emma and Anna die horrible deaths as a result of their quest for passionate love. Married women who chose to betray their husband sexually in literature were being held to higher standards than real women, who now at least under the law stood a chance of marrying their lovers. 'Early Adultery fiction, mainly female-authored and by no means centred on the adultery of wives, is concerned above all with problems that arise from marriage as an institution constraining women's social and affective aspirations,' writes Bill Overton in his history of *Fictions of Female Adultery*, 'while nineteenth century adultery fiction, written almost exclusively by men, is concerned much more with the role of the wife and its potential for social disruption.'

The new Court for Divorce and Matrimonial Causes established by the Act of 1857 was seismic in the history of adultery, challenging the principle of the wife as sexual property of a man, for both could now sue for divorce in a public court. The double standard remained, however. A man could sue for divorce if he could prove his wife's adultery. By contrast a woman had to prove an additional crime such as desertion, incest, cruelty, bigamy or rape as well as adultery. 'It had ever been the feeling of that House,' said the Lord Chancellor, introducing the bill in the Lords, 'indeed it was a feeling common to mankind in general that, although the sin in both cases was the same, the effect of adultery on the part of the husband was very different from that of adultery on the part of the wife. It was possible for a wife to pardon a husband who had committed adultery; but it was hardly possible for a husband ever really to pardon the adultery of a wife.'[3]

Months of heated debate in the Houses of Parliament had taken place before the Act was passed, by just two votes, at the end of a long, hot summer. 'The principal object of the act was to reduce the amount of unregulated adultery, and by improving the legal position of wives, to shore up the family from the threats that surrounded it,' writes Lawrence Stone in *Road to Divorce*. Yet it was the legal sanction endorsing the importance of monogamy in wives which seemed particularly to matter. 'Much time was spent in debating reactionary old proposals, dating back to the late seventeenth century, to make adultery a criminal offence punishable by fine or imprisonment,' continues Lawrence, 'and to forbid the guilty wife in a divorce suit from marrying her lover.'

A wronged husband was still entitled to sue his wife's alleged seducer for damages, assessed by a jury and paid over to the judge, who would use his discretion to divide up the payment between maintenance for the wife, endowment for the children and legal costs and reparation for the husband.[4] The concept that a husband required compensation for the 'loss of his wife and for the injury to his feelings and the hurt to his family' continued well into the twentieth century. In April 1964, for example, Mr Edward Taylor agreed to pay £6250 in damages to his lover's husband and son. Opposition began to grow. The *Daily Telegraph* suggested in December 1968 that 'a provision as undignified and equivocal as that which places a price on a woman, as though she were a work of art or a consumer durable, should go'. And finally it did, with the Divorce Act of 1969.[5]

The double standard over how men and women could sue for divorce over adultery was only eliminated with the Matrimonial Causes Act of 1923. Changes to the law in 1937 extended the grounds for divorce for both sexes from just adultery alone to include cruelty, insanity and desertion. Even so, until the end of the Second World War, divorce was only available to those who could afford it. The majority of working people could get separation orders awarded by a magistrates' court but these prevented remarriage. Many resorted to creative solutions to marital unhappiness such as discreet adulterous relationships, or cohabiting with a woman who had changed her surname by deed poll to that of an already married man as his 'illegal wife'.[6]

As the Second World War came to an end, countless British soldiers returned home to find that their wives had changed or been unfaithful. For those serving overseas marital fidelity had been a source of anxiety, for letters revealed that their wives were now working for the war effort, earning money and enjoying leisure activities as independent women, going to jazz dances and the cinema. Soldiers, however, in both World Wars were allowed their fun with prostitutes and local girls to relieve them momentarily of the immense stress of fighting for their country. The worry was over the spread of venereal disease and not their moral conduct, and as soon as a reliable condom was developed in 1942 it was hastily dispatched to the front and to married soldiers. Troops were warned about the dangers of brothels and 'amateurs', but blame for the spread of venereal disease was laid firmly at the feet of the women they slept with.

Almost one third of all illegitimate children born in the last two years of the war were to married women. The percentage of illegitimate children born to married women in Birmingham, for example, tripled between 1940 and 1945. Illegitimacy was a sure sign of a woman's moral failure.[7] A woman needed her husband's consent to offer up their baby for adoption, so it was difficult to disguise the mishap. Some husbands returned and accepted the new baby as their own, but for others it was too much to bear and the divorce rate soared. The state even offered these men financial assistance to divorce, while poorer wives received no such help until legal aid was introduced in 1949.

The divorce system has always been predicated on the notion of marital fault. One of the couple has to be found guilty of breaking their contract to both innocent spouse and state. 'Someone has to behave impurely in order to uphold the Christian ideal of purity,' laments Lawyer Boom over an oyster lunch to his client in A. P. Herbert's *Holy Deadlock*, a satirical novel of 1934 attacking the contradictions and hypocrisy of divorce law at that time. 'Someone has to confess in public to a sinful breach of the marriage vows in order that the happily married may point at him or her and feel themselves secure and virtuous.'

A. P. Herbert was himself a lawyer as well as an independent MP who went on to achieve reform with a vigorous campaign for the Divorce Act of 1937, which established new grounds for divorce: desertion and cruelty for more than three years, and insanity. However, adultery continued to be the easiest 'crime' to prove or fabricate for a successful divorce, with 48 per cent citing it in 1950, 56 per cent in 1960 and 70 per cent in 1970.[8] The burden of proof was high and the legal requirement regarding adultery was that there must be evidence that sexual intercourse had taken place. An industry of private detection and false evidence mushroomed around the 'Brighton quickie'. Photographic evidence or witness statements from hotel managers (who often demanded a fee), waiters and chambermaids were required to prove adultery in order to dissolve a marriage. The important thing was that someone walked in with a breakfast tray and found you in bed together with a lover, even if you were fully clothed under your dressing gown, as Tony Last was in Evelyn Waugh's novel *A Handful of Dust*, published in 1934. His wife has been having an affair and wants a divorce, but it is Tony who behaves like a gentleman to preserve his wife's reputation.

A great many new acts of infidelity had to take place in order to achieve a legal separation. And a great many people perjured themselves in court, conspiring with each other to separate legally, making a mockery of the law. L. C. B. Gower, Professor of Commercial Law, estimated that over half of the cases which went undefended in the upper income brackets were based on falsified claims.[9] Many couples who wanted to part amicably had to come to an agreement as to who would take the rap as the villain in court so that they could go on to openly consort with another lover. 'The law regards physical fidelity as the vital element in the marriage bond. Thus without an act of adultery on one side or the other it is impossible to obtain a divorce,' continues Boom in *Holy Deadlock*. 'If you violently knock your wife about every night the ordinary person will conclude that you have not much affection for her; but the law requires you to prove it by sleeping with another woman.'

As the divorce rate began to rise after the Second World War, concern mounted during the late 1940s and the 1950s about the possible resultant collapse of the family and life as we know it. The Royal Commission on Marriage and Divorce was set up in 1951 as a response to pressure both within and outside parliament on the need to reform the 1937 Matrimonial Causes Act so that relationships could be ended once they 'broke down' rather than as a consequence of matrimonial offence. But the Commission had such a wide remit, embracing preparation for marriage, saving marriages as well as divorce, that it was hopelessly divided and recommended no change. Removing the idea of 'fault' from marital breakdown was too radical an idea, because it seemed to undermine the whole moral fabric of the nation. Individuals couldn't be trusted to behave responsibly. The siren temptress of adultery was always there just around the corner now that sexual morals were beginning to loosen.

Politicians and women's organisations such as the Married Women's Association and the Housewives' Association mounted searing attacks on the seemingly common practice of 'illegal wives' and the easing of access to divorce where a legal wife could be passed over without financial security. 'The fact is that a woman living with a man, who is not her husband, taking his name by deed poll, though his wife may be alive and her husband alive, is a threat not only to the moral structure of society but also, in many cases, to the well being of legitimate and illegitimate children,' maintained the Housewives' Association Chair, Mrs Gertrude Carrington Wood, 'and a cruel embarrassment of injustice to a spouse whose rights and true position are overthrown by an imposter.' Or rather, by another woman.

The concept of a woman suffering more as a result of her own infidelity lingered on too. Many divorcing wives in the

1960s feared they would lose their children if evidence of their own lover came to light, for the courts tended to remove children from the party guilty of breaking their marriage vows, irrespective of mitigating circumstances. A divorced woman was stigmatised and if she was a mother she was also a single mother and likely to be a poor one, once the need for maintenance was diluted by the 'clean break' Matrimonial and Family Proceedings Act of 1984. A divorced man, however, exuded the excitement of experience, and was likely to be richer after a divorce than his ex-wife, for there was little the law could do to force him to pay for the true costs of bringing up children. 'When a woman wants to leave a marriage because she is having an affair it is usually a disaster and I try to chain them to a chair,' a leading divorce lawyer told me. 'They feel they have to be the one to leave the children because they have been so bad. There is still this sense that there is something unnatural about a woman who has met someone that she wants to leave the marriage for and she is still severely punished for it, particularly by her children. Whereas with a man this is standard behaviour. In fact we get a lot of repeat business.'

Blame continues to influence divorce petitions today. The words '"no fault" divorce' may be bandied about but people still need to prove either adultery or 'unreasonable behaviour' if they want to divorce within two years, with one of the pair petitioning as the wounded plaintiff. The grounds for unreasonable behaviour can be pretty loose, such as devoting too much time to a career or having no common interests, which again makes a mockery of the law's attempts to sanction behaviour within our private relationships or pass judgement on whether or how we separate. Significantly, under the new civil partnership legislation, couples of the same sex cannot cite adultery if they want to divorce within two years, although all of the other reasons still apply. So the age-old notion of adultery being solely the province of a wife and vessel for the inheritance of genes lives on. Or perhaps there is an inbuilt stereotypical assumption that homosexual sex is so much more promiscuous that the partners aren't going to mind. It is also interesting that you 'cannot obtain a divorce due to adultery if you have lived for more than six months in total with your husband or wife after discovering the adulterous act', according to the separation and divorce self-help kit supplied by Lawpak, 'unless the adulterous relationship is continuing or there are other acts of adultery discovered'. The law continues to reinforce the notion that if infidelity is to sever a marriage it has to be immediate, whereas most couples need a substantial cooling-off period just to be able to assess what went wrong, let alone what they might want to do about it.

'I find sometimes that I have to shoehorn people into filing petitions for adultery,' another divorce lawyer told me. 'You have to work much harder to prove "unreasonable behaviour" because you then have to state what that was. That often upsets people and can be contested. But you don't even have to name the third party now to file for adultery and no judge is really interested in why a marriage has broken down. What we ought to have is "irreconcilable differences" for under two years instead.' Another family lawyer agrees that it is time to widen the reasons for divorce into something so all-embracing that the notion of 'fault' lying with one of the pair disappears for good. 'The worst acrimony in cases tends to come when there has been an affair. It's just so toxic as they try to come to terms with what has happened and women want all the gory details to come out; they often want a man's betrayal to be borne witness to. They want others to know what their husbands have done.'

For me, as a practising family mediator helping separating couples to split their assets and make arrangements for the children, the idea of 'fault' and reparation is always all too apparent in the room. It never feels fair to the person who has been left to have to split their assets, lose their home as well as the future they had imagined they would have when they never chose any of this. 'Why doesn't he have to pay more when he is the one who left? Why do I have to lose day-to-day contact with my children and pay her anything at all when she chose to break up the marriage by having an affair?' For Marianne, who has always been the main breadwinner throughout their twenty-year marriage while her husband earned very little as an artist, coping with the financial aftermath when he left her for another woman felt particularly unjust. 'The law was surely meant to protect women who have given up everything to stay home with the children and have literally nothing. But that isn't the way it was for us. He could have helped me out and earned more money when the children were small but he didn't. And he wasn't even there for the children all day long, like I would have been had I been at home, because we had a nanny. Now I am the one who has to hand over half of everything we have to him.'

As women began to enjoy greater equality with men the sexual double standard shifted to one of differences in male and female desire. There has been greater advancement in the social, legal and economic status of women in the past one hundred years than in any other century of our history. Women gained the vote, the right to an education and to work in all of the same fields as men, earning their own money, and enjoying sexual pleasure outside marriage thanks to safer contraception and legalised abortion. With women increasingly seen as equals, marital relationships changed slowly to more mutual, companionate partnerships. So the arguments used to defend the sexual double standard and a man's right to stray changed too, as men began to lose complete power over their wives. Once a woman was just as capable of enjoying extramarital dalliances, and ending a marriage because her husband was 'playing away', absolute fidelity in both sexes became paramount to seal commitment.

When women gained the legal right to divorce under the 1857 Matrimonial Causes Act, a man could no longer think of a wife as entirely his to abuse or neglect. Greater emphasis began to be placed on marriage as a 'contract for the development of mutual comfort and domestic happiness', according to Lawrence Stone in *Road to Divorce*, and adultery was no longer just a question of trespass and a threat to the line of inheritance. There were now more interior differences between a man and a woman which meant that a man could still have his mistresses. 'The double standard now rested on a theory about a fundamental difference between male and female sexual psychology,' continues Stone. 'A man commits adultery as an act of pure sensuality, for instantaneous physical gratification; a woman commits adultery only as a by-product of a deep emotional commitment.' This argument, that a man can compartmentalise his emotions, that if he has sex with another woman it is just sex and therefore meaningless, whereas for a woman any sexual encounter has to be linked to love, is still very much with us today.

That a woman has sexual desires has never been in dispute. 'Ever since the dawn of western civilisation it has always been presumed that women were the more lustful sex,' writes historian Faramerz Dabhoiwala in his book *The Origins of Sex*. 'Though lust was a universal temptation, females were mentally, morally and bodily weaker than males – less rational, less able to control their passions, less capable of self discipline.' It was after all Eve who tempted Adam in the Garden of Eden. 'Throughout the Middle Ages women had been considered the lusty sex, more prey to their passions than men,' concurs historian Stephanie Coontz in *Marriage, A History*. 'The older view that women had to be controlled because they were inherently more passionate and prone to moral and sexual error was replaced by the idea that women were asexual beings, who would not respond to sexual overtures unless they had been drugged or depraved from an early age.'

With rising discussion of the rights of women, romanticism and greater value being placed on the welfare of the child within the family during the nineteenth century, a new mythology around the weaker sexual desires of women began to take hold culturally, reinforcing patriarchy and the sexual double standard. Sexuality resided entirely now in the male penis. An article in the *Westminster Review* in 1850 remarked that, save in the case of fallen women, sexual desire in women was dormant, 'always till excited by undue familiarities; almost always till excited by actual intercourse'.[10] During parliamentary debates on the 1857 Divorce Bill, Gladstone maintained that there were two very different motives for adultery between a man and a woman. 'I believe that a very limited proportion of the offences committed by women are due to the mere influence of sensual passion. On the other side, I believe that a very large proportion of the offences committed by men are due to that influence.'[11]

'Good' mothers and women were naturally chaste and pure. A woman was morally superior to a man and kept him in check. 'The best mothers, wives and managers of households know little or nothing of sexual indulgences. Love of home, children and domestic duties are the only passions they feel,' wrote the gynaecologist William Acton in 1857 in *The Function and Disorders of the Reproductive Organs*. 'As a general rule, a modest woman seldom desires any sexual gratification for herself. She submits to her husband, but only to please him.'

To keep the better class of woman free from too much sexual invasion, or too many pregnancies (although not sadly from the transmission of venereal diseases), a husband was doing his wife a positive favour by taking his sexual needs elsewhere, to the legions of servants and 'fallen' women among the lower orders. There were large numbers of unmarried women in England in the latter half of the nineteenth century. Factory work or life in service was hard; prostitution was much more profitable. Large numbers of prostitutes – approximately fifty-five thousand in 1841, or one for every twelve adult males – worked London's streets, bars and theatres.[12] Prostitutes were not just inevitable but considered by many to be beneficial, a necessary evil as a buttress for the morals of the rest of society. 'On that one degraded and ignoble form are concentrated the passions that might have filled the world with shame,' noted W. E. H. Lecky in his *History of European Morals*, published in 1913.[13] The sexual double standard applied even to these women too. 'We may at once dispose of any recommendation founded on the principle of putting both parties to the sin of fornication on the same footing by the obvious but not less conclusive reply that there is no comparison to be made between prostitutes and the men who consort with them,' stated the *Report of the Royal Commission upon the Administration and Operation of the Contagious Diseases Act* in 1871. 'With the one sex the offence is committed as a matter of gain: with the other it is an irregular indulgence of a natural impulse.'[14]

A whole class had to be described as depraved to justify Victorian sensibilities, with the new ethos of purity not necessarily extended to working-class women. 'The respectable family man who at home was a paragon of sexual propriety might also keep his lower class mistress or frequent the flagellants brothel,' writes Steven Marcus in *The Other Victorians*. 'The masses were not necessarily expected to subscribe to the same sexual morality as the proper bourgeoisie, or the raffish aristocracy.' Prejudice and wild exaggerations masquerading as sociological fact were exploited to suggest that most factory girls were unchaste. Friedrich Engels, in his 1844 survey *The Condition of the Working Class in England*, deplored the 'unbridled sexual intercourse' of industrial workers. William Acton, the great Victorian authority on the subject of prostitution, concluded at a popular London dance hall that a third of the girls there must be whores simply from their appearance. By the second edition of his work *Prostitution* in 1870 he was certain that they were 'of course all prostitutes'.[15]

Sigmund Freud, the founder of psychoanalysis, vigorously endorsed the fashionable Victorian notion that civilised men commonly needed sexual release with women whom they despised of a lower social order, for they were unable to fuse the separate threads of love and desire with the same person because visceral reminders of childhood triggered fears of incest. 'Where they love they do not desire and where they desire they cannot love,' he writes in his essay 'On the Universal Tendency to Debasement in the Sphere of Love'. They 'seek objects which do not lead to love in order to keep their sensuality away from objects they love', he adds, endorsing the view that men are simply unable to find complete sexual satisfaction within marriage. With women such an incestuous association was, Freud maintained, more likely to take the form of frigidity. He also desexualised women with his theories of penis envy and the need for a healthy woman to transfer the seat of her sexual satisfaction from her clitoris to her vagina, because of course all she really wants to do is have babies. By giving up the clitoris, she gives up sexual pleasure for motherhood.

When it comes to sexual desire there are plenty of reasons, historically, why a woman might have been reluctant to express her libido. With little in the way of contraception, fears of unwanted pregnancy were very real. Childbirth could kill or leave a woman physically undermined, lacerated, with gynaecological problems or exhausted through anaemia. Life was hard for many working mothers and sex was the last thing that many wanted at the end of a long day, just as it is for many working mothers today. The taboos on sex before marriage remained powerful for women up until the 1950s. Parents issued dire warnings, particularly to their daughters, and most sex education books prescribed abstinence and chastity for the unmarried. Sexual ignorance was common. Sex was forbidden fruit and few men and women had the chance to experiment and explore the full range of premarital sexual pleasures in the way that young people expect to do today.

All that began to change in the late 1960s with the arrival of the Pill, the boom years of the Beatles, the miniskirt and a new sense of sexual empowerment for women. Jenny Diski describes in her book on the 1960s how a girl in the school where she taught was not prepared to stick her fingers into her vagina to remove a tampon because she considered that part of her anatomy to be dirty. But with pioneering books such as *Our Bodies, Our Selves* from the Boston Women's Health Collective, where women were encouraged to get to know themselves a little better, sexual emancipation as a woman's right slowly began to spread. A new culture emerged in which a woman's right to an orgasm became paramount and a man no longer just had to please himself. Moreover a woman could, science asserted now, be 'multi-orgasmic' and therefore potentially insatiable, denting the fragility of male sexual competence still further. And a woman did not necessarily need a man to have a good time at all. 'At the very moment the pill made intercourse safe for the unprotected penis, intercourse was deemed irrelevant,' writes James Petersen in *The Century of Sex*. 'On the other hand a woman could ride an erection, a tongue or a vibrator all night.'

The idea of a woman 'finding' herself through sexual infidelities took hold in a plethora of popular fiction such as *Diary of a Mad Housewife* by Sue Kaufman and *Fear of Flying* by Erica Jong in the 1970s, little more than a decade after D. H. Lawrence's *Lady Chatterley's Lover* was thought sufficiently corrupting in its portrayal of female sexual passion to be put on trial for obscenity. In cinema, too, attitudes towards infidelity began to reflect the times. Laura, in *Brief Encounter* (1945), finds it hard to countenance consummating her passion for Alex James, a married local doctor, and returns to suburbia and her marriage even though she is unhappy. Just a few years later, in the swinging sixties, the adulteress is glamorised in *Dr Zhivago* and *The Graduate*, before the ugly reality of the 'bunny boiler' came vividly to life in *Fatal Attraction* in 1987. Now, should a happily married man stray for just one weekend of recreational sex, he is likely to find that brief indulgence will come back and haunt him, wreaking havoc with his family life.

Women began to be able to 'exercise a hitherto unknown degree of control over their reproductive capacities', Claire Langhamer writes in 'Adultery in Post-War England'. 'Whilst the married woman, unlike her single sister, was constructed as a legitimately sexual individual, fears that her sexuality might not be containable within marriage coincided with her increasing participation in paid employment and movement beyond her immediate domestic sphere.' So the landscape shifted again to suit men's needs. Sex appeal replaced sexual submission as a woman's primary responsibility to her man as the miniskirt and the new pornography objectified women sexually in *Playboy*. A good wife now had to continually excite her husband to stop him from straying and every woman had the right to enjoy heterosexual pleasures, the way a man liked them. As unmarried sex became increasingly acceptable, men could enjoy a feast of activity for free and the numbers of prostitutes fell sharply. The agony aunt Virginia Ironside remembers the 1960s as 'An endless round of miserable promiscuity when often it seemed easier and believe it or not politer to sleep with a man than to chuck him out of your flat.'[16]

New ideas about free love began to pervade the relationship ethos, benefiting men once again if they could twist the argument to their advantage and still stay married as the boundaries of commitment were stretched to accommodate infidelity. 'You couldn't own someone or get everything you needed from one person, so you were entitled to seek it elsewhere,' a female publisher now in her seventies told me. 'Monogamy or the idea of faithfulness was backward and not progressive enough and it didn't matter if people got hurt in the process because responsibility or consideration was not part of that ethos. Jealousy was ownership.'

Pat married her second husband in the early 1970s. When she found photographs of him engaging in threesomes, she challenged him and then promised to think about joining in foursomes to keep him loyal and happy. 'There was a lot of swapping going on in those days. We would meet people in country pubs and I would either say I didn't fancy the other man or they would come back and nothing would happen because if it was your house it was your prerogative to decide whether or not you had sex. He tried to trick me into it once by arranging a supper date and then all these duvets came down and were arranged on the floor, so I walked out of the room. We were also very close to another couple and the wife was keen to stop her husband from wandering, so we had four-somes with them for quite a while. My husband liked the exhibitionism but I always found it quite peculiar.'

Absolute fidelity in both sexes began to emerge as the most important symbol of commitment in this new age of promis-cuity. As a more companionate togetherness slowly became the all-embracing ethos of a loving, lasting relationship through the twentieth century, relationships became more exclusive. As couples began to share more, as lovers, companions and con-fidants, 'Emotionally and in every other way, the prospect of sharing any of the aspects of this with others outside the marriage became more difficult and threatening,' write psy-chologists Martin Richards and Jane Elliott in their essay 'Sex and Marriage in the 1960s and 1970s'.[17] 'There is the added threat that an extramarital relationship might also be a com-panionate one.'

Sexual incompatibility could now make or break a marriage and with the rise of a more overt sexualised culture expec-tations of fulfilment rose, as did rates of perceived sexual malfunction. The likelihood of forging an extramarital bond with a social equal rose too as men and women began to mingle more at work or socially. Having a child became an even bigger crisis point for an affair because children and family life intruded so much more on new expectations of loving togetherness. And as premarital sex became the norm for women as well as men, the fashion for big weddings grew as a very public way of marking off the monogamy of marriage. We also became less accepting of the idea that with time a sexual relationship often turns into a domestic friendship. 'Marriage became increasingly based on love but there was little expectation prior to 1960 that it would (or should) last throughout marriage,' write Richard and Kris Bulcroft in their paper 'The Management and Production of Risk in Romantic Relationships'. 'In previous eras, individuals could rely on extended family relationships and same sex friendships as a hedge against loneliness. In late modern society, such alternatives are more limited. The implication of not being in a long-term romantic relationship is loneliness . . . ' Marriage, or a committed relationship, matters more as a means of meeting all of our emotional needs. Infidelity is consequently far more threatening, for both sexes.

It is hard to assess whether more people were in fact being unfaithful than they used to be as the twentieth century progressed. However, public perception was that sexual betrayal had to be growing as the divorce rate and those citing adultery (the easiest way to end a bad marriage) rose. Social disapproval of infidelity therefore began to grow as a way of keeping two people true to each other – social checks and balances perhaps to protect the sanctity of marriage and the family unit. 'There is some evidence to suggest that infidelity (particularly on the part of the husband) was more likely to be tolerated and seen as less of a threat to marriage in the 1950s and early 1960s than in the 1970s,' continue Martin Richards and Jane Elliott.[18] In 1949 a Mass Observation survey in Britain found that extramarital relationships were acknowledged by one man in four and one woman in five but that the majority seemed surprisingly tolerant of that fact. Social historians such as John Gillis and Joanna Klein believe that factors other than sexual fidelity mattered more to the health and welfare of a marriage – such as good housekeeping or managing to earn a living in the earlier half of the twentieth century.

Geoffrey Gorer conducted two large-scale studies of attitudes in the under-forty-fives in England. The first study, *Exploring English Character*, was published in 1955. The second, *Sex and Marriage in England Today*, which asked many of the same questions, appeared in 1971. In the 1950s Gorer found that infidelity was rarely perceived as being the worst crime that a spouse could commit and that only a minority believed it should automatically end a marriage. If it happened both men and women emphasised that discussion about what went wrong as well as self-examination was important and the subject warranted only one chapter. By the late 1960s, however, Gorer found in his cohort of two thousand men and women that 'comradeship and doing things together' was now considered to be the most important ingredient for a happy marriage whereas it had been lower down the list in the previous survey. He also found that sexual fidelity was much more central to the idea of marital happiness. Two chapters were now necessary: 'Fidelity and Casual Adultery' and 'Serious Adultery, Separation and Divorce'. The idea that the betrayed spouse should look into their own heart to see how they might have contributed to their own betrayal was also no longer a popular strategy.[19]

Studies of letters in women's magazines also reflect a hardening of attitudes towards infidelity. Claire Langhamer found plenty of evidence of adultery in *Woman's Own*. 'The adultery stories presented on just one problem page in August 1955 provide examples of: a woman in love with her brother-in-law and pregnant by him; a wife who wanted to adopt the child which her husband had fathered through an affair; a woman who suspected her brother-in-law of having an affair; a wife who suspected her husband; and an eighteen-year-old conducting an affair with a forty-five-year-old married man.' This was a pretty average week at that time and yet it was deeply reminiscent of many of the stories that Verity the infidelity detective told me in a small hotel bar in 2011. The advice in the 1950s, as Gorer also found, was to talk about it, perhaps in conjunction with the new marriage guidance experts. Women were likely to be advised by Mary Grant in *Woman's Own* not to confront a husband's infidelity, for this was just 'an infatuation which would pass with time'. By the mid-1960s, the idea of minimising the effects of affairs on married life was in decline. Some women were even advised to leave if their husbands would not end the affair, for they now had the power to do so.

From the 1970s onwards sexualised imagery and pornography began to percolate through culture and the state's hold over our private lives and public morality loosened. The large-scale prosecutions for pornography in literature were now history and different social checks and balances emerged, with new codes around sexual behaviour. When men were entirely dominant at work, the boss having 'a thing' with a secretary or a subordinate was accepted as normal. Once women and men began to mix more equally across all levels in a wider range of occupations, a more sanctimonious policing of office affairs developed. Sexual relationships at work are now considered to be a major disruption and some companies have policies requiring people found having an affair to leave.

New codes of conduct developed around sexual harassment, suggestive comments and unwelcome flirting in any mixed-sex or public place. Sex had to be negotiated and there emerged a new awareness of the definition of rape as any non-consensual intercourse both within and outside marriage. These new codes established firmer boundaries around sexual contact and the old romantic notion of seduction and untamed passions, full of fraught potential, risk and the unexpected, needed to be replaced with clearer communication, perhaps making the thrilling transgression of an infidelity all the more exciting.

Paradoxically, the safer some of us feel, the greater the temptation to rock the boat. Just beyond those walls of marital certainty there is always the drama of a grander passion, the illicit thrill of a secret sexual dare that could destroy everything. 'Sex is allied with death,' writes Erica Jong in her introduction to a collection of women writing about sex, *Sugar in My Bowl*. 'Danger is part of the excitement. That may be why adultery still flourishes and why we are titillated by news of others' adulteries. Risky behaviour is thrilling. Walking the tightrope of desire is more spine tingling when the tightrope is stretched over a chasm.'

An entire relationship or marriage is seen now as being flawed if an affair comes to light, rather than inappropriate behaviour by one partner. Several surveys in western Europe have shown that we are less tolerant of extramarital sex. American disapproval of affairs as 'always wrong' increased from 70 per cent in 1973 to 82 per cent in 2004. Americans were also found to be more approving of polygamy and human cloning than they were of adultery in a Gallup poll.[20] Survey evidence in Finland has found infidelity to be less accepted in the 1990s and 2000s than it was in 1971.[21] British disapproval of infidelity as 'always wrong' has stayed remarkably high at 85 per cent in the surveys conducted by British Social Attitudes since it began in 1983. We just don't like it. And the young dislike it even more, partly because of their parents' behaviour, a subject which will be explored in Chapter 8.

Sexual betrayal has become the number-one crime in a relationship and there are usually no second chances. Prohibition does not prevent people from finding others attractive; it merely makes it harder to talk about that fact. With the new ethos where all should be confided in a healthy, loving relationship, another contradictory tension emerges, for we have to become more skilled at hiding any extramarital flirtation. An act of infidelity undermines our understanding of what love should be more than it ever used to, if we are to be each other's everything. The sense of being betrayed is greater, for we were not loved enough by our partners for them to say 'no'; as is the guilt and shame for the one who has transgressed. If our understanding is that affairs are always wrong, it is much harder for us to be tolerant of human frailty and accept that it often takes three people to provoke an infidelity. Ultimatums, threats and acts of revenge are the sole weapons of those who feel powerless or threatened. The new sanctimony surrounding infidelity makes these weapons all the more prevalent and powerful, as we intensify our attempts to preserve the monogamous ideal.

Historically, such a high level of institutionalised infidelity among men could only operate for thousands of years in Europe when men were omnipotent and women were worth less. Today, thankfully, that power balance has shifted. It is a sense of power and entitlement which often opens the door to illicit sex and a distinct pattern of inequality between the 'haves' and 'have nots' is still apparent. Those higher up the social scale have less to lose should they be discovered. In Britain one in sixteen men in social classes 1 and 2 reports having two or more concurrent sexual partners in the past year, compared with just one in forty men in social classes 4 and 5.[22] It is interesting that Gorer also found in his second survey of sexual attitudes that people lower down the social scale tended to be more rigid and unforgiving of any infidelity. A large survey of mate poaching in fifty-three nations found that men and women from higher socio-economic backgrounds in cultural regions with greater resources tend to engage in extramarital activity more, while in 'resource poor environments, it appears that humans pursue more long-term, monogamous mating strategies'.[23] People who enjoy success in other areas of their lives are more likely to believe that they can get away with infidelity. They can buy immunity with their privilege. The better educated are also more likely to be able to afford an affair, with perks and expense accounts to disguise their activities as well as greater opportunities for travel.

The sexual double standard is still alive and kicking. The most privileged sections of society still tend to be male, and there money attracts opportunities for sex like a magnet. 'A search for power often coincides with the search for sex,' writes Emily Brown in her textbook on infidelity for marital therapists *Patterns of Infidelity and Their Treatment*. 'Common arenas for seeking power are politics, law, entertainment and religion.' We don't have to think very hard for well-known examples in all of these categories. 'From what I hear on the couch, it seems that some professions are more prone to it than others, the Law, for instance,' says couples counsellor Liza Glenn. 'Obviously for those who have to travel the loneliness of the hotel room at the other end of the world plays a part, but alcohol does too. There's the drink after work and then ... People lose control.'

Those lower down the power scale have less income, education and occupational status. The risk of divorce and losing everything is high when people depend so much more upon each other in a familial way, particularly mothers at home full time with their children. Those lower down the social scale are less able to buy in support if their relationship has broken down because of an affair, whereas a wealthier woman abandoned by her husband has better prospects when it comes to getting out, rebuilding her life and finding a new partner. The richer infidel may risk losing a great deal financially and emotionally but he or she has more to begin with and dabbling with danger feels like a less threatening risk. Women tend to be more afraid of the repercussions of discovery, whether that is guilt about their spouse's hurt, or fear of a violent reaction or being slung out of the house. She is less safe than a man because she stands to lose more, for when a woman reveals an infidelity her marriage is more likely to end than a man's.[24]

Unsurprisingly, infidelity by women is rare in countries such as Iran, Somalia and Saudi Arabia, where they can be stoned to death for it. Honour killings are often connected to accusations of adultery and continue to be legal in many other countries, including Argentina, Ecuador, Jordan and Syria. The double standard by which only a woman can be prosecuted for adultery still exists in India and the Philippines. In some Muslim countries, such as Saudi Arabia and Pakistan, adultery is a crime under the Hudood Ordinance, which requires a woman making an accusation of rape to provide strong evidence from no fewer than four witnesses in order to avoid being charged with adultery herself. Well into the 1970s judges in France and the US states of Texas, New Mexico and Utah viewed crimes of passion, where a man killed his unfaithful wife, as a temporary insanity deserving of far greater leniency than murder. All over the world the mere suspicion that a woman is interested in a man other than her husband provokes countless acts of domestic violence which never get reported, tyrannising women and compromising their freedom. 'Women caught having an affair, in contrast to men,' concludes the psychologist David Buss in his book *The Dangerous Passion*, 'suffer a greater risk of physical abuse, more severe damage to their reputations, a higher risk of being shunned by family and friends, a greater loss in self-esteem, and a higher vulnerability to abandonment.' No wonder then that their rates of sexual straying are lower.

However, in societies where women have greater parity with men, where the penalties for infidelity are not greater for women and where they have access to political power and economic resources, the rates of female sexual straying rise, implying that the differing rates between the sexes have a lot less to do with the presence of testosterone and the male 'need' to spread their seed as widely as possible than the evolutionary psychologists suggest. A large study of 'poaching' other people's partners in fifty-three nations found that men are more likely to have poached or succumbed to being poached than women in all of the countries surveyed. However the survey also found evidence that in more egalitarian societies female rates rose.[25] 'Overall, the influence of culture on human mate poaching appears to be profound. Although proportionally more men than women seek short-term mate poaching across all regions,' concludes David P. Schmitt, the author of the survey, 'this effect is tempered by cultural factors. When in resource-rich environments – both men and women tend to engage in more short-term mate poaching.'

A man is still more likely to divorce his wife after the discovery of her infidelity than she is after the discovery of his. A
woman is still more likely to blame herself and be blamed for
her husband's affair, for not being kind or sensitive enough to
his needs, for not having enough sex or working hard enough
to keep him loyal. But if she strays it's all her fault too. A
woman is still likely to lose more financially than her husband
through divorce, whoever has strayed, so it is hardly surprising
that she should be more forgiving of his extramarital affairs
than he is of hers and that she should be better at concealing
her own dalliances until she is absolutely sure she wants to
leave. Pat felt she had no choice but to put up with years of
compulsive philandering from her husband. 'What could I do
with two small children when I knew he had already gone
through a very acrimonious divorce with his first wife? There
were constant fights with her over money and he was incredibly mean to her so I took a cold-blooded decision and decided
to hang on in there.'

In men, sexual straying is regularly excused as just 'how
men are'. They help themselves because they cannot help
themselves, feeling their behaviour is justified by socially
semi-accepted notions of male sexual entitlement: 'She has
broken the marriage contract by not wanting as much sex as
I do,' or: 'Sex isn't the same with a woman once she becomes
a mother.' Men *need* sexual diversity and novelty as a natural
consequence of all that testosterone but that doesn't mean,
the notion goes, that they can't also love their wives, or that
they want to leave. Women, on the other hand, always want
relationship. Not just to get their rocks off with some stranger.
When a woman has an affair the assumption is that she must
be deeply unhappy in her marriage. Why else would she risk
everything?

A man would, according to comedian Lenny Bruce, screw mud if he was on a desert island, while 'A girl doesn't understand this: "you'd do it to mud – you don't love me" – sex is a different emotion for women.' A woman who has similar urges, or one who merely wants more sex than a man, is called a nymphomaniac. No such term for a man exists. When it's a woman who strays, the reaction is often vitriolic. A mother of three children only has to express the escapist thought that she is feeling attracted to another man on a thread on Mumsnet for a torrent of righteous indignation to tumble down, isolating her as evil. 'I expected a certain amount of hostility,' the American author Julie Powell told me in an email exchange after the publication of her memoir of infidelity, *Cleaving*, 'but I was surprised by the vehemence of the response. Women mostly stuck with "selfish bitch" and chastised me for "defiling the sanctity of marriage", but men called me a whore, a cunt, they wanted me to die. One guy told me to "go fuck a knife". People seemed to take it very personally, as if I was threatening *their* marriage with *my* infidelity, as if adultery were a contagious and invariably fatal disease. It wasn't just that people were offended by what I had done, it was that I had written about it, that I had dared to describe what infidelity is like, how it happens and how, in the moment, it can feel wonderful. It scared them, like publishing a book on how to build an atomic bomb out of common household objects.'

The popularity of evolutionary psychology and Mars/Venus theories about the gendered differences between men and women feels like a last-gasp attempt to preserve male sexual privileges. Evolutionary psychology roots human behaviour in our Neanderthal, animal past. Women have lower sex drives than men because, it is argued, of the reproductive imperative.

Women risk more with any sexual encounter and therefore they are more picky. They need protection from men as they bring up their children and are therefore much more jealous of any emotional rather than sexual infidelity in their partners. Men, on the other hand, cannot be entirely certain that their progeny is theirs, so they guard women with a higher reproductive value more intensely, they inseminate more sperm after a separation from their wives in which a possible infidelity could have occurred, but they also have an inbuilt biological need to spread their seed widely to preserve their own genetic inheritance and propagate the species. 'Almost all studies have shown that the sexes are equally jealous,' writes David Buss in his 1995 paper 'Evolutionary Psychology: A New Paradigm for Psychological Science', 'but evolutionary psychologists have long predicted that the sexes will differ in the event that activates jealousy. Specifically because fertilization and gestation occur internally within women and not men, men over evolutionary history have faced an adaptive problem simply not faced by women – less than 100% certainty of parenthood ... the female's certainty of genetic parenthood is not compromised if the male has sex with other females.'

Any argument which roots our behaviour in the purely biological is attractive. Evolutionary psychology speaks to us in the broadest human terms. It turns the individual and specific into generalised and highly gendered stereotypes of male and female. It reduces people to their reproductive drives and ignores the effects of culture or disparities of power. Hormones clearly play a very important role in determining our sexual desires and our behaviour as men and women. But that is only part of the story, for we are much more complicated than the sum total of our biology. We do not have sex just to reproduce;

we usually try to avoid that outcome. 'If we take the socio-biological argument to its logical conclusion, this would suggest that those with the best genes – the ones of most value to the human race – are the Don Juans of this world – those who are most irresponsible, selfish and unable to make decent human relationships,' writes marital psychologist Warren Coleman. 'The socio-biological argument is able to tell us nothing about the reason why Don Giovanni is eventually pulled down into hell.'[26]

As the numbers of women 'cheating' appear to rise, elements of the media persist in looking for Venus and Mars causes such as higher levels of oestrogen, apparently discovered by a University of Texas study, or a variant of the DRD4 gene which increases sexual risk-taking. Surely, though, it is more likely that women dabble in extramarital sex for all of the same reasons as men and that their numbers are likely to increase once they have the means to do so. Recent bestselling books such as *Sex at Dawn: The Prehistoric Origins of Modern Sexuality* by Christopher Ryan and Cacilda Jethá and *The Monogamy Gap: Men, Love and the Reality of Cheating* by Eric Anderson justify male infidelity as normal and acceptable, ignoring the profound weight of the sexual double standard throughout history which still rests on our shoulders, where any sexual activity by a woman either before or during marriage was heavily controlled by men and sanctioned by the state. 'We didn't descend from apes. We *are* apes,' write Ryan and Jethá. 'Like bonobos and chimps we are the randy descendants of hypersexual ancestors.' Sexual variety is everything and essential. 'Despite the love, history and intimacy that men share with their partners after 6 months or sometimes 2 years of being together, they begin to strongly desire sex with someone else,' writes Anderson. 'Frustration towards one's partner

grows because men (even if subconsciously) view their partners as stopping them from having the sex they desire ... this
is akin to asking a gay man to remain in the closet: the emotional consequences are devastating.' Really?

It is always easier, and safer, to retreat behind the gendered
stereotypes around reproduction than it is to construct something new within the unique alchemy that two people create
when they form a relationship. Women and men are of course
different and we like to accentuate that, perhaps to enhance
erotic appeal. At the end of *Adam's Rib*, a wonderful film about
the sexual double standard, Spencer Tracy says, 'Vive la
différence' to his wife and fellow lawyer Katharine Hepburn
as he draws the curtain around their bed. Some sexual drive is
inevitably rooted in the animal instinct but we are human beings
too, with a conscience, rights and responsibilities towards each
other, and we need much more from a mate than just a parent
to bring up our children. Relationship is far more important to
us than just a vessel for the survival of our genetic code and
infidelity threatens any loving relationship and our sense of
security within it. There is so much more that unites us as
human beings than ever divides us through our gender.

However, the weight of historical double standards around
sex and infidelity is so immense – as I hope this chapter has
shown – that we can all be a little forgiving of ourselves and
each other when we conform to stereotype, for concepts of
gender penetrate far deeper than we ever really recognise.
'Gender is a prism through which all of our lives are lived,'
writes Susie Orbach. 'It is ever present and yet taken for
granted. It affects the language we use, the way we move, our
conception of relationship, even the emotional states to which
we have access.'[27] When we allow those stereotypes to domi-
nate our love lives, we run the risk of failing to see the real

person beneath and losing them to another as a result. A remarkable revolution has taken place in the new egalitarian way that we expect to conduct our relationships. Inevitably, as with all revolutions, there are problems in adapting. As state sanction and control over how we conduct our private lives falls away, it is up to us to take the reins and drive loving partnerships towards the commitment that so many of us need, armed with greater knowledge about each other and a more holistic understanding of the life course of a long relationship. It is this honesty and parity, not gendered pre-sumption, which lays foundations solid enough to limit the likelihood of betrayal.

# 4

# SEXUAL DESIRE

There has never been such a stark contrast between the fantasy sex we are told we could be having and the reality of what most of us are getting. It's a truism that once a relationship becomes familiar and predictable, sexual desire wanes. The first passionate throes of eroticism cannot help but change into a very different kind of sex within a long, loving relationship, and many find this equally or even more nourishing. However, the particularly narrow interpretation of the erotic offered to us as a constant stream of romanticised sexual fantasy by advertising, films, magazines and pornography highlights all-consuming lust as the only sex worth having. 'Good' sex is always presented as a passionate, athletic and orgasmic encounter between two perfect, youthful specimens. Most of us cannot ever hope to match their performances within the stability and familiarity of a long relationship. So the lure of forbidden fruit grows.

The 1949 Mass Observation survey mentioned earlier found that only one third of people believed that sex was crucial to a relationship. Then, during the second half of the twentieth century, regular and enjoyable sex gradually became the lifeblood of marital stability. Nowadays we rarely question the fact that the natural opiate of orgasm unlocks repression, flooding the body with health and good feelings. Orgasm is nature's free drug, an entirely healthy way of soothing away all of our anxieties and the dim reality of life. When we have 'bad', unfulfilling sex or no sex at all for a while, we are some- how incomplete, and being failed. This is not the sex we were led to believe was essential, the sex that other people must be having, the sex we see constantly portrayed as earth-shatteringly ecstatic.

A multi-billion-pound range of industries including premium- rate phone lines, lap-dancing clubs and illicit dating agencies for the married has stepped into the widening gap between our heightened expectations of sex and the reality. Any infidelity, from the frisson of a text flirtation to a full-on sexual affair, also has more of a purchase on our imaginations as the solu- tion when things get tough or, increasingly, just because it's there, with little other than our own inner restraint in the way to stop us.

The most important defining feature of couple life now is sex, even when there is no sex. With the rise of the 'science' of sexology through the twentieth century, spawning a clutch of new sex surveys and the sex labs of Masters and Johnson, people had new norms of sexual behaviour against which they could compare their own sex life. Widespread assumptions about frequency of sex and number of sexual partners could be made, backed up by 'data'. A new definition and awareness of 'healthy' sexual activity emerged that made many people feel inadequate. US psychologists now accept the definition of a sexless marriage as one in which a couple has sex less than ten times a year, according to Kathleen Deveny in her article 'No Sex Please, We're Married',[1] and that describes nearly one fifth of all American couples, according to the National Health and Social Life Survey.[2] But surely the true definition of a sexless marriage is one in which there is no sex at all.

'Good' sex has become one of the most important and openly discussed indicators of a successful relationship, yet paradoxically many, if not most, people do not manage to find the courage or the words to talk about what sex might mean for them as individuals, even in their most intimate moments. Obviously the only sex we know is the sex we have experienced. We know that the sex we see others enjoying on the screen, for example, isn't real, but it's almost impossible not to imagine the seductive possibility of stronger orgasms and a more colourful sexual palette with someone else. This is especially true as soon as couples slide into a familiar, and probably less frequent, pattern of sex.

Thousands of sexual self-help books, magazines and websites emphasise performance, techniques, novelty, spontaneity and incredible orgasms as the key to 'great' sex, and offer instant solutions to problems we never knew we had. The implication is that you are almost entitled to seek greater pleasure elsewhere – if things aren't working for you and alternatives are easy to find. In the past, if you wanted to pay for sex you had to look for coded messages in the lonely hearts columns. Now you can book a prostitute online as easily as a flight, and read reviews, complete with starred ratings of their sexual performance, as if you were checking out a hotel on TripAdvisor. You only have to scroll down a blog offering you support after you've discovered your partner has been unfaithful to find an advert for one of the many 'have a discreet affair' websites, which plant the idea that you too can have one as a means of revenge.

'There's a lot of money to be made out of sex,' says David Williams of lovinglinks.com, who admits that he regularly uses sex surveys to sign up clients. 'I have one coming out next week on what constitutes cheating and last month we did a survey from the ministry of the bleeding obvious – do you have more sex before or after marriage? The survey companies make money out of it and present you with a list of suggested survey topics together with sample press headlines and then the results get picked up by online media, which leads to Google hits and then you get the clients. Or take those ridiculous phone-sex ads on late-night TV with three girls in their undies rolling around laughing on a bed for £2.50 a minute. These girls just don't exist.' He adds, 'I have friends who work those lines. One is a lovely woman in her sixties who is eighteen stone, with a cut-glass voice, who has a great time winding these guys up because it's all total bloody fantasy.'

The messages of sexual entitlement are so constant and pervasive that fidelity struggles to compete. But that's a very recent development. Any discussion of sexual desire or display of sexuality was taboo or censored up until the late 1950s. Mass Observation's 1949 sex survey (which was never published) discovered that only 11 per cent of their sample received any sex instruction from their mother; and even less, 6 per cent, were given advice by their father. Only 8 per cent of the entire sample had learned about the 'facts of life' by reading a sex manual.[3] Ignorance was probably seen by parents as the best way of controlling or postponing the developing sexuality of their sons and daughters and if it was discussed it was usually as something either sacred or disgusting. Sex education books prescribed chastity for the unmarried and chemists often refused to sell contraceptives to single people. Social workers had the power to place 'promiscuous' girls in institutionalised care and unmarried mothers were often humiliated and sadistically treated in infirmaries, workhouses and mother-and-baby homes. Sexual exploration for the young was impossible indoors, so they went outside, experienced hurried 'knee-tremblers' in alleys and doorways, or if they could afford it they might hire a taxi. Police and vigilante patrols such as the Voluntary Women's Patrol, established in 1914, warned or even arrested young people who became too amorous in parks and public places. 'If they caught you, they took you to the police station and they would class her as a prostitute, though she wasn't,' remembers Bill Phillips of his courting days in the 1920s in Steve Humphries's oral history *A Secret World of Sex*. 'Then once they were branded prostitutes they'd always be a prostitute.'

There was no sexual imagery in advertising or on television. The BBC during the 1920s and 1930s under its founder and first Director General, Lord Reith, would not broadcast anything with a whiff of sexual unconventionality about it, nor would he employ a divorcee. At the cinema, bedroom scenes were heavily censored, with 'one foot on the floor at all times'.[4] So it would not be an exaggeration to say that the premarital sexual experience and knowledge of many would have been limited. While many growing up in overcrowded slums would have heard or witnessed others making love, Steve Humphries maintains in his book that most sex took place in an atmosphere of ignorance, guilt and fear. Young men discovered the 'facts of life' by watching animals mate, or from prostitutes if they were lucky, well into the twentieth century. Young people got married just to be able to have sex legitimately.

Once they were wed, periods of sexual abstinence were common and accepted as a form of birth control by both men and women, particularly in the early years when they were trying to establish a home, in the later years of a woman's fertility when they were trying to limit the size of their family, or after a difficult confinement, often on the advice of a doctor. In Simon Szreter and Kate Fisher's oral history of intimate life in England between 1918 and 1963, *Sex Before the Sexual Revolution*, abstinence was 'presented by interviewees as a natural, spontaneous and temporally specific response to the pressures and challenges of their busy lives'. They add, 'It was a response that was indicative of the strength of the loving relationship, in which both partners were sensitive to each other's feelings and desires.' Lorna, one of their interviewees and a weaver married to a valve tester with two children born in 1942 and 1945, talks of how a new sexual love emerges which is sensitive to tiredness and each other's work burden. 'Dr Howarth said "no more babies", so that were when we were extra special careful … but he (husband) respected me really and he knew my fears so he controlled his— and he was a controlled man.'[5] Men bore the main responsibility for contraception, largely through withdrawal, until the arrival of the Pill in the 1960s. Withdrawal, as anyone who has tried will know, isn't particularly easy or safe, so for many men it was simply less frustrating not to try and to go down to the pub instead.

Most people never saw each other naked and physical attractiveness was gauged largely by behaviour, dress or perhaps the hair. 'The body, defined as specific shapes or forms, was not what they admired in either sex,' write Szreter and Fisher. 'Most interviewees enjoyed a sexual relationship during their marriages without sexualising or eroticising particular physical aspects of their bodies' until the post-Second World War years, when there was a marked rise in the sexualised nature of the female body and desire became flesh.

When it came to pornographic imagery in the 1950s, magazines had to be secreted home in a brown paper bag. 'Getting them into the house was almost more exciting than the magazine itself,' commented Howard Jacobson at a recent debate on pornography in London. Then, in 1964, with the publication of *Penthouse* and *Mayfair*, the landscape changed, bringing an eroticisation of the female form that had never been seen before as well as a new sexual permissiveness to the text. Sales soared. It's interesting that the minute women won the right to their own sexual freedoms with the Pill, they found themselves portrayed as bunny girls and sexual objects.

As public discussion about sexual matters increased throughout the 1960s, pornography mushroomed and jumped into the vast gap between people's ignorance, their lack of sexual experience and sexual fantasy, cranking up expectations of 'great' sex and narrowing our understanding of erotic desire. Pornographic images of women and explicit sexual activity have infiltrated popular mainstream culture. We have lap-dancing clubs and sexualised pop videos. We are bombarded daily by advertising images of naked, beautiful people in steamy situations, used to sell a wide variety of products from perfume to cars. Sexualised clothing such as thongs, padded bras and high heels are now considered the norm in fashion for young girls, and growing numbers post sexually suggestive pictures of themselves on Facebook and on one another's mobile phones. Hardcore pornography has therefore had to become more extreme and violent to distinguish itself. It percolates freely through the internet, into the television set of every hotel room and through the airwaves on to handheld devices such as iPads and smartphones.

Pornography is big business and increasingly seen as another form of entertainment to be consumed without consequence.

'The industry boasts its own annual trade show and trade publication; it employs lobbyists, lawyers, accountants, marketers,
internet gurus and industry analysts. Pornography businesses
trade on the NASDAQ and the New York Stock Exchange,'
writes Pamela Paul in her book *Pornified*. They have helped to
drive the technological revolution, from streamed videos to file-
sharing on the internet, which in turn expands their own
market. Young men do not crave iPads and iPhones to watch
porn. They want the gadgetry for all of the other advantages
and then cannot avoid it.

Pornography works by detaching sexual acts from loving
relationship and real people. In the 1970s pornographic films
were based on conventional narrative forms. The boring bits
of *Emmanuelle* or *Deep Throat* had to be sat through publicly
in a cinema just to get to the sex bits. Now the internet and
the DVD market allow pornographers to cut together hours
of sex scenes without any narrative around them and then
market them according to proclivity – anal sex with blondes
or young black men, lesbian threesomes, take your pick.
Consumers no longer need a story on which to base their
sexual fantasies: they can fast-forward to enlarged imagery
of moving body parts and watch them over and over again.
Google too allows people to just tap in numerous different
sexual preferences, such as 'sado-masochism', 'erect clits' and
'anal fruitshakes', just to see what comes up, detaching sexual
acts from the intimacy of a real human being. 'The difference
between old-fashioned porn and internet porn is like the difference between wine and spirits,' writes Damian Thompson
in *The Fix*, his book on the new addictive culture. 'Digital
porn is the equivalent of cheap gin in Georgian England: it
provides a reliable, dirty hit that relieves misery and boredom.
You don't know how strong it is until you've tried it – at which

point you may discover, too late, that you're wrestling with obsessions that until a few years ago you thought were confined to ferret-faced men in raincoats hanging around school playgrounds.'

While porn can be erotically pleasing for women, the main market panders to male fantasies. In Pornland a woman wants sexually what a man wants, all of the time. In Pornland women with pouting lips, surgically enhanced breasts and very little pubic hair have explosive orgasms in three minutes after vigorous vaginal pounding without foreplay by men who can call them 'slut' or 'cum dumpster'. In Pornland women want sex with more than one partner, with all three orifices preferably filled at the same time. In Pornland woman-on-woman sex bears very little resemblance to real lesbian sex. Even that is perverted, hetereosexualised, to suit male desires.

With pornography a man can retain complete control over his own sexual satisfaction with an unattainable woman who is always up for it. Porn is easy and it feels safe, compared with what could happen with a real woman or even with the viewer's wife. The only person you have to please is yourself, and that must be harmless. The evidence appears to suggest otherwise. The more we watch pornography, the more we seem to believe that sort of sex to be real. So the orgasms the actresses are faking become genuine. It's all right to watch because this is 'good' sex and the women are enjoying themselves. The established truism is that pornography is harmless. Those who complain are strait-laced prudes, hell-bent on ruining other people's fun. Yet there is substantial evidence that watching porn tends to leave men and women feeling inadequate about their own bodies or their penis size, or the real-life body of their partner. Pornography objectifies women as a series of body parts, detached from a real person, and therefore legitimises, even accentuates, a man's emphasis on the visual as his primary source of desire. It degrades men just as much as women, raising huge doubts over their sexual performance when they fail to provoke so swift and dramatic an orgasm in a real woman.[6]

There is also mounting evidence to suggest that pornography is becoming self-defeating, dampening real desire within a relationship rather than raising it. Research on men who have been exposed to popular erotic imagery such as *Playboy* centrefolds have subsequently found their partners to be less sexually appealing and rated themselves as less in love with their wives.[7] Men and women exposed to popular, non-violent porn in hourly sessions over six weeks were found subsequently to be less satisfied with their partners' physical appearance and performance, and they placed increased importance on sex without emotional involvement.[8] Other research found that prolonged consumption of porn fostered greater callousness towards women, led to depression and social isolation, financial difficulties and greater acceptance of extramarital sexual relations, as well as the idea that unrestrained sexuality was wholesome and healthy.[9] Yet it is a growing kick, with 66 per cent of men between eighteen and thirty-four looking at internet porn several times a month.[10]

Regular consumers of porn can find they get into difficulties with their relationship as they disconnect from family life and their partners by masturbating alone in front of the computer. Such an orgasm may provide relief but there is no one beside you to hug, or share it with, and it is the sharing of sex which fosters attachment, the essential ingredient in relationship. Pornography endorses the paramount importance of orgasm to good sex, when it is only one aspect of sexual pleasure. The more we focus narcissistically on the importance of our own orgasm, the more the other person drops out of the equation. Regular users of porn in Pamela Paul's *Pornified* had trouble reaching orgasm with their partners and tended to reproduce the acts they had seen, rushing to intercourse or forced oral sex without foreplay. There is little caressing or kissing in explicit erotic material even though these supposedly more 'feminine' aspects of sex give pleasure to men too. Sadly, real sex, with its tenderness, fumbling and false starts, as well as the joy that comes from giving pleasure to another human being one cares for, loses much of its magic.

Many use pornography for the same reasons others have an affair – as a form of cruelty or to avoid dealing with sexual and emotional problems in their relationship. This isn't cheating, they believe. This is acceptable, for men have always enjoyed the visual treat of pornography. Another myth, for avid consumers of porn are just as vulnerable to all of the same problems as those who have full extramarital liaisons: guilt, shame, betrayal as they turn away from their partner to an outside source of stimulation which is secret.

Laura only discovered that her husband had an addiction to porn – films and a stream of premium-rate calls – after they had separated. Her husband never said he was unhappy with their sex life or suggested new tricks. 'I knew our sex life wasn't ideal but if anything my libido was higher than his. Often he was the one who didn't feel like it. Sometimes I felt like I was having sex with a robot, he was completely unemotional, lacking passion until he had an orgasm, when he made a few pleasurable noises. Then when I was pregnant he found that sexually off-putting but he couldn't ever talk about that so I had no idea. He never once said in five years, could we have oral sex, or could we hire some soft porn and watch it together? – I'd have been fine with all that if only he had said.

You would think watching porn would make him a more adventurous lover in that it would make him want more but actually it did the exact opposite.'

Instead of finding ways to reconnect with Laura sexually, Tim continued to look outside his marriage for thrills and had an affair with a younger, childless woman. Laura imagines they must have had fantastic sex, which makes her feel even more inadequate as a tired mother of two small children. 'His porn addiction and his affair went hand in hand because both were forbidden and therefore hidden from me. It was only after we separated and were talking through our computers about whether we could get back together again that he said, "I have never been satisfied with our sex life. I like talking dirty and I want deep throating and if I come back to you, you will have to promise to do deep throating on me." I had no idea what that was! I had to ask a friend, who said she didn't think that was healthy in a normal, loving relationship.'

Pornography is desensitising. People grow tired of watching the same material repeatedly and then seek out extra thrills through novelty to get the same hit. The boundaries of what is thought to be erotic can get pushed to such extremes of brutality or perversion that non-consensual sex is considered normal. Pornography and cultural representations of sex as always passionate magnify the split between sexual desire and marital love. They ramp up hopes of perpetual ecstasy and invade the sexual fantasies inside our heads. They make it seem impossible to merge lust with loyalty as sex with the same body inevitably turns into the same sort of sex over time. Growing numbers of young people learn about sex primarily through watching porn, hardly an accurate representation of real sex and not always the nicer kind for women. Large numbers of people believe that once the sex goes a relationship is over, and that this is enough to break a marriage and make one or both partners crave new sexual sustenance elsewhere rather than seek to understand how sexual boredom or loss of desire is symptomatic of deeper difficulties.

The true nature of erotic desire and sexual intimacy is far deeper and richer than pornography or cultural representations of 'good' sex suggest. Erotic desire is enigmatic. It stems from somewhere very deep and hidden inside, from the give and take of unfolding relationship. We have little in the way of research into the outer reaches of sexual experiences. 'None of us is ever quite sorted out in the area of sex,' writes couples psychotherapist Francis Grier, 'and it is perhaps both a torment and a comfort to realise that we never shall be.'[11] It's reassuring perhaps to note that he is referring as much to his colleagues working with couples in difficulty as he is to human beings in general.

One research paper I found, 'The Components of Optimal Sexuality: A Portrait of "Great Sex"' published in the *Canadian Journal of Human Sexuality* in 2009, surveyed people of different ages and sexual orientation and in both short- and long-term relationships, throwing up some interesting findings. The two factors which cultural sexual myths seem to endorse – lust and chemical attraction as well as the physical sensations and orgasm – were considered to be *minor* components of the sexual experience.[12] Instead the research found that people emphasised the connection and the sense of alignment they felt with the other person, where they almost lost a sense of their own boundaries. The best sex was meditative, all about being lost in the moment, focused on touch, feeling wanted and cherished. The respondents talked of a heightened sense of communication and empathy, a place where they could drop their guard, say or be anything, be selfish as well as emotionally available to the other. They also talked about needing a sense of humour, for the times when certain positions are either impossible or seem ludicrous.

Popular culture promotes achieving great sex through techniques, suggesting that to find it one almost has to look outside oneself and learn the art. By contrast, those taking part in this survey found great sex had much more to do with their own mindset, or with their own intent both as a person and as a couple. Great sex is deeply rooted inside us, in the psyche, in how we feel about ourselves as well as each other, in our use of sexual fantasy and in being comfortable enough in our own skins to be totally present and let go. The trouble is that we also have to find the strength and the courage to relinquish the popular stereotypical sexual scripts inside our head. 'Good' sex is not about performance, props and positions. It is something less tangible.

There is a very different kind of sex, a better experience in many ways, when you make love to someone with the carefree abandon that can only come with the knowledge that you are well and truly known. It can be far more tender, more sensual and satisfying when each partner feels safe enough to be able to abandon the rational and more conscious borders of their physical and psychic identity and play. That is the hard core of intimacy. But this kind of real sex is rarely depicted. Perhaps that is because it doesn't pander to the fantasies of chase and sexual conquest which shore up male and female self-esteem. Perhaps that is because it doesn't sell magazines or spice up fiction or television dramas with the hunger of pursuit and longing.

Sex with a new body and sex with someone one you share a life with are two entirely different things. We have to lose the former in order to gain the latter. The very idea that one could ever hope to enjoy constant passionate ecstasy and new sexual thrills throughout a long relationship is both laughable and an exhausting thought, particularly as one gets older. The early frenzy of extreme sexual passion has a drug-like, intoxicating quality that makes lovers feel cut off from the rest of the world and reality. Their sense of self and self-control disappear for a while as obsession with the other magnifies that person's importance. Such excitement cannot last because it is based on an idealised illusion rather than on the true, flawed and probably very ordinary human being one has fallen in love with. It is dangerous both for our psychic stability and for the health of a relationship for this essential, initial period of bonding to last too long.

Romance becomes riskier the longer it continues. The more one loves, the more one stands to lose should it all go wrong. Our longing for safety and our thirst for passion seem to pull us in opposite directions and yet there is also a sense that the longer a relationship lasts, the more destabilising and dangerous the deepening erotic attraction feels. What seems on the surface to be boredom with the same kind of sex with the same old body might in fact be a subconscious form of insurance against the pain of loss. We pull away from each other at the point where we cannot cope with the growing strength of sexual intimacy between us, when what we might need is a leap of faith and imagination.

Commitment can be very sexy indeed. In short-term relationships, lovers worry more about their performance and are often anxious about where the relationship might be going. They are also less likely to have developed their own unique wordless form of communication or knowledge about each other's desires. There is mounting evidence to suggest that we

choose people as mates because there is something of the
familiar to them which we feel we can trust, not just as co-parents to children but also as sexual confidants. Neuroimaging
studies appear to show that orgasm in females, in particular,
requires enough of a sense of safety to be able to yield and surrender sexually with the deactivation of the hippocampal
regions in the brain associated with anxiety.[13] 'With a husband
or boyfriend, there is the delicious certainty that pleasure will
be both given and received,' writes Susan Cheever. 'Sex feels
like a series of shared secrets, a passage through a maze leading to the most wonderful feelings available to human beings.
With a long term partner, I can relax. He is not surprised by
the moles on my back, nor is he self conscious about the hair
on his shoulders.'[14]

Sexual desire is mysterious, complex, fragile and rich. There
is always some element which remains deeply private and is
never revealed. Desire is never a fixed entity or predictable,
because there is always a sense of other possibility to it since
it is an act of imagination. These are the reasons why we
continue to find sex so alluring, for there is always another
sensation we could be experiencing, deep in the unknown. We
assume that sex must feel the same for everyone but the
research seems to show that people can have very different
definitions of desire and different levels of arousal. It is not
necessarily spontaneous either, but needs tender stoking over
time to flourish. Some research suggests that desire is circular
and expansive, less a forerunner to sex than an afterthought. It
is rooted in the whole person, mind, body and soul, in a sense
of yearning for the other, in memories of past sexual encounters, prolonged eye contact, dancing, massage, holding hands,
the mere caress of a cheek. Desire is the most elusive of passions, easily ignited and extinguished by too strong or rough a

move, or the sound of a child crying. Desire is not necessarily an essential, natural prerequisite for sexual arousal either. It can be triggered by seduction, which is in some ways a much more 'feminine' way of looking at sexual behaviour and worlds away from typical pornographic material.[15]

The assumption that the drive of desire is linear – starting with a spontaneous biological urge, then requiring the stoking of genital arousal and intercourse to provoke an orgasm – is a very limiting definition of what sexual exploration can be. Female desire is seen as a pale imitation of male desire and consequently a woman usually fails, either in not wanting as much sex as a man, or in wanting a different type of sexual experience. A woman's sense of desire appears to be deeply influenced by how she feels about herself and her body, by the way that the desexualised roles she inhabits during the day as mother, home-maker or worker seem to be so incompatible with the sex goddess she is expected to be in the bedroom at night. A woman can feel desire and enjoy that feeling just for its own sake. She doesn't necessarily need prolonged multi-position intercourse. But rarely is that considered true desire. We see loss of desire as a female condition rather than as a relationship problem because we compare everything against the male standard and the new cultural imperative to have a lot of vigorous, penetrative sex three times a week for life.

Research from a new breed of female sexologists in the US and Canada seems to show that sexual desire in women can be vibrant and all-encompassing. Meredith Chivers, Psychology Professor at Queen's University in Ontario, has studied how men and women respond to a variety of visual sexual stimuli from images of naked men and women to images of full intercourse. Straight men tend to be aroused by straight men and women having sex; gay men by watching gay men having sex. Women, on the other hand, of all sexualities appear to be aroused by any image and any sexual activity by either gender.[16] Women show signs of genital arousal to things which they reported did not turn them on and can experience lubrication, even orgasm, without any apparent signs of sexual desire.[17] They respond to all manner of stimulation: flowers, small kindnesses, compliments, considerations, a man doing the vacuuming.

The more male, orgasm-orientated approach does not necessarily lead to the best sex. In 1979 Masters and Johnson published their book *Homosexuality in Perspective* after five years of studying the sexual behaviour of straight, gay and lesbian couples in laboratory conditions. Many of the participants were having sex with complete strangers, having left their long-term partner at home. They were being observed qualitatively, and two different portraits of sexual activity emerged. There was efficient, goal-orientated sex. But this was not the most amazing sex. 'The best sex going on in Masters and Johnson's lab was the sex being had by the committed gay and lesbian couples,' writes Mary Roach in *Bonk: The Curious Coupling of Sex and Science*, 'not because they were practising special secret homosexual sex techniques, but because they "*took their time*". They lost themselves – in each other, and in sex.' That's the kind of democratic and considerate sex which women still crave in their relationships and rarely get.

Loss of desire, particularly in women, is presumed to be a common prelude to extramarital infidelity, implying that one or both partners no longer desire the other. The flames of erotic passion have simply died with time. However, there are numerous reasons for loss of desire which can affect both men and women equally. It can be biological because of medications or illness; psychological because of stress, depression or psychiatric disorders; developmental because of a history of difficulties as a child; cultural because of religious beliefs; environmental because of living conditions, lack of privacy or a sense of safety; or because there are problems in the relationship which are not being addressed. Statistically men are just as likely to suffer from loss of desire as women, if you include physical manifestations such as erectile difficulties.[18] Research conducted at the University of Chicago found that less than five hours of sleep a night reduced testosterone levels in men, which in turn reduced sex drive.[19] Stress, shift work and over-work are notorious libido killers affecting men and women equally and yet loss of desire in a woman is still primarily thought of as a 'natural' consequence of her gender, because of motherhood and the plummeting hormones of menopause. The fact that there might be relationship difficulties, or that a woman might want more than her partner can give, is often overlooked. And certainly the fact that she might crave a very different kind of sex from the narrow interpretation that macho porn now offers is not factored into surveys of sexual frequency.

Pregnancy, bringing up children and the menopause can dampen desire in women, but the same is true for men. Both men and women tend to want less sex as parents to young children, for they simply crash into bed exhausted and want to sleep. Both men and women tend to want less sex as they get older. 'Sex goes up and down inevitably because it is part of life and life isn't constant, but there is definitely a slow climb upwards in that it gets better overall. We cuddle each other more than we have ever done in forty years of marriage,' says Naomi. 'There's a lot more touching and fondness. There are times when there is no sex at all but there are also times when we have come back from the cinema and felt so turned on by something we have seen we have had sex in the car!'

One major study of those aged forty to fifty-nine in the US found that as the gendered sexual stereotypes faded with age, men valued relationship and delved more into feelings rather than techniques now that they felt less of a need to present themselves as sexual stags and masters of the universe. Women could find themselves enjoying sexual pleasures more as sex got safer once the risk of pregnancy had faded and they felt more in control.[20] The lives of men and women became more similar the longer they were together, united more by their age and their shared history than they were divided by gender. Survey results from the Massachusetts Male Aging Study found that 40 to 70 per cent experience a 'consistent and significant decline with age in sexual thought and dreams and in the desired level of sexual activity'.[21] This is part and parcel of growing older, not just of having been with the same person for a long time. 'Let's run upstairs and make love,' suggested his new young lover to Micky Dolenz of the pop group the Monkees. 'At my age,' he replied, 'it's either one thing or the other.'

So how do we maintain sexual intimacy in a long relationship within a cultural climate where the notion of 'good' sex and sexual desire is so heavily distorted? First of all, it helps to recognise that there is no definition of either 'good' or 'bad' sex. The only thing that really matters is finding ways to be content with the sex that we can have with our partner. Growing numbers of people visit their doctors concerned about low sexual desire. In many cases there is no obvious pathological reason for their withdrawal other than a general disillusionment and reluctance to dive deeper into psycho-sexual intimacy with the trust of a committed relationship. For many people daily life becomes routine and their lives as a couple have become so entwined that they feel they know all there is to know about each other and pull away sexually at the point when intimacy hits the deepest of raw nerves. It is then easier to look wistfully back to a more passionate past, or outside that relationship for someone else, than it is to face their deeper sexual demons with each other. 'Many of the couples I see have no idea how much tension exists while they have sex because it's there every time they do it,' writes sex therapist David Schnarch in his book *Passionate Marriage*. 'Exploring your sexual potential isn't just easier to do as you grow older; it's a necessity if you want to keep sex a vital part of your life.'

With so many sexual handbooks and websites on improving erotic techniques it is easy to forget that sexual emancipation is recent. Most couples rejected the idea that sexual relations should be consciously worked at or that they should ever turn to external sources such as advice books or doctors for help, for this was such a deeply private matter. Those reservations are still felt by many couples today. Countless people in established relationships find it difficult to talk to each other about what turns them on or about a temporary celibacy if loss of desire begins to take hold. 'When people struggle with sexual desire I think that is predominantly linked to the fact that they carry an enormous sense of shame about their bodies,' says psycho-analyst and couples counsellor Brett Kahr, 'all those anxieties about the "down there" bits which are the same parts involved in excretory and birthing functions, parts of the anatomy that we are told as children must be covered and cleaned.' The idea of talking to anybody outside that relationship about so private

a matter, when 'good' sex is now the expectation and bench-
mark of a happy relationship, is still horrifying for the majority
of couples.

Pornography and the constant lure of sexual alternatives
feed off that inability to talk about our sexual needs and widen
still further the gap between the seemingly opposing needs of
lust and loyalty. They prey on people's deep sense of sexual
inadequacy and make it harder to integrate feelings of love and
erotic desire towards the same person. Pornography has cre-
ated hundreds of thousands of new addicts out of those with
childhood attachment difficulties, who find it easier to get their
sexual kicks met by anonymous and distant erotica than from
a living human being, for dopamine, the brain's natural aphrodisiac, is highly sensitive to novelty.

The trouble with these raised sexual expectations is that we
risk losing love as a result. If sexual desire is solely about the
selfish pursuit of pleasure, a narcissistic solitude where only 'I'
and my needs matter, then we are truly alone. There are only
so many permutations of pleasure. Swinging from the rafters
with an orange in your mouth while masturbating may well
trigger a more explosive orgasm, but there is such a deep loneliness to such an experience, as there is to solitary sex in front
of a computer or sex with an anonymous stranger for whom
you are just another body. In these ways we reject love and the
sharing of our deepest selves, for surely the point of sexual
desire is that it connects us to another human being in a unique
and very private way. Sexual attraction may bring two people
together, but it is love with its growing sense of attachment
which allows them to fathom even greater depths of erotic intimacy within the safety of commitment.

Our sexual needs and erotic hinterland are intricately
connected to relationship, both past and present. With the

intimacy of relationship we use the sensations and exploration of sex to reinforce our sense of self as an individual, validated by the touch and appreciation of the other. Over time we give and receive love and a sense of caring which build up enough trust to allow us to reveal ourselves a little more sexually each time we touch. While research shows a strong connection between early attachment problems in childhood and our ability to expose ourselves erotically as an adult, a fascinating subject explored more fully in the next chapter, this is not necessarily an irreparable situation. There are indications from early research into 'security priming', where people are repeatedly exposed to images of security or are told to keep thinking of people who have made them feel loved, that an adult relationship which builds over time can heal some of those childhood wounds. Sexual satisfaction and emotional sustenance are so intertwined that they feed off each other. We can improve both by simply applying a little consciousness to how we relate physically as well as emotionally, instead of buying into the myth that sexual desire is an entirely natural and spontaneous human hunger, like our desire for food.

Familiarity, the safety of relationship and the fact that someone is available to us doesn't have to dampen desire. It is up to us to find ways to fathom the erotic in marriage. To do that we have to be more honest with ourselves and each other, for often it is what we are *not* doing sexually with each other and *why that might be* which is more significant than what we are doing. New positions, techniques and toys might enliven sex for a while but opening the mind and expressing feelings of both love and hate with each other physically will open the door into an entirely different psychic landscape, for it is in the sexual play of fantasy that we can act out our difficulties. Better sex is not necessarily about doing something new, it's more about being conscious enough to stop what might have become habitual sexually and then seeing what happens in that void.

Sexual desire reflects the complexity of marriage. It shouldn't be sidelined or reduced to merely a recreational activity. The more fused we feel as a couple and therefore lost as an individual, the more we tune out from our partner during sex and focus on our own bodily sensations. We disconnect emotionally in order not to feel swamped, which can mean superficial or brief foreplay and less intimacy such as kissing or gazing into each other's eyes. We focus on techniques and the genitals rather than on the emotional connection between us. And we use the sensations of sex as a self-soother, for the release of orgasm, rather to build the bonds of relationship.

When couples feel that there is enough differentiation between them to come together as two individuals there is enough mutual respect and personal integrity for the balance of power to be more equal. Sex is then not about coercion or withholding desire in order to exert control over the other; it becomes a means of deeper personal exploration as well as of forging deeper attachment. It is then not your partner's fault that you no longer have sex with other people. It is an active personal choice because the erotic and the emotions of intimacy become more fused. To betray that by having an affair would be foolish, because we would be losing more than we would gain. As the actor Paul Newman, who had a long and monogamous marriage to Joanne Woodward, once said, 'Why go out for a hamburger when you can have a steak at home?' With enough of an imaginative leap, who knows, you could even have a whole cow.

It is simply weak and not good enough to just throw up our

hands at the difficulty of achieving fidelity within a lasting relationship because we are surrounded by so many seemingly stringless sexual opportunities and there is the excuse that 'the sex just goes'. We choose to forget that overcoming obstacles is essential for sexual excitement and that finding enough space for the possibility of seduction is key to that challenge. We can inject greater erotic distance between us by challenging the straitjacket of gendered stereotypes associated with desire, where the male is active and the female more passive and submissive sexually. Few things are sexier for a woman than a loyal, loving, considerate man who adores her every sag and wrinkle as she ages. Few things are sexier for a man than the woman he loves throwing sexual innuendo into the mix, spicing up the routine by getting 'dirty'. A woman who retreats sexually as she ages or has children may be throwing down such a gauntlet not merely off it with a headache because of the waning biological imperative to reproduce. Excite me. Seduce me. Try harder. Perhaps it is men too who retreat behind gendered roles by heaving the blame for dwindling interest in sex on to women, so that they can go for what feels must be the easier option – someone else.

Research shows that couples who can talk about sex are more likely to maintain a deepening erotic interest in each other, acknowledging each other's needs and fantasies. They nurture an erotic distance within their togetherness and heighten desire by mentioning what they would like to do to each other or remembering past sexual encounters when they are fully clothed and apart.[22] Other research has found that couples who adopt more traditional gender-stereotyped roles in their relationship tend to have more traditional sex. If the presumption is that it is always the man who should take an active sexual lead, this can make things difficult for a woman who does not like to feel out of control. Couples who share roles more equally are more likely to experiment sexually because they are used to discussion and negotiation and less likely to make gendered assumptions about who does what. Both partners are more likely to feel that they have a right to suggest or refuse sexual encounters, and play with gendered role reversals.

'Good enough' sex in a healthy, happy relationship is the kind of sex which allows each person to feel accepted in their entirety, with their physical and emotional weaknesses as well as strengths. Each is allowed to keep a sense of distance in order to enjoy their own arousal and venture deep into their own imagination at the same time as giving pleasure and trusting that the sensations of merging and melting into each other will not annihilate their sense of self. In 'good enough' sex each is allowed to lose control through orgasm, to be selfish and wallow within their physical sensations before they pull away from the other. They do not have to maintain the illusion of finding everything in their partner overwhelming in its attraction and can relax more during physical encounters as a result. 'Good enough' sex – perhaps even 'great' sex – flourishes when men and women feel equally free to pounce rapaciously or to be submissive without feeling threatened or threatening. This is sexual play, delving into the darker, more dangerous nether regions without it being misinterpreted as a personal attack.

Both pornography and extramarital sex are the easy way to get our sexual needs met without having to battle for them in a relationship. The key to better sex is not to look out, to a world of false promise, but within ourselves. The lure of sexual novelty and pornography is now omnipresent. The answer is not to censor it, but to match it with greater honesty about the complexities of sexual desire from childhood onwards. If we start to fill in some of the vast void left by sexual taboos, then romanticised and pornographic notions of sex have less allure as the key to fulfilment. They are less able to sell dreams and unrealistic fantasies to those who are unhappy and unfulfilled. And greater honesty makes it easier to dispel the myth that 'good' sex has to be spontaneously passionate, frequent, always orgasmic and vigorously athletic. 'Good enough' will do but to live with that we have to be strong enough to resist the pull of unrealistic sexual expectations and recognise that there is no one right way but a myriad of sexual energies and play. We have to seize back the initiative and reclaim sexual pleasure as a very private and personal act of intense intimacy between two people who care deeply for each other. Only then will the lure of extramarital adventure seem less desirable.

# 5

# WHAT DOES AN AFFAIR SIGNIFY?

The assumption tends to be that the root cause of most sexual infidelity is sex – people needing more than they already get, or a very different kind of sex with someone new. However, the underlying causes of affairs are usually more complex. 'I think the erotic aspect is usually the least significant component to an affair,' says Brett Kahr, psychoanalytic psychotherapist and couples counsellor. 'Not everyone is a highly proficient lover and given the intensity of the porn-ography market most people do not have terribly satisfactory sex, in which case sexual novelty can then seem like a kind of cure. But I also think that large numbers of people suffer from low-grade depression. The safety of commitment feels like deadness. The affair then gives people the illusion that they have become enlivened.'

It is easy to delude ourselves that sex is somehow detached from real life and without consequence, when it is publicly celebrated as 'no strings attached' or 'friends with benefits'. However, an extramarital liaison is rarely just about getting your rocks off; it's almost always about what that illicit encounter signifies and the fact that it could be discovered. An affair is an attempt to solve a problem. For some that is a means to escape responsibility and the constraints of family life. 'I just wanted to be someone other than a wife and mother,' says Kristen, who had a six-month affair with a younger man when her children were five and three years old. For others an affair is a means of escape from a relationship which doesn't seem to be working. 'The friendship's gone and there's lots of bickering, tit-for-tat childish arguments where neither of us will budge and that has just snowballed into a position where we are not getting on at all,' says Oliver, who has been married for ten years and has been having an affair with a married woman for six months.

'Research confirms that poor communication and unresolved marital problems are linked to affairs,' writes Emily Brown in *Patterns of Infidelity and Their Treatment*. 'Affairs can make or break a marriage. They're sexy, but have little to do with sex – and a lot to do with keeping anger, fear and emptiness at bay.' Brown categorises infidelity in five basic ways. There is the multiple adulterer, the sex addict with a neurotic compulsion to conquer. There is the 'conflict avoider' who is so eager to please that he or she channels all of their resentments into an affair rather than an argument. The 'intimacy avoider' feels uncomfortable depending entirely on just one person. With the 'split self' affair a person does the right thing by their family but loves someone else more passionately. And finally there is the 'exit' affair where the infidelity doesn't provoke the end but merely confirms that the marriage or primary relationship really is over.

My research shows that affairs often transgress these boundaries and can be a mixture of two or three of Brown's categories. We know too that there are common triggers at various points in a relationship: early on, when a person might be struggling with issues of commitment and intimacy, after the birth of children, or at other key transitions such as children leaving home, illness in a spouse, mid-life or the death of a parent. When you then add to these common life pressures the evidence that our own individual family history also appears to play a significant role, affecting not just the quality of our most intimate relationships but also our ability to withstand these transitions, the possible causes of an affair become even harder to unravel from such a heady mix.

Physiological and biochemical drives are clearly important. For instance, men with higher levels of testosterone tend to marry less frequently, have more affairs when married and divorce more often, perhaps as a consequence of these affairs.[1] Many women detect significant shifts in levels of sexual desire around their menstrual cycle. Our psychosexual drives reach to the very heart of our erotic life and that core begins with the earliest sensations of childhood, with skin against skin, sucking and the sheer warmth of being held. The ability to enjoy sexual pleasure appears to have strong links with childhood attachment patterns and our resilience to feeling threatened. 'A secure person's comfort with closeness, self disclosure and interdependence creates a positive foundation for sexual relations, which are among the most intimate of human activities because they require unusually high degrees of physical closeness, potential vulnerability and personal disclosure,' write Mario Mikulincer and Phillip Shaver, two distinguished professors of psychology who have conducted a series of ground-breaking studies of the links between early attachment and adult relationships.

The ability to integrate erotic desire with our love for and prolonged sense of attachment to a particular person is a sign of health, and those seeds are planted in childhood. In addition family patterns of secrecy, abuse, avoidance of difficult topics of conversation and betrayal contribute to our emotional hard-wiring and can influence the nature of our relationships. With poor self-awareness and emotional intelligence about their own individual family history, a person can be more easily tipped towards an affair when they encounter problems in their relationship which they don't know how to solve.

Our earliest experiences of feeling secure seem to provide the emotional scaffolding for adult intimacy and can inhibit or distort aspects of sexual pleasure and commitment. When a child feels that a parental figure is responsive to their needs, they grow up believing that the world is generally a safe place and that it is possible to explore and engage with other people. They also learn that at times of distress others will come to their support, which generates self-confidence and trust in others. Secure foundations also seem to equip people as adults with greater skills when it comes to finding joy in a relationship and handling negative emotions or stressful situations.[2] The surer our sense of self, the less preoccupied we seem to be with our sexual performance and the more able we are when it comes to trusting the other enough to let go, maximising orgasmic pleasure.[3]

When those foundations are less stable, life becomes complicated as our emotional armour gets pierced by another person trying to love us, or make love to us. Those with a more negligent upbringing tend to trust less, and have poorer conflict resolution skills and more negative expectations of their partner. With a lower sense of self-worth people have a tendency to be more clingy, controlling and needy, and may have learned how to use their distress, or sex, as a way of keeping someone close. They may avoid conflict, fearing they will lose their partner completely, or shy away from expressing any negative emotion such as anger because they have learned as a child that these normal human reactions produced pain or punishment. Those who have suffered deep rejection in childhood can be reluctant to commit, pushing anyone who gets too close away to confirm what they already know instinctively, which is that they are unlovable. And once they are committed in a relationship they are more likely to want to spread their emotional resources as a means of avoiding the depths and therefore the risks of an exclusive intimacy.

The chaos of a triangular relationship feels more comfortable because unpredictability was the one thing that was predictable in their difficult childhood, where coping meant being on guard and keeping enough distance to make rejection less painful. Those who grew up in an environment characterised by rage, either expressed or repressed, can be eager to please and do anything to avoid confrontation. When resentments begin to pile up, the pressure builds, because one of the pair cannot talk or the other doesn't appear to 'hear'. So the tension grows, and without an understanding of the blueprint of their past or the verbal means to resolve these intimate difficulties in their relationship, people are more likely to seek sustenance and escape them through the secret, and comparatively safe, fantasy world of an affair.

There is a great deal of accumulating evidence to suggest that those with more insecure attachments as children don't have sex just to enjoy its pleasures: they are more likely to use sex as a means to meet their unresolved attachment needs. Those with a more 'anxious' and 'enmeshed' pattern (from inconsistent care-givers) 'tend to sexualise their desire for acceptance, affection and security' and use sex to find love, according to Mikulincer and Shaver. Fear of rejection and of not being good enough sexually can make relaxation and erotic abandonment difficult. Sex can consequently be less intense or pleasurable. Those with more 'avoidant' patterns of insecurity (from insensitive or rejecting care-givers) seem to approach sex in ways which make intimacy or interdependence unlikely. They report less enjoyment of kissing, touching and cuddling, are more likely to be dissatisfied with the physical aspects of sex, are more likely to engage in one-night stands and are less likely to be involved in sexually exclusive relationships.[4] 'Avoidant people's discomfort with closeness and negative models of others sometimes cause them to abstain from sexual intercourse, rely on masturbation, engage in casual uncommitted sex, experience various forms of discomfort during sex, forgo mutual sexual exploration, and seek self enhancement or peer admiration through sex,' continue Mikulincer and Shaver. 'In other words, avoidant people's sexuality may be focussed on their own narcissistic needs, combined with dismissal of or blindness to a partner's sexual needs and preferences.'

Both 'avoidant' and 'enmeshed' patterns of childhood insecurity appear to be associated with less positive appraisals of one's sexual being, less enjoyment of sex generally and less willingness to use contraception and safe sex, talk openly about sexual matters or experiment sexually within a relationship – not good foundations for a lasting physical intimacy, particularly when both people come from deeply insecure backgrounds. Sex becomes more important in a relationship when it is being used unconsciously to master unresolved issues with a parental figure than it does in a more stable relationship where sex is just one aspect of the numerous threads of intimacy which unite a couple.

All of these aspects associated with deep childhood insecurity are capable of undermining the quality of couple life and contributing to separation and/or infidelity. Some research has found that attachment anxiety is associated with intimacy-related motives for having extramarital sex – 'I was lonely/feeling neglected and needed to feel cared for.' Someone with attachment anxiety is also more likely to become obsessed with a third person. Conversely, those with a more 'avoidant' pattern of attachment were more likely to say, 'I wanted more freedom/space from my partner,' or 'I don't do intimacy.'[5] Other evidence suggests that those who are more 'avoidant' reveal a greater proclivity to poach or be poached. And perhaps most interesting and important of all, 'These associations between avoidance and sexual promiscuity could not be explained by variations in libido or sexual drive.'[6]

If there is also a history of infidelity as well as distrust in the family, 'There can be an assumption that it will happen to you too sooner or later,' says psychoanalytic psychotherapist Jenny Riddell, 'so some people will either provoke the affair in their partner or have one themselves just to get it out into the open because it's a pattern of behaviour they understand, and feel might be inevitable. Often when you unpick what has happened, the person who has had the affair was feeling very insecure and doesn't want to feel abandoned. There is this deep feeling that you have to spread your eggs in two baskets to protect yourself. The irony is then that they often provoke the abandonment they were so terrified of when that affair gets discovered.'

These are not hard-and-fast rules. There are bound to be individual differences, depending on character, temperament and degree of emotional intelligence. However, research shows an empirical connection between childhood difficulties and problems merging love, interdependence and sexual desire with one person. It's all about triangles, and triangles are of course the lifeblood of affairs. All three protagonists – lover, betrayed spouse and 'cheater' – play their part in perpetuating the spaces between them, influenced by their own personal attachment history.

The first triangle most of us experience is a formative one – as a child standing on one corner while our parents stand on the other two. Psychologists believe that our ability to merge intimacy with sex, as well as tolerate our position as a separate being, stems from that primary triangle. With a more secure base, people grow up accepting the paradox that they stand outside their parents' relationship as a couple but are also somehow an integral part of it. Consequently when they become adult they can be 'involved with romantic partners without attempting to recreate the oedipal situation', according to Mikulincer and Shaver.[7]

Those with unresolved issues about a parental figure are more likely to unconsciously equate their lover with that parent, as loving and being cared for triggers visceral reminiscences of the broken trust they experienced in childhood. 'It didn't matter how much money I made, nothing was ever good enough and in retrospect I think she turned me into a father figure, someone she could stick two fingers up to, but then she also expected me to provide for her, just like she had always done with her dad,' says Philip. He eventually separated from the mother of his two children because the intense acrimony between them was beginning to upset the children and his partner was in a prolonged affair with another woman. 'She has a lot of insecurities and used to say that she had a lot of anguish in her life as a child because her father would ignore her and move them around a lot, but then she was always happy to take the money he offered her.' Philip is certain that his ex-partner had one-night stands with other men while they were together. 'It was a childish need for short-term satisfaction and comfort, I think. She is very immature. I hoped things would calm down or that she would grow up a bit but I now think there was something back in her childhood which has affected her and won't ever go away.'

Strong feelings of rage and hostility can surface as people try to master that primary hurt the second time around, this time with their partner rather than a parent. Sex or sexual infidelity can become a means of expressing power or aggressive control over the other, or avoiding the mutuality and deepening intimacy of good sex. In line with all this theory, I have also noticed, without really looking very hard, a connection between childhood insecurities and adult sexual infidelities in the interviews I conducted for this book as well as those for my earlier book on relationships, *Couples*.

Pat's second husband was serially unfaithful to her throughout their thirty-five-year marriage, with prostitutes, occasional lovers and at least two long-term mistresses. 'He usually had two or three on the go, which may also be why he was made redundant several times,' she told me.

When I asked her whether she felt his childhood had influenced his sexual behaviour she was unequivocal. 'He will never be faithful. His mother sent him to stay with relatives in South Africa when the Second World War started. He was just four years old and when he came back his sister had died and he had a younger brother. His mother seemed to give all her love to this new baby. He was then packed straight off to boarding school. She was always "Mother". She was a cold and formidable woman. I never saw her kiss or hug him and all I ever got was a cold peck on the cheek when she arrived.' Each time Pat uncovered extramarital liaisons, her husband would go down on his knees and 'beg like a schoolboy, promising that it would never happen again but each time he lied. He is very immature emotionally, likes to push the boundaries as far as he can, just like a child, and then be punished for it, which just made me furious in the end because I don't want to be put into that position.'

For some couples, such as Pat and her husband, infidelity is one of the key weapons in a complex abusive cycle, where both are locked into the drama. If there is a climate of general belittling, put-down or violence, sexual betrayal is another powerful way to assert dominance and to wound. Once that affair is uncovered, the victim then regains some power in the relationship through their ability to punish or determine the future. Even though this is unlikely to have been the first major betrayal, and even though friends, family and their own children get sucked into the drama and profoundly affected by it (as we shall see in Chapter 8), each cannot pull free from their role in this scenario, often because of their own family history.

Pat now believes that her husband is a sex addict, who will never seek therapy because he is in his seventies. According to Emily Brown, 'Sexual addiction does not refer to a frequent desire for sex per se ... but to the compulsive pursuit of sex to assuage inner pain and emptiness.' Sex becomes a means of soothing, just like food, drink or drugs for that dopamine high, but also a means of conquest in the hope of gaining love and an enhanced sense of self-worth. 'I have always felt alone,' writes Sue William Silverman in her memoir of sex addiction, *Love Sick*. 'The more distant I grow from my workaholic husband, the more I believe I need a man, then another man to fill the expanding emptiness I feel.' But it is not just the highs of the quick sexual fix which matter. It is also the subsequent more familiar sense of guilt and shame, feelings which pervaded the emotional texture of the person's childhood as they were made to feel less worthy of being loved, as my interviewee Pat describes.

The glamorised stereotype of the Don Juan seducer who loves sex and enjoys pursuing women does not help, for while the common assumption is that most affairs are fuelled by this drive, just 10 per cent of men surveyed who have affairs appear to fall within the definition of a sex addict. One study estimates that as many as 81 per cent of them may have been sexually abused as children and have at least one other addiction.[8] As with every other addictive behaviour, one sexual encounter is never enough. Getting that 'fix' and fulfilling one's own immediate needs become more important than others' feelings. What drives their behaviour is a selfish narcissism coupled with the foolish grandiosity to believe that it can be hidden. Sexologist Susan Quilliam says that there are big differences between someone who can be defined as a sex addict and those who claim to have the affliction so that they can justify sleeping with a lot of people. 'With cheating a person chooses to have an affair. Sex addiction is where cheating dramatically interrupts your life. It's compulsive, making silly choices and not thinking of the consequences. Once a sufferer has done it, they feel bad and guilty and that drives them to have sex again to feel better. It's a vicious circle – unlike cheating.'[9]

The intimacy of sex distinguishes a couple from other close relationships. This is their world and only the two of them get to touch and open up to each other in this way. So it is sexual infidelity which will also wound the most, shattering the protective membrane around that intimacy. There is a host of possible reasons for infidelity. A sexual transgression can be a means of injecting distance and a sense of danger into a stifling relationship. It can be an indirect way of saying to your partner that things have to change. It can be a means of ending a relationship without taking responsibility for walking out of the door, for the affair both confirms that the relationship is over now that absolute monogamy is king and can be blamed for upsetting the status quo. A secret sexual adventure can also be a very powerful way of wounding our spouse, because we know how devastated they would be if they were to find out. It may remain hidden, but each time you feel under-appreciated, misunderstood or diminished by your partner or your situation, you can relish the memory of what you have done. Often just the fact that the other person can sense an intangible change in the quality of your intimacy is enough for the dynamic between you to shift.

Jean had two short affairs when she felt diminished to less than an equal in her marriage. Her husband was in severe financial trouble with his business but refused to discuss any of his problems and cut himself off for days on end. Jean recognises that his own family history played a part. 'He was sent away to boarding school when he was seven and was used to containing his emotions and sorting out his own problems. However, I found it very difficult,' she told me. 'When I said to him that we should be sharing this he said he had to sort it alone and that he didn't want to worry me, whereas I thought that was one of the worst things he could say because I worried more and I felt he wasn't noticing me. I remember saying at one point, "I could move out and it would be a week before you'd realise." I kept telling him that I had to feel a part of this marriage and not just the person

who gets up at the crack of dawn to get the kids off to school,
does a day's work, all the shopping and cleaning, organising
the doctor's appointments, and then you expect me to be gag-
ging for it when you come to bed? That's just not fair. The sex
wasn't any better with either of these men. No one has ever
been a better lover than my husband, and maybe if one of
them had been a fantastic lover you could understand it,
but at least they were totally focused on me when we were
together. My husband suspected and I denied it, and even
though he never found out the truth, I think it did help me to
realise that things had to change. He broke down in tears
during one conversation and begged me not to leave, which
meant I could tell him that I had to feel a part of this marriage.
Did I use the affairs as a weapon? Maybe. I shouldn't have
done it but I had tried to speak to my husband and this felt like
the line of last resort.'

When I met Rachel, an attractive married woman in her
early thirties, she was quick to tell me that she was highly sexed
and loved it. However, the more she told me about her life, the
clearer it became that she could be a sex addict, using the edge
of illicit sex in exactly the way that professional textbooks on
infidelity describe. She had been sent away to boarding school
when she was twelve and hated it. She was a long way from her
home in Canada, where her parents still lived and worked. 'I
felt totally abandoned and learned how to cut off my emotions
because you have no choice. You can't cry all the time. You
have to get on with your life.' Rachel told me that she had a history of being unfaithful with boyfriends. 'I'm sure it goes back
to my father, I never felt he gave me enough love or approval
in that nurturing kind of way that makes girls feel confident, so
I think I was looking for affirmation and attention through
sex, that I am attractive.' Her father was a strict Catholic who

abhorred sex before marriage and took her to a priest for confession when he found her kissing a boy. 'He would not talk to me for a whole year when he discovered I had a boyfriend at university.' In *Patterns of Infidelity and Their Treatment*, Emily Brown explains that an influence of this kind in childhood can be key to later serial infidelity. She writes that it is common in therapy to see 'the emphasis the sexual addict's family placed on sexuality, either directly or by rigid avoidance of anything sexual. Addicts report growing up in families where no one is allowed to talk about sex or in which a family member is dedicated to controlling all expression of sexuality, or in families where sexuality runs rampant.'

However, in Rachel's philandering there were also signs of intimacy avoidance and disillusionment with the romantic dream, a reluctance to accept her husband totally. She loves him and their life together as a family. 'We get on and we work well together as a team but emotionally I feel we are not on the same wavelength. I don't feel an emotional connection with him, he doesn't "get" me and I have to explain everything about how I am feeling or why things might matter. I got married because all I ever wanted was a family and a home with a picket fence because that has to be easier than working crazy hours in banking as I used to. He seemed to tick all the boxes, good father, financially sound, kind, but he never gets the fact that I feel so let down by him.' Rachel has found a trainer at the local gym to fill in that gap in her life. She has the time for an affair. She is bored as a professional, intelligent woman at home full time with a nanny and excuses her need for a lover with the fact that he is her emotional 'rock – I know he isn't going to leave me and he doesn't want to break up my family, but I also know that I can talk to him about anything and rely on him emotionally in ways I find hard with my husband.'

If the expectation now is that relationship should be perfect and love should make us happy, the numbers of those who feel unhappy with their marital lot is bound to rise when couples hit what marital psychotherapist Warren Coleman calls the 'inability to tolerate the state of being ordinarily contented'. We want, indeed feel, we are owed more individual happiness without really knowing what that is. When a spouse does not tick every single box within the unrealistic romantic ideal of total compatibility we feel more justified in seeking that unfulfilled need elsewhere.

Clive's repeated philandering throughout his thirty-year marriage with casual encounters while working abroad and illicit dating sites here at home could also be defined as a sex addiction. Yet he also exhibits signs of a 'split self' affair, conflict and intimacy avoidance as well as boredom. 'You could say I am a serial adulterer on an opportunistic basis probably driven by a high sex drive and goodness knows what psychological entourage comes with that, but I am also good at compartmentalising stuff because that's what business teaches you to do, put stuff in boxes.'

Clive spent his twenties and thirties climbing the career ladder and providing for his wife and sons. He has an active, intellectual and enquiring mind, reads history books and political biographies and goes to the theatre whenever he can. He loves his wife in that he cares for her, admires and respects her as the mother to his children but feels she doesn't challenge him intellectually. He has worked hard to provide for his family but 'Most of the business stuff is repetitious and crushingly dull. If I could find something that interested me and get well paid, wouldn't that be a dream come true?' He has escaped that boredom with infidelity. 'I think it is curiosity and conquest, a kind of craving for new blood and flesh almost on an intellectual basis, testing out my interpersonal skills, and if we are both consenting adults, then who are we hurting?' It was safe. Nothing was going to bounce back and hurt him. He could compartmentalise his life in a businesslike way and his wife never found out.

Then Clive's sons grew up, left for university and he hit mid-life. 'You lose one of your parents and the mortality thing kicks in.' His wife grew fatter and depressed. The tedium of his job and living in suburbia began to grate even more. At that point he fell madly in love for the first time in his life, with a woman whose intellect he felt matched his own. He could escape boredom, family commitments, grief for his mother and fear of his own death with a younger woman who seemed to tick all of the boxes. 'I had never had this crazy feeling for anyone before, even for my wife. That opportunistic, more mechanical, gratification sex no longer interested me and I had this incredible feeling of calmness: I didn't have to go hunting any more. We had so much to talk about. There would be this two-day oasis when we were together and then all I could think about was when I was going to see her again. It was sort of an addiction where everything else pales into insignificance, but it rattled my cage big time because I never realised that you could have this level of excitement and engagement on a daily basis with one person where you connect so completely, with your head, your heart and your genitals.'

Clive's world suddenly became far from safe. His wife discovered that he was having an affair and was devastated. His mistress began laying down ultimatums, as she wanted a proper, exclusive relationship with him. 'Leave your wife or you lose *me*. Tell her you love *me*. Choose *me*.' It was an overt display of female rivalry which his wife could do little to compete with other than threaten to kill herself. When Clive prevaricated his mistress cranked up the pressure. She rang one of his sons to tell him of his father's sexual betrayals. She sent abusive letters and made threatening phone calls. Suddenly Clive's controlled and stable world of serial infidelity had vanished, replaced by a dramatic soap opera ripe with the raw, uncontrollable emotion he had denied himself for so long.

He had either not seen or ignored the numerous signs that he had fallen in love with a deeply unstable woman, and he was now a tortured man. For he was faced with what he believed to be a stark choice between two women who seemed to offer very different things: the hedonistic, dangerous excitement of pursuing 'true love' with his 'soul mate' and the calmer stability of family life. What Clive was perhaps also facing up to was his own indecisiveness between doing the right thing as a family man and feeding his own emotional self, what Emily Brown would describe as the classic 'split self affair'. 'There is the pursuit of happiness at one end or what you think will make you happy,' says Clive, 'and then on the other side you have responsibility, guilt, obligation, family and money because my family depends on me to generate the wealth and clearly it would cost a great deal to separate and we would all lose out. I would have been happiest if she could just have carried on being my mistress, box it and go back to my wife and my life but she wasn't prepared to do that.' Clive had never tested the affair with the reality of daily life, so it remained an escapist, romantic fantasy until time began to heal the longing.

Clive is still with his wife and has gone back to a more controlled life where he continues to seek out sexual liaisons through infidelity websites. 'It's almost like depression management,' he told me when I met him again several months later. 'Women are not difficult to find. But I am loved out now and unlikely to ever find someone like her again.' He knew he had fallen in love with a woman who showed signs of being unbalanced, 'But that doesn't stop you from loving them if the chemistry is there. It's true that you can't expect to find everything you might want from one person, but that doesn't stop people from wanting to try.'

In spite of the apparent ease with which we can divorce these days, people still live with a great deal of marital unhappiness. When you consider that it takes a couple seven years on average to get to the point where they might even consider couples counselling, I think it would be fair to say that people often allow their love life to stagnate and drift, in the hope that one day it will just get better by itself, before they even attempt to salvage something better from the wreckage or end up separating. Some people simply don't know how unhappy you have to be before you can leave. Others cannot afford the financial costs of divorce or are reluctant to put their children through the emotional upheaval. An affair then offers the sense of being enlivened, a temporary escape. It seems like an easier answer than leaving. The romantic allure of being able to find everything you might need in someone other than your partner beckons as an easier solution than trying to delve deep into the psychosexual chemistry of your relationship and beginning to address the difficulties.

It takes three to create a love triangle and inevitably the third person brings their own family history into the equation. When someone embarks upon an affair with another person who is already married, the chances are high that they too will be replaying their history and the Oedipal hurts of their own childhood within this new triangular situation, in an effort to master them. Many choose a married lover so that they can

avoid the intimacy of commitment and the risk of being abandoned, and feel safe. It isn't necessarily just happenstance.

Anyone could slide unknowingly into a relationship with
someone who already has a partner. However, if this is a regular occurrence, then both lovers might do well to consider
why that might be. A third party may present themselves as
independent and highly choosy, but an affair with a married
lover provides an arena in which he or she can replay all of the
unresolved issues of their past, such as dependency, denial of
self, abandonment and abuse. And sometimes when a woman
has an affair with a married man it is a useful medium in which
to replay unresolved issues with her own mother by inadver-
tently attacking another woman – his wife. 'Some form of
Oedipus complex – the desire to oust the mother in order to
enjoy an exclusive relationship with the father – does seem to
come into play in a large number of women who become, or
have become mistresses,' writes Victoria Griffin (a mistress
herself) in her book *The Mistress – Myths, Histories and
Interpretations of the Other Woman*.

Emily Brown writes that typical childhood experiences of
the persistently unmarried third party include the absence of
the same-sex parent, being closer to or receiving inappropriate attention from the opposite-sex parent, and having
emotional needs consistently ignored or ridiculed. In having
an affair with a married person the third party constantly feels
the rejection of never being quite good enough, never knowing when or whether they will be accepted and completely
loved, just as they felt when they were young. With their nose
pressed up against the window of another relationship they are
spared the humiliation of comparison with their rival because
they never have to share normal life or responsibility. Moreover, they might kid themselves that they hold all the power

because they share a secret with their lover, but that power is compromised if they can only see each other on their married lover's terms. They may rationalise that they are just in it for the sex and that they don't want a serious commitment, but in that case why not go for someone unattached to make life even less complicated?

For some 'mistresses', an affair with someone unavailable is a form of protection from deep hurt. Clara is in her mid-thirties and has embarked on a series of impossible relationships with men who are either attached or living in another country. She had an unhappy childhood with parents who fought bitterly when her mother became deeply religious. Her parents were self-absorbed, her mother depressed, and Clara admits to suffering depression too. She had a nervous breakdown when she decided not to observe religious practice proscribing physical contact before marriage, and she then suffered hugely when her first boyfriend ended their relationship. 'I never wanted to go through that kind of hurt again and decided that from then on all my relationships would have to be less intense. I think I am afraid of being able to love completely and all my relationships have been dysfunctional on some level. There was no real commitment from any of the men.' Clara wants to break that pattern from now on. 'I don't want to carry on with such foolish behaviour and it is foolish because I only hurt myself.'

For others it is the potential triumph of conquest which motivates an affair with a married partner. 'I think that in attacking the spouse of their lover they are often attacking their own mother or father by trying to steal their most prized object away. There is something very destructive and Oedipal about getting their own back,' says Jenny Riddell. 'We talked about his wife – because that is the thing about stolen love, it is important to know who you are stealing from,' writes Anne Enright in her novel of adultery, *The Forgotten Waltz*. Again gendered distortion often surrounds the third party. When it is a woman she is seen as a home-wrecker, the bunny-boiling femme fatale, whereas the married man is more readily excused for succumbing to the primary male weakness of seduction by the charms of an evil temptress. When that third person is a man his predatory tendencies are often presumed to be less threatening, for as a man he is surely in it just for the sex.

Childhood insecurities in particular can have a profound effect on the nature of a person's adult relationships. But that does not mean that a poor start will automatically condemn someone to a life of marital difficulties and infidelities. Our emotional make-up is not a fixed entity. We change through life as a result of our experiences as well as the new insights and emotional security which a good adult relationship can offer. Our attachment needs do not begin and end with childhood; they are constant throughout life. Recent research on 'security priming' has had interesting results. Exposing people repeatedly to a security-related word such as 'love' or 'hug' and to pictures representing secure attachment, for instance a mother hugging her child, before asking them to recall positive memories seems to ease anxieties and aggression and improve mood and compassion. Other studies where people were asked to imagine themselves in a problematic situation, surrounded by supportive people, found that 'Repeated security priming had positive effects on participants' views of themselves and their relationships.'[10] In short, these experiments lowered attachment anxiety but had less effect on those with a more 'avoidant' disposition. The longer the exposures, the stronger the effects appear to be. Over time these 'brainwashing' techniques helped individuals to lower their defensive positions and strengthen their sense of self.[11]

Imagine then the healing power of another loving person, who really hugs and touches and cares. These early scientific forays confirm what we all know deep in our hearts: that loving and caring for each other is crucial to our health and sense of well-being. While these concepts have yet to be woven into a therapeutic process, they fit with what we already know: support from a wide network of friends and family is crucial if we are to get through life's difficulties. And among these is living through the aftermath of an infidelity.

While sex may not be the main motivation for infidelity, for some couples an affair can be deeply useful sexually. It can reignite eroticism, injecting the thrill of danger and the threat of loss into a sex life that has become routine. The disclosure of an affair forces many couples to reconnect intimately – by fighting, screaming, crying, putting their entire future together on a knife edge of danger. 'If a couple want to make a go of their relationship after an affair has been revealed, one of the first things that happens and signifies a good prognosis is that their sex life dramatically improves,' Jenny Riddell tells me. 'Whoever has been betrayed desperately needs reassurance and the person who has betrayed also needs reassurance through forgiveness – they have realised what they could lose.' Many a woman with a straying partner finds she suddenly loses a great deal of weight. 'I also found him so deeply attractive I couldn't get enough of him,' one woman told me. 'I wasn't going to let her have him.'

Some of those who seek and discover a more exciting sex life with a lover inevitably bring some of these new tricks back into their marriage. What often leads to illicit and more adventurous sex is the desire to free oneself from the restrictions which seem to inhibit our sexual pleasure. Many feel they have to take their body away from what has become familial in order to get aroused because so many associations with family are steeped in a sense of shame, guilt, fear or helplessness. When that external lover then offers something deeply satisfying denied to them by their partner, such as oral sex, the sexual strayer then feels more torn and finds it harder to part with them. One of Jean's lovers was a married man. 'I think I did things his wife didn't do, different positions, using sex toys. When he wanted to leave her for me I told him that all he needed to do was to communicate with her a bit more. It's all that naughtiness, turning up in a trench coat with just your underwear on, silly things, but sometimes that's easier to do with someone who isn't your partner.'

However, if a couple want to recover from the damage caused by an infidelity they are going to have to delve deeper into the psychosexual history of their relationship and begin to fathom what caused the distance, and why it wasn't possible for either of them to express themselves sexually to each other in a more open way. When her husband left her for another woman Naomi bought a vibrator and learned how to give herself pleasure. 'The sex has been better since he came back because he must have learned a thing or two while he was away, so why not benefit from it? He was a bit shocked that I had bought a sex toy but why not? The sex we have now is much more tender whereas before it was just intercourse with not much foreplay. I used to say, "Just pretend I am dead or a hole in the wall" and that's a terrible thing to say and I never do that now.'

Others get off on the thrill of the illicit nature of what their partner is doing. I have met men who have enjoyed being told through a flirtatious text by their wife that they were about to have their brains fucked out. Men can find they have a more powerful erection, as 'They engage in an unconscious competition with their rival which in a paradoxical way helps them to feel less jilted,' says psychoanalytic psychotherapist Brett Kahr. 'Many people are secretly aroused by the fact that there has been or is a third person in the bedroom. From clinical practice I know that many people will masturbate to thoughts of their spouse with the other partner and that has a multitude of meanings depending on their particular biographical histories. Some have complicated contra-sexual identifications with the male spouse, say, being excited by the idea of another penis being in his wife's body. That can be an unconscious means of engaging in homosexual behaviour, knowing that your penis and his penis were very close by in the same location.'

For some of those who stray, the affair rekindles their sense of self-worth because they have been desired by another. They then feel such guilt that they return home to make love to their partner with even greater aplomb. Others find that just the thought of their spouse making love to someone else inflames their desire. Genevieve has had several affairs but has often found the occasional one-night stand to be far from satisfying. 'Sex is only really good, I think, with someone you have an emotional connection with and it is good with my husband. I often have fantasies about him making love to another woman when we make love. He knows that and thinks I am mad but I find him more attractive that way. I suppose I feel it's a strength to be a bit of a womaniser,' she told me.

Sexual betrayal may wound more than any other betrayal, as we shall see in the next chapter, but sex is in many ways the least significant aspect of an affair. The quality of our sex life reflects the quality of our relationship and when one of the pair chooses to stray sexually they are delivering a very specific message to their partner. How we discover, reveal or choose to interpret that message has an impact on the future of our relationship, together or apart. Infidelity, marital strife and the separation that so often follows can also have a profound effect on the stability of our children and influence the nature of their own intimate relationships once they become adult. It is to these crucial issues that I now turn in the second half of this book.

# 6

# BETRAYAL

Society focuses on the pain and powerlessness of the one who finds themselves betrayed after an infidelity through, apparently, no fault of their own. Research on the impact of various marital problems such as drink and drug abuse, or aggressive controlling behaviour, has found that extramarital sex is the biggest predictor of subsequent divorce, that it hurts, with an impact which is twice as large as any other problem and that any subsequent separation is likely to be messier and more vengeful as a result.[1] In the emotional vortex which surrounds the discovery of infidelity, simplistic notions of the seducer as 'villain' and the betrayed as 'victim' often trigger extreme reactions of rage, revenge and instant separation, masking the causes of such a deep betrayal and making recovery even more difficult, either together or apart.

What is less well understood is the extent to which having an affair can be a means of wielding power when a person feels powerless. The balance of power in any couple relationship is rarely on an entirely even keel. It shifts according to circumstances – family issues, health, stress or success at work, having babies. Couples with the most successful relationships are aware of this, of how at different points one of them might be more powerful economically, in their careers, or in the home over the welfare of the children. When couples find it hard to accommodate or even talk about their differences and the way that this delicate balance of power shifts between them, resentments can fester for years. For some an affair then becomes a very powerful means to reinstate balance in the relationship. It seems to fill an immediate need, either sexual or emotional, and it is typically entered into in the delusion that it can be kept secret.

Many men and women come to feel so crushed, neglected and threatened in their relationship that an extramarital affair holds a multitude of attractions. It is not unusual for men to stray when their wives have just had babies, when they feel vulnerable at encroaching mid-life or when their partners are terminally ill, because of a deep need for comfort at a time of acute stress and impending abandonment. Others need to assert their sexual potency when they feel aspects of their place in the world challenged, if their business has just gone bust or their partner is suddenly earning more money than they do. It is common for men with a castrating and difficult male boss to have fantasies of revenge by sleeping with the boss's wife. Others pursue that sense of conquest more actively. 'I had one client who used prostitutes in an addictive way,' says psychoanalytic psychotherapist Jenny Riddell. 'I asked him if he could correlate his use of prostitutes with times when he lost a lot of money and he could. It made him feel empowered again. He might be paying out more money but he was definitely getting something for it.'

For those who are feeling powerless, an illicit sexual encounter seems to inject a sense of omnipotence. They feel and see the effects of their presence or absence on someone else who might want them more than their spouse seems to. They feel special enough to have two people they can call their own. They share a secret from which their spouse is excluded with some-one outside their relationship, and this can be a particularly devastating form of cruelty and revenge, because their partner is likely to know them well enough to sense that something has changed. Whenever their spouse dares to ask, 'Are you having an affair?', that truth is vehemently denied, exacer-bating a sense of suspicion which can build into a feeling close to madness. 'It's as if you are wearing an invisibility cloak, you believe that nobody could possibly notice that you are behaving differently, which is ridiculous,' says Jean, who had an affair when she felt badly under-appreciated by her workaholic husband. 'I became completely provocative, going out at unusual times. I even went to pick up my lover from the airport once. I wouldn't have let my husband step out the door at those hours but he let me. I would have said, "Where the bloody hell have you been?" but he didn't, and the more they allow it, the more you think you can get away with. You want them to see and to stop it.'

The greater the emotional upheaval integral to maintaining the deceit, the greater the sense of self, at first, in the one who strays, for this turmoil is the product of their actions. With the emotional chaos they create, they now control the texture of their relationship. Previously it was the one withholding sex or over-exerting their authority by determining how they should live who held most of the cards. Now, for the betrayer, the scales of their relationship are tipped back into a sense of balance. Seeing the effects on those around them, they feel more powerful, a particularly attractive scenario for anyone who has been made to feel powerless as a child.

Patrick grew up as an only child with an alcoholic stepfather who got violent with both him and his mother regularly. He says he was terrified of him for most of his childhood because his behaviour was so unpredictable. He met his wife Naomi when they were at school and feels they found comfort in each other's shared sadness and married young. According to Naomi, 'We cleaved to one another, which isn't healthy.' When Naomi became severely depressed, Patrick felt desperate about his inability to help her. 'Sometimes she would just sit there and I just couldn't get through to her, but I loved her so I just kept on working at trying to make her happier. As a man I like to be able to solve problems but there was no way in which I could solve this one. The minute she saw other people she would smile and try and behave normally, but with me she just sort of blanked me and scowled, refused to talk to me or tell me what was wrong, so in the end I just thought I must be the problem.'

When a woman at work, 'one of the most affectionate and tactile people I have ever met', began to lavish her attention on Patrick he couldn't resist. 'I think I just got very lonely and here was someone who made me laugh and flattered me in a sense in that I realised I was still quite attractive, at least to somebody. I didn't realise it at the time but I was basically swapping the deep relationship that I had built with Naomi for nearly thirty years for the gratification of affection and I deeply regret that now.'

Patrick behaved in exactly the same way as many of those who stray: he dithered, uncertain as to what he really wanted, returning home before leaving again on several occasions, maximising the impact on Naomi of his betrayal, along with his own sense of guilt and self-loathing for his behaviour. Patrick still feels remorseful even though he has been back with Naomi for years. 'It isn't that you are evil but you are so out of control that you do these evil things. I had to travel a lot for work and I remember once building a long weekend out of it so that this woman could come with me to see if we could work out a way to be together permanently. Naomi drove me to the station to see me off without any understanding of the significance in that I might not be coming back, and I still feel terrible about that. On one level it is incredibly immature in that I couldn't make a decision. I didn't want to hurt anybody, I just didn't know what to do and in the process of being so indecisive you drag out the pain for everybody. It was the first time in my life I had been this cruel and consequently I didn't know how to deal with it, and the guilt of that still hurts to this day.'

When I met Oliver his torment at feeling so powerless in his marriage and so guilty for having embarked on an affair was palpable. 'She never holds back from letting me know that I am a shit husband in that I probably go to the pub a bit too much and I am probably not supportive enough. She is always on at me about earning more money but she never lets me see how much she is spending on her credit cards. We have probably had sex twice in the past year, which isn't enough for me. There has always been this feeling that she doesn't like me much or want to be near me.'

Oliver was seduced by an attractive married woman and the occasional sexual encounter soon stretched into a regular rendezvous at her house while her husband was at work. 'The sex wasn't even that good to begin with, over and done with in seconds because I had no confidence or self-esteem. I wasn't quite broken but I was feeling very needy and sorry for myself, in need of loving. With hindsight my personal needs should have taken a back seat and that is part of being a grown-up. I

never thought I would be the sort of person who would have an
affair once I was married, and I have let myself down. I was
proud of the fact that I was trying to be a good husband and
a good dad, and I should have been a stronger person and
never gone down this betrayal route. I don't want sympathy
and I am going to have to learn how to live with what I have
done, but it also has to be said that I am quite a simple beast to
keep happy and my wife didn't bother to even try, she just sort
of gave up on me. However, I am also sleeping with someone
else's wife and that makes me feel even worse because he is a
good guy and I have been at his house playing with his son and
that has just felt horrendous.'

Nareen felt an acute sense of powerlessness within her marriage because of her husband's refusal to have sex with her for
the past four years. She is an attractive woman in her early thirties who has been married for nine years to a workaholic
husband. She has tried all of the traditional sexual fix-it solutions offered by the plethora of self-help books, from sending
suggestive texts to buying sexy underwear, but her husband
will not respond. 'He can get an erection and he does masturbate but he doesn't seem to want to do it with me, so either he
doesn't fancy me or he is gay,' she told me. 'I will never forget
the shame of prancing around the living room in some really
nice underwear and him saying, "Mmm, nice" before settling
down in front of the telly. I had to put my dressing gown back
on. I am seen as the villain because I had an affair but what no
one seems to get is that his lack of desire for me makes me feel
completely unacknowledged as a woman. Why is that not
worse when it has felt like a form of controlling behaviour,
abusive even . . . ? If he had been hitting me people would say
that was unacceptable behaviour, but denying me sex isn't?
He doesn't see our lack of sexual intimacy as a problem. He

doesn't miss it and for him cuddling up in front of the telly is enough.'

Nareen began to neglect her appearance and question it constantly: 'Am I too skinny, do I need bigger boobs? Why should I give a shit about myself and then all it takes is one guy flirting with you at a party to wake you up to the fact that yes, I am a sexual being.' Her brief and discreet affair with another man gave her back her sense of herself as someone others might desire. 'It's more than the sex, it's being made to feel beautiful again because the sex is good, but I have had better. He makes me feel pretty and so wanted again. And he makes me tea. I can't remember the last time my husband made me a cup of tea. He doesn't do anything that caring or kind. I have bought myself nice new clothes and he hasn't even noticed, and that's weird too. I want him to notice me, to want me.'

Alice had two short affairs when her husband made her feel less than an equal in their marriage. He was going through severe financial difficulties with his business but refused to share any of the details with her. The sexual frisson of an extra-marital affair was consequently exactly the right method of punishment, wounding him back in the way that would hurt most should he ever find out, and Alice behaved provocatively enough in order to create suspicion by staying out late or going out at odd times. 'When you have an affair they are totally focused on you at that moment. I think now there was some pathetic immaturity in me which enjoyed that tension because I was jeopardising a whole lot as a wife and mother. I loved my husband, I could never imagine leaving my children, and you are intelligent enough to know that six months down the line you will be washing your lover's underwear instead and life won't be any better but still I did it, twice.' With the second affair Alice found an additional flattery in the fact that she was being hotly pursued by someone half her age when she was in her mid-forties. 'But even then it wasn't that I looked at him and thought, God, you're gorgeous. It was the fact that he seemed to find me so attractive. I remember saying to him once, "What's with this Mrs Robinson syndrome?" and he replied, "Mrs who?"'

Years after she had ended the second affair, Alice's husband died in a road accident. She discovered, to her horror, that he had no life insurance or mortgage protection and that he was substantially in debt. Alice had to sell their house, pull their youngest child out of private school and move away from friends, 'Which was doubly traumatic for them because they didn't know why and I didn't want to tell them. I didn't want them to think worse of their father when they were already griev-ing.' It could be argued that her husband's inability to confide in her and share their difficulties was a worse betrayal, for he left a mess that Alice had to unravel after his death, complicating her feelings of deep grief. However, she still feels that her betrayal of him was worse and only ever confided in one friend before she told me her story. 'In spite of all this I loved him and I know he loved me and I would never have left him, so there is still a part of me which feels so guilty about being unfaithful. It seems like such a huge betrayal in a way that nothing else is. There's a very large and old-fashioned part of me which believes in the sanctity of marriage and I shouldn't have done it.'

In many affairs there is an element of unconscious revenge for some other marital offence, for feeling overlooked, diminished, controlled. It's an aggressive act of pre-emptive defence, because it demonstrates that you are still desirable, effectual, important to others, even if that is a hidden message since your partner never finds out. The more threatened the transgressor feels, the more they are tempted to dangle that weapon tantalisingly in front of the other's nose, and then there is additional cruelty when the infidelity is actually disclosed or discovered. 'The primary reason for having an affair is usually not that you have just met the most beautiful woman and you just have to have her body,' says psychoanalytic psychotherapist and couples counsellor Brett Kahr. 'We want to hurt our partner. We want the affair to hit home even though we might claim that we have to do everything possible to prevent them from finding out because they would be devastated.'

If a person really wants to keep an infidelity secret from their partner they choose someone from another city, another country, somewhere far removed from their family, and never bring those two worlds together. Most people, however, choose someone much closer to home because of happenstance, as a way to wound or to emphasise the fact that the former relationship is over. 'There are numerous ways of being discovered and all of them contain a barbed arrow aimed right at your partner's heart,' continues Kahr. 'That's the communication of sadism. Some people smash plates, which is a much more honest and direct way of saying you want to smash their head in. People can find it very hard to know how to convey their fury towards their partner so they go off into this subterfuge because we are all terrified of both our partner's aggression and the aggression we are capable of projecting on to them – "I would like to be able to tell my wife that she is a bitch but because she is a bitch she will chew my head off and life won't be worth living so I will just go off and have an affair with my secretary instead."'

While the secrecy inherent in deceit can be exciting and empowering for the one who has dared to transgress, it can also happen that over time the lying diminishes their sense of self-worth. 'My God, the lies! I never knew I could lie this well,' Nareen told me. 'I have this wonderful, sensual time with my lover and he is caring and kind, but he asks a lot of questions about my marriage so I am deliberately vague with him. I feel guilty and I hate the constant lying. It's hard work, you have to remember all of your stories and it would be so easy to slip up. But the really scary thing is facing up to the music if my husband were to find out.'

Maintaining the fiction of fidelity becomes increasingly stressful the longer an affair continues. You have to engage regularly with your own dishonesty, remembering what you have said before, covering your tracks, erasing texts and emails, finding time as well as places to meet and inventing alibis. The affair itself might heighten feelings of adventurous escape, but the longer it goes on, the more you have to confront your own dishonesty towards both lover and partner and the more that initial adventure can feel like a betrayal of self. Ambivalence is integral to the deception practised in any substantial infidelity: the feeling of wanting all of the lying to stop but also wanting to avoid hurting their spouse. In many cases the eventual result is that the person feels their sense of enhanced power dwindling away and an even greater self-loathing because of the deceit. Lying may be essential to maintaining an affair but over time it can erode our dignity and distance us even more from the person we are lying to.

'I often get people telling me they are having an affair and asking me if they should tell their partner because they have no one else to talk to,' says relationship counsellor and psychosexual therapist Evelyn Cooney. 'I ask them what they hope to gain from that. Is it that the relationship is really over, or is this just a way of offloading everything on to their partner because they can't cope with the responsibility of having such a secret alone any more?' Is telling yet another form of cruelty, wanting to witness the hurt of your betrayal? Is it perhaps a way of forcing your partner to end the relationship so that you don't have to, or placing them in the invidious position of having to decide how your future as a couple should be, together or apart?

The person having the affair often deludes themselves about their conduct and their integrity by seeing only the best of themselves reflected in their lover's eyes. But, once their transgression is discovered, they have no choice but to face up to the hurt they have caused and cannot avoid the subsequent feelings of guilt and shame. They may have never thought they could be the sort of man who would have an affair while their partner was pregnant or the sort of woman who would cope with her difficulties by compounding them with yet more. Sometimes the pressure cooker of deceit and denial within a relationship builds to such an intensity that the only way out *is* to get caught through some flagrantly stupid act – making love in the marital bed, knowing that their partner could come home; leaving tell-tale notes or presents lying around. Kahr tells me extraordinary stories of discovery – of men being found asleep in front of their computers with their trousers around their ankles; of love letters being inserted into favourite books just waiting to be found; of cleaners being included in private intimacies before they are sacked by their female employer, which gives them plenty of ammunition for retribution. Kahr says he has heard of at least ten cases of mobiles in handbags and trouser pockets ringing home mysteriously on speed-dial. The owner's partner then picks up to hear them making love to someone else.

'It's like any obsessive behaviour such as gambling or

drinking which gets out of control,' says Jenny Riddell. 'The higher the stress levels, the more you lose insight and the ability to judge or control your behaviour.' So, people give out more and more clues as a cry for help. They can't cope with this great secret or with their addiction any longer. 'How much can I get away with? What do I have to do to make you see how wayward I have become and stop me?' 'Everybody wants to be found out,' continues Riddell. 'People often question how others could keep such a secret for so long, but the question you need to ask is, why have they revealed this now?'

It's even harder to see how a sense of powerlessness could be motivating the third, unmarried party. There is such an overt sense of superiority to the one who is apparently free to bed whom they like within a culture where sexual promiscuity is celebrated. But the reality is often very different. The lover's needs come last, as Victoria Griffin writes in her book on mistresses. As the mistress she is the one who 'springs up in joy when my lover rings the doorbell, who makes me abandon all my plans for a work-filled morning if he suggests meeting for coffee, who urges me to cancel any appointment in order to make love in the afternoon, who encourages me to go on spending money on meals and holidays with no thought of the morrow'. Oliver, like many, does not just feel he is betraying his wife for reasons which have been explained above, he also feels powerless as the third party because he is having an affair with a married woman. 'I never thought it would be possible to love two people but I do. I have no powers over her and she still sleeps with her husband while I don't sleep with my wife, and that troubles me but that's just how it is. But there also seem to be so many other men in her life, so how would I know if she was sleeping with them too? There's a part of me that feels like I am just another fly caught in her web with a load of other little flies scattered around.'

Once the affair has been uncovered it is often the third person who feels the most powerless and abandoned. They may have felt like the special, chosen one, relieving the tedium of family life with their powers. They may have deluded themselves that over time their lover would change, that they alone hold enough charisma to keep them faithful once they leave their partner. When the secret is out, however, the bubble of delusion bursts. They are either abandoned entirely as their lover attempts to repair the damage with their spouse, or they cannot decide what to do and the narcissistic injury of rejection cuts even deeper than it did each time they left their lover's bed for home. Whatever they might have said in the heat of a passionate moment, they did not love that lover enough to leave everything. All they have left are a few mementoes, expensive presents if they have been lucky, and the dirty feeling of having been used.

One of the saddest people I have ever met while researching for my books on relationships and family life is Clara. She is in her mid-thirties, has a history of depression and has always found it difficult to form relationships. She has a pattern of being attracted to or courted by men who were either married or so far away from her geographically that a lasting relationship was unlikely.

When the husband of a friend came on strong he confessed he was unhappily married and had been sexually abused as a child. She knew he had a pretty dysfunctional past, but felt such a strong emotional connection that she succumbed and fell in love. 'I felt he was someone who was deeply hurt. He didn't feel worthy of having a normal relationship and he also didn't have the strength to leave his marriage. He told me that he loved me and if we saw a child on the street he would say things like, "We could have such a beautiful child together." But then at other times he would say, "This is just sex." He played emotional games with me.'

Then Clara discovered that she was pregnant and understood exactly how her lover really felt. She was still upset by his reaction as she told me her story five years later. 'He became very threatening and told me to have an abortion. I expected him to be more caring and I suppose on some level I wanted him to say that he wanted to be with me.' Clara went to a clinic to have a termination but decided against it at the very last minute. While she had never wanted to be a single parent, she also could not get rid of a child fathered by someone she loved, 'even if he hated me'.

She gave birth to a son, who lives with her parents in the north of England, while she works and lives in London. Clara stayed in contact with the father of her child. 'He asked me several times if he should leave his wife. I told him that I wanted to be with him but that he had to decide what he wanted for himself. I need to be with a man who knows that he wants to be with me.' When his wife discovered through a mutual friend that her husband had fathered a child with Clara, she kicked him out. But still he didn't come to Clara. 'I feel like someone who has been through a divorce even though he was married to someone else. I was devastated by the way that he turned on me and blamed me for everything when the affair became public knowledge, when we were both equally guilty. That was all so very painful.' To this day Clara has not told her religious parents that their grandchild is the product of an adulterous affair because she knows how horrified they would be, incredulous that their own daughter could be guilty of such a sin.

Sometimes the third party feels so powerless and so doubt-ful that their lover will ever leave their partner that they try to gain the upper hand by forcing the issue. They decide to reveal details of their spouse's infidelity themselves, either by telephoning the news or simply sending a devastating text. When lovers know that their relationship is likely to be doomed, some seek revenge by telling the spouse that their partner doesn't love them but is too much of a coward to say so. I heard several tales of vengeful lovers trying to stir up as much trouble in a marriage as possible in a desperate last attempt to draw someone closer – the woman who tried to mirror the wife's miscarriage by feigning pregnancy and then a miscarriage; the mistress who threatened to drive two hundred miles and into the front garden of their house unless he left his wife, forcing him to phone his wife and explain, as he was away.

Verity the infidelity detective has even been hired by third parties to stir up trouble as a means of revenge. One of her clients was having an affair with a married man but knew that he was also sleeping with someone else, 'cheating' on her too. She gave Verity information about restaurants and hotels she and her married lover would meet at illicitly and wanted Verity to take pictures of them in compromising positions so that these could then be sent on to his wife. She wanted to punish her lover for having another lover by revealing her own affair with him to his wife. 'I asked her afterwards if she felt any better,' Verity told me, 'but she said that she didn't feel joy or retribution, just a sense of emptiness.'

Affair partners with a greater sense of their own self-worth would surely not stoop to such low tactics but move on to find someone new. Ultimatums are a desperate form of screaming a sense of powerlessness to effect change in any other way –

'Leave them, or . . . ' – and are just as often issued by the third party as by the betrayed spouse. When Andrew was visiting his son's boarding school with his wife to watch him play in a football match, he received a text from his mistress saying, 'I am taking more tablets. Goodbye.' She had threatened him previously that she would tell his wife because she 'knew he didn't love her' and had presumed that their night away near their son's boarding school was romantic rather than parental. Andrew had no choice but to send an ambulance to her house and cut short their visit. 'My wife knew by this time about the affair and had herself threatened suicide, so I had to drop her home and then go on to find that she had taken an overdose but that it wasn't fatal. I realised then that this was way too extreme and possessive. She wanted me to nuke my wife basically – you leave and then you never go back there.'

When Andrew ended the affair, his ex-mistress cranked up her attempts at revenge. She sent to his workplace packages with the word 'adulterer' written on the envelope. She rang the police and tried to get him arrested on charges of sexual harassment. 'She tried to amplify everything to cause maximum humiliation and damage to me and my family, which just devalues any love she might have had for me.'

Threats and ultimatums force people into defensive positions where they are likely to be more guarded emotionally and aggressive. Such tactics also have a nasty habit of backfiring. Pat's husband has been serially unfaithful to her throughout their lengthy marriage. His long-term mistress spent a week with him on holiday and enjoyed herself so much that she decided she had had enough of sharing and insisted that he leave Pat within twenty-four hours of their return or else their affair was over. 'When he told me that their liaison had been going on for close to twenty-five years I was so shaken I just gave up and let him go,' Pat told me. 'But then he discovered a whole lot about her that he didn't much like. She smoked and he never knew that, which is astonishing given how long he had known her. She thought it was going to be like being his mistress the whole time and that he would take her out, not just sit morosely in front of the telly. So he came back to me like a shot!'

For the betrayed partner it isn't usually just the fact that their partner has had sex with someone else which hurts. Infidelity attacks an essential human need – to feel special to another human being – and raises primal anxieties about being abandoned. The person we trusted most to have our best interests at heart now threatens our entire sense of self, place, purpose and security. Sexual betrayal feels like an unravelling, a rejection of all that you are – 'I was not good enough to keep them faithful.' There can be uncontrolled rage and jealousy as well as an overwhelming sense of impotence where the only way to raise yourself up again is to distance yourself entirely from the betrayer. 'It's like a bereavement for a lot of the couples I see,' says relationship counsellor and psychosexual therapist Evelyn Cooney, 'and people go through the same stages as they do with grief, for the loss of the relationship they thought they had. What's not talked about is the humiliation. People don't want to talk about it to their friends and often I am the first person they tell.'

Those who experienced deep rejection as a child can find that their feelings of self-loathing are particularly acute, for the only way they could rationalise their parents' behaviour as a child was by believing that they themselves were bad: 'If I was good they would not be abusing me in this way.' The

symptoms of those who discover they have been betrayed sexually can resemble those of post-traumatic stress disorder.
Every assumption about their partner, the meaning of their
relationship, and themselves has been shattered and they
need to recount the experience over and over again. 'It was
always there, this constant gnawing pain,' says Naomi, who
married her husband Patrick when she was nineteen. Her
childhood was dominated by her parents' violent arguments and as the only daughter with two older brothers she
was smothered by her mother's efforts to fulfil her own
emotional needs. Naomi's marriage was enmeshed. They did
everything together. With an emotionally chequered childhood of his own, Patrick then left Naomi for another woman
when his business began to fail. She recalls, 'All of that childhood insecurity came flooding back and I spent a lot of time
crying. Our lives had been so intertwined for so long that it
was like losing half of me. I also lost four stone. And Patrick
couldn't decide what to do. He said he wanted to stay with
me but that he couldn't tell the other woman on the phone,
so he went to see her, then decided to stay with her and rang
me to tell me. The double standards of that really hurt. It was
like he had turned into this stranger even though we had
been married for so long.'

For others the months following the discovery of infidelity
are so fraught with rage, uncertainty and emotional turbulence
that it is hard to find a way through the chaos. 'I felt bewildered, I couldn't understand why she would jeopardise
everything we had built together in such an uncaring way when
I would never consider doing such a thing. It was emotional
torture which went on for the best part of a year,' says John,
whose wife left him and their children for another man and
then came back on several occasions. 'I was really upset,

worried and scared. I lost a lot of weight.' Jan says she 'went back through our relationship and unpicked everything. How could I have been so stupid, so blind? I guess I wasn't able to face up to who he really was until we had this crisis.' Confidence in oneself as a sexual being is shattered. It can rock belief in every other aspect of life and relationship to the core. 'You suddenly have no sense of reality,' writes Nora Ephron in *Heartburn*, 'you have lost a piece of your past. The infidelity itself is small potatoes compared to the low-level brain damage that results when a whole chunk of your life turns out to have been completely different to what you thought it was.'

There tend to be multiple layers of treachery, wounding us where we are most vulnerable. For men that can be the humiliation of not being 'man enough' to satisfy a woman completely. 'Of course it's a sexual rejection,' says John. 'But I try not to dwell on that too much . . . ' But the deepest betrayals seem to centre on our emotional vulnerabilities and our dependency on each other, for instance after the birth of a child, when male infidelity is particularly common, or when we are ill or rendered less significant by society through unemployment, or as we age and lose our firm flesh and youthful looks. 'I think it attacks a person's sense of self-worth because they have let so much of another person in,' says psychotherapist and couples counsellor Liza Glenn. 'And of course a woman has also let that person in physically.'

The impact of a man's betrayal is often mitigated by the notion that men can more easily disassociate sex from love. 'I thought there might be some extramarital sex because we had married so young,' says Naomi. 'But I never thought that he would leave or fall in love. That's when it really hurts, when it is someone else's mind.' There is also a difference between the most casual sexual assignation discovered quite by chance and the discovery of a lengthy affair, where a parallel life has been disguised and denied, and where we are doubly humiliated for being so foolish as not to have noticed anything untoward going on for so long. If we are in a relationship with a serial philanderer, each time we take them back and forgive them their failings the sense of betrayal cuts deeper as we recognise that we are not loved enough for them to change, and that we have only two choices: to stay and put up with it, or leave and be alone.

For Candy it is not her husband's extramarital sexual activity which is the real betrayal: it is the absence of a sexual relationship with her which has really hurt. They have had a tacit open relationship for much of their thirty-year marriage. She is in her late sixties and is still a very attractive woman. She says that a high libido fed her promiscuity, but being desired by other men is also clearly important to her. Her husband's sexual dalliances never caused her enough grief to consider divorce. It is the fact that he did not accompany her to the hospital after she had a stroke two years ago and has announced that he will not make love to her because she is 'too fat and I do not fancy you any more' which has sent her running to counselling and a lawyer. Candy has tried to arouse him sexually but he pushes her away. 'He is cruel. He rushes around frantically working all the time, trying to make money, and he has said that he is scared of getting old, which is, I think, the reason why he didn't want to cope with my illness, but that doesn't make it any easier for me. I also know that he has had sex with other women and that really pisses me off. He won't do it with me any more but he will with other women . . . younger women.'

For Isabel too it is not the extramarital sex that feels like a betrayal. She and her husband had been married for over twenty years. Isabel had a brief affair when her children were small which he never discovered and 'I have always thought fidelity over a long time to be an impossibility in most marriages. In a way it is none of my business if he wants to go and fuck someone else and morally I didn't have any problem with it. It was a shock and it made me very angry, of course it did, but that was because I didn't know whether or not he would leave me for her. And that raises all sorts of other issues. I don't want to be on my own or bring my children up on my own. I don't want to have to sell the house and have my life turned upside down and I didn't want to be without him because he intrigues me, makes me laugh and I am never bored. I love him. The real betrayal came when I discovered that I was being lied to in that the affair was still going on, when he had said it was over. That completely undermined my trust and then all the classic reactions came into play. I was very, very angry, bitter, upset and behaved like the classic wronged wife.'

For Amanda, who is thirty-four and left her home in Kenya to study in Britain and has been with her husband ever since, there are multiple layers of betrayal to his infidelity. He disclosed his affair with a younger, white woman when she was pregnant with their first child and then left her. He then said the affair was over and came back to Amanda when she had a miscarriage. While they had been separated he had visited his sister in France with his family during the summer. When he came back she found highly explicit photographs on his laptop which showed that the girlfriend had been there too and that his family had omitted to mention that fact. The other woman then announced that she was pregnant – a massive wound to Amanda, still mourning a miscarriage – and her husband said that he couldn't leave his lover. 'But he could leave me pregnant,' she told me over a coffee. Her sadness at the end of their marriage was palpable. 'I deserve more, someone who is capable of loving me properly and putting me first, and what is really painful is that he was so selfish that at no point did he seem to consider that he might lose me. The image of them together haunts me, not just the explicit ones, but he had taken loads of photos of her when they were out and about, like you do at the beginning of a relationship when everything is so WOW, and that hurt a lot because he didn't want to take lots of pictures of me, but then why her, clearly such a piece of trash? What does she have that I don't?'

There is a profound sense of powerlessness in discovering that you have been betrayed. The one who has decided to transgress by having an affair seems to hold all of the cards. They have betrayed trust by sharing intimacies with another. They seemingly have the power to decide whether to stay or go, and have someone else to go to. The uncovering of an affair can provoke such a crisis that neither partner can see beyond it. Many assume that once the bond of monogamy has been broken, the relationship is over. Research indicates that an infidelity can be particularly distressing and damaging to the health of a long-term relationship when there are already other difficulties such as unemployment, health problems or very young children. An affair can feel like a soother for these stresses, which is why they are common triggers. However, there is already such a serious lack of stability in the relationship because of them that an affair is much more likely to tip that partnership over the edge completely.

If you have been betrayed, the sense of bewildered hurt can be so immense that you can only focus on the drama of the affair and the fact that you have been betrayed, rather than on the wider picture of the story of your relationship. Some avoid confronting the issue at all; others kick their partner out instantly, making any dialogue impossible. But probably the best advice at this early stage is not to do anything which could be regretted later. Marianne knew that her husband of more than twenty years was unhappy, but was devastated when she discovered that he was having an affair. 'I was in such shock I couldn't sleep, I couldn't speak, but I also knew that I didn't want him to go. So I just tried to live through it day by day. Then I got really upset because he wouldn't come on holiday with me and the children. He wasn't prepared to leave her for just one week and I thought then, what is the point of even trying, and told him to go. The thing is, I am not sure where we might be now as a couple if I hadn't done that.'

Some people try to regain the upper hand by becoming hyper-vigilant, monitoring their partner's every move with an obsessive jealousy. 'The worst aspect of the whole experience was becoming a suspicious person. I hated the woman I had become, going through the rubbish, the computer, his mobile phone,' says Isabel, who discovered her husband was having an affair twenty years into their marriage. 'I wanted to go through all the bank statements and receipts. I wanted to look at the parking payments stuck to the windscreen of the car to see where he had been. You become this pilfering, long-nosed person poking in places you shouldn't, and that's a dereliction of self. You are out of control and the only way to regain control is to say you will have no truck with this person that you have become and when I did that things got better.'

Others try to restore the balance of power in their relationship with actual or imagined revenge whereby the one who has strayed is made to feel equally humiliated. It is often the third person, the one who dared to trespass, who bears the brunt of it, for they are such an easy target. 'I have three ongoing fantasies of what I would do if I passed her on the street,' says Isabel, even though her husband's affair ended several years ago. 'One involves ignoring her entirely. In another I slap her hard across the face. But the most common one involves sitting down with her over a cup of coffee and making her tell me everything that happened, everything that he won't.'

Laura fantasises about telling the parents of her husband's lover that their daughter has had an affair with a married man. 'She has stolen my life. She is in bed with my husband at night and having a fantastic time with him while I am here looking after our kids alone. When I think about the fact that she has been here and touched my children it makes me want to harm her physically. We're in a car together and I ask her if she realises how much damage she has caused to me and then I pull her out of the car by the hair and start banging her head against the ground.'

'It's probably illegal but I would want to humiliate him,' says John. 'I would want to show him the same utter lack of concern for his life and his emotions as he has shown for mine. I might enlarge his face and put it on a billboard with the word "adulterer" across it. Or hire some guys to chuck him in the back of the van, get him really scared before chucking him on to the street miles from his home, bound, gagged and naked.'

When Julie Metz discovered, only after her husband's death, that he had had a series of affairs throughout their marriage, she couldn't vent her rage at him, so it was his lover, her former friend and neighbour, who became the focus of her frenzied imagination. 'A gun was too swift, too merciful,' she writes in her memoir *Perfection*. 'I wanted a sword to slit her end to end and then, with one hundred more cuts, dice her body into small pieces and leave the bloodied, quivering remains of skin, muscle and soulless guts on her front lawn, arranged in a gruesome scarlet letter.'

Society tolerates, even expects, an explosive reaction from the spouse who has been betrayed. Revenge is a powerful way to feel vindicated, to right the balance and restore a sense of justice, to soothe our injured sense of self after a betrayal, for we see the immediate visual impact of our actions. It's a cathartic release and adds yet more drama to the narrative of the affair. However, there is evidence to suggest that we resort to revenge when we cannot verbalise the hurt of rejection and the loss of public face in any other way. Anger may be a natural and visceral response, but it is primarily a defensive measure which tends to mask all of the emotions swirling beneath, such as guilt, shame and the profound pain of feeling abandoned. Anger is one of the most difficult emotions to control, particularly when it is combined with a sense of having been humiliated, for not to be seen defending yourself against such a shameful slight could be construed as showing even greater weakness. Excessive hostility is not good for our health. A meta-analysis of forty-five published studies shows that hostility raises blood pressure and is an independent risk factor for coronary heart disease and premature death.[2] Anger may be natural but it is in our interests to find ways to control it. Revenge may feel good in the short term but it is unlikely to even the score, for how can you ever compare the pain felt by two people?

It is natural for those who discover an infidelity to feel so hurt and humiliated that they want to rage and shout, to send crockery flying, to ruminate over every detail of the affair, to ask thousands of questions daily as they try to understand why it happened. To take that rage a stage further into a form of violence which will wound someone we profess to care about is a transgression born of the delusion that any of us can own another human being. Nothing brings about the end of a relationship faster than exacting revenge. It may feel good in the moment, but it usually diminishes us more. 'A man that studieth revenge keeps his own wounds green, which otherwise would heal and do well,' Francis Bacon wrote in his essay 'On Revenge' in 1625. 'Certainly, in taking revenge, a man is but even with his enemy; but in passing it over, he is superior.'

Nor does revenge right the balance between two people: it usually distorts and poisons a precarious situation even more. Revenge isn't justified by the misguided notion that right is on our side as the victim, or that 'love' vindicates a crime of passion. Such an attitude condones the countless acts of domestic abuse that occur all around the world when a person feels so powerless that they have no other means left to reassert control over someone who seems to be threatening them profoundly. It is estimated that, in the US, as many as half of all those who have been murdered by their partner died when they tried to leave the relationship, whether or not they were leaving it for somebody else.[3]

'Jealousy is the most absurd pain of all,' laments Charles in Elizabeth Taylor's novel *A Game of Hide and Seek*, 'the public indignity, the private pain. The shock of it lays dreadful waste in one's soul; it discolours the whole world, cancels every remembrance of tenderness.' Delusional jealousy, sometimes known as the Othello Syndrome, is a sign of mental illness. It can affect both sexes but is appreciably more common in men and is a major contributory factor in domestic violence.[4] The tiniest things, such as a new perfume, a tie done up the wrong way, being slightly late, losing a handkerchief that was a gift of love, become exaggerated symbols of infidelity. The suspicious mind is never at rest. The innocent partner is interrogated over and over again. Physical threats are used to extract a confession, but this merely supports the deluded person's own warped sense of reality, for nothing untoward has actually taken place. Mild jealousy may be a healthy sign of love. Obsessive jealousy raises uncomfortable truths about our own weaknesses – our resentment and envy of what others have, our sense of helplessness and deep fear of being excluded – rather than revealing anything about our partner's presumed misdemeanours. 'When I am jealous I suffer four times over: because I'm jealous, because I criticise myself for being so, because I'm afraid my jealousy will hurt the other person, because I have allowed myself to be dominated by something so banal,' writes Roland Barthes in *Fragments d'un Discours Amoureux*.

An obsessive jealousy which feeds revenge is so highly reactive that it blinds us to the rational and reduces our ability to cope. It means that we can hurl all of our resentment with life and the relationship at the target of our revenge. It allows us to hide permanently in the powerless role of innocent victim, and alters our perspective so radically that it becomes difficult to conceive of any clear-headed path through intense personal difficulties to some sort of resolution. Obsessive jealousy means that we confuse love with fusion, unable to tolerate the separateness of our lover as a human being, and are likely to drive them away. 'Sexual jealousy is widely accepted as grounds for moral indignation in our culture,' writes Ayala Malach Pines in her book *Romantic Jealousy*. '"Feeling jealous" serves as an explanation or excuse for a wide range of hostile, bitter and even violent actions. Without the legitimizing context of jealousy, these actions would be taken as severe pathology and derangement.'

Obsession with the details of the affair may seem like a natural consequence of sexual betrayal but it isn't helpful. It freezes a person into a kind of stasis where they can avoid some of the deeper, more painful emotions such as fear of being abandoned completely. It means they can avoid facing up to their part in the slow, corrosive acrimony, in the distancing that must have taken place to have allowed a third person in. And it allows them to maintain the upper hand in the power balance of the relationship, forcing the other into their own corner of guilt and appeasement, where no amount of apology can ever be enough.

An obsessive need to get even lurks within the most habitual couple reactions after the disclosure of an affair. Take the woman who says she has forgiven her husband the transgression, but remembers to bring it up at every dinner party, or the man who now sees no reason not to parade a new interest in excessive public flirting in front of his wife. Others take revenge by refusing to show even the tiniest act of kindness or courtesy, because they have already given too much to someone they feel showed little kindness to them. They refuse to comfort their partner through the tortured indecision as to whether to leave or stay, or the grief of giving up a lover they cared for, or the guilt they feel for having hurt their partner and ruined everything. They brought it upon themselves. They must now pay, continually.

Stan had an eight-month affair five years into his second marriage and not long after the birth of their first child. 'I should have had the strength to say no, I know that now but at the time she was attractive and confident and she sort of controlled me and I kept thinking that Iris would never find out.' When Iris did find out she was devastated. Stan's first wife had engaged in a series of affairs but he hadn't left her because of the children and Iris believed that, having lived through such an ordeal himself, he would never do the same thing to her.

Rather than talking with Stan about the root causes of his infidelity and finding ways to forgive each other and move on, Iris spent the next fifteen years punishing him by allowing almost no sex and by saying that she couldn't love him any more because of the betrayal. 'I felt that if I put too much into it he would think, oh good, she's got over it, and I couldn't allow that because I was still so hurt,' she told me. Stan spent those fifteen years trying to avoid answering Iris's questions about the details of the affair because he didn't want to hurt her any more. He also bought her anything she wanted to keep her happy, but nothing was ever enough. 'She's never got over the fact that I just went back to work and carried on with my life, playing golf and going to the football. I wasn't unhappy like she was unhappy.'

When the wounds of hurt and humiliation freeze into this kind of cold and clinical revenge, the entire relationship suffers. Men obsess over sexual betrayal every bit as much as women. It's another form of revenge, pouring energy into refusing to be nice, or spying on every move their partner makes, hiring infidelity detectives, fanning the flames of blame and the drama of the affair, rather than looking at the relationship with an open mind. 'How could *you* do this to *me*? How could you lie to me like that? What does s/he have that I don't?' Nothing the straying partner says or does could ever be enough to answer such questions adequately, but they are asked over and over again. In this way the betrayed person punishes their partner by reinforcing their guilt, giving them little choice but to apologise repeatedly and ask for forgiveness rather than speaking out about why they think they might have strayed. The affair becomes a black hole, 'Trapping both parties in an endless round of bitterness, revenge and self-pity. These couples endlessly gnaw at the same bone,' writes Esther Perel, 'reiterate the same mutual recriminations, and blame each other for their agony. Why they stay in the marriage is often as puzzling as why they can't get beyond their mutual antagonism.'[5]

It is easier to focus on the drama, to have an affair with the affair so that you can vent all of your rage and frustration about everything else you hate about the relationship or the person, than it is to delve into some of the hidden, more difficult emotions that a couple might have been avoiding for years. They may not even be aware that there are any. Those who like to avoid conflict or intimacy are more likely to separate at this stage. Obsession with the affair as the reason for the end of the relationship then becomes an essential means of defence against the painful knowledge that the betrayed spouse might have had a hand in their own rejection, for the end of the marriage is usually even more devastating emotionally than the discovery of the sexual infidelity. 'Obsession with the affair is the betrayed spouse's biggest enemy – spouses who stay stuck in the obsession end up bitter and often alone,' writes Emily Brown in her textbook for marital therapists. 'Some become lifelong victims, focussing their life on the fact that their partner had an affair. The spouse is usually less aware than is the straying partner that he or she has issues to face.'

People betray each other regularly in relationships in all sorts of ways. They violate trust by lying, embarrass each other in public, make unilateral decisions and spend at the pub or on handbags money they do not have in the joint account. Most of us accept that someone we care for might make mistakes or slide into drinking too much. Flawed behaviour can rock a relationship but it is only with sexual infidelity that many feel they should operate a policy of immediate zero tolerance. 'If you have a husband who spends lots of time on sport, neglects you, falls asleep in front of the telly, shows little affection and devotes himself to causes outside the home, why is that viewed as normal and OK, yet meeting up once a week for some enjoyable sexual activity in as responsible a way as you can is viewed with outrage and derision?' laments a mother on a Mumsnet thread. 'It seems to me that the former is far more reprehensible than the latter.'

Infidelity threatens the monogamous ideal and the foundations of coupledom, family life and society. The more socially accepted responses of betrayal – the rage of revenge, the self-pity of being a victim and the deep, deep guilt of the villain who requires punishment and atonement – are rarely questioned. However, these reactions tend to exacerbate the degenerative cycles which exist in any relationship and rarely help a couple in trouble to find their way out of such a deep crisis. Such reactions may be common and seem understandable but they force people to take defensive positions. The danger then is that the deeper resentments, unhappiness and feelings of powerlessness which may have provoked the betrayal in the first place are never addressed because that would be even more painful. Each spouse assumes the other to be more powerful than they really are.

Infidelity can provoke the spectrum of negative emotions – fear, anger, sadness, self-contempt, shame, jealousy and guilt – in both the one who has strayed and the one who feels betrayed. Negative emotions narrow the mind and mask the deeper truths of what might have been going wrong between two people who probably still care for each other. If the affair is an easy way to end a relationship that was in terminal decline before any sexual infidelity, then so be it. But for most couples the drama of a discovered affair induces such a state of panic that neither really knows what they want or what to do next. There is just an overwhelming sense of emotional chaos and impotence. Blame then mushrooms, clouding the picture still further as it is heaved back and forth. That is the subject to which we turn next.

# 7

# WHO IS TO BLAME?

Blame is integral to our current understanding of infidelity. The one who transgresses and breaks their marital vows is almost always seen as the guilty one, the one with the problem, the 'cheater' vilified by friends, family, their community. If they are in the public eye the press takes its stand too. Proving guilt or innocence may be an essential aspect of maintaining law and order and appropriate for the crimes of burglary and murder, but these are entirely inadequate concepts for the intricate and very delicate alchemy of relationships and family life. In fact the whole notion of blame for sexual transgression does far more damage to the chances of a relationship recovering from an infidelity than the actual act of sexual betrayal itself.

The prospect of a 'no fault divorce' may be touted by the legal profession, but assigning blame to someone for marital breakdown is still where proceedings start. The concepts of betrayal and blame are often used by lawyers to frustrate a fair settlement and discredit the notion that the straying parent should be allowed equal access to their children. Countless separating couples would prefer some external party labelled 'justice' to make a judgement over their lives and those of their children. But the idea that anybody, whether a judge in a court of law, friends and family or society, with its rigid endorsement of monogamy, should decide what might be right for us as a couple is absurd and deeply unhelpful. Even so, couples find it easier to blame each other than to take responsibility for examining the failure of the romantic dream, where two people who once loved each other could have drifted so far apart.

It is easy for the one who has strayed to blame their spouse for failing to make them happy, for not being that perfect mate, rather than looking into the heart of their own unrealistic romantic expectations of both happiness and relationship. It is much easier for the one who has strayed to blame the baby or the fact that their sex life has died than it is to look into why they might have withdrawn sexually or felt so threatened and abandoned by the existence of their own child. It is also easier for a mother to use the children and the endless work of caring for them as a shield and blame the father for not understanding this than it is to do the harder task of re-establishing a separate relationship with him. 'The saddest cases I think are when the kids are involved,' Verity the infidelity detective told me. 'The one who is cheating tries to manipulate the kids by making out that it is all the other parent's fault, which then makes it very difficult for the children to know who they can trust. The other partner is not only losing someone they thought would be a lifelong partner but they are also finding that their kids are being slowly turned against them.'

The narcissistic injury of rejection and the dashing of all their romantic hopes and dreams can be so immense for the betrayed partner that they feel justified in withdrawing to lick their wounds, confident they deserve the support of every friend or family member they choose to tell. It takes great courage to look honestly at what happened and to listen to how we might have contributed to our own pain by our behaviour with the relationship. 'When I first started couple work I had the naive notion that you would find 99 per cent of the fault in the man who had seventeen prostitutes or mistresses while the wife just cleans and cooks, or perhaps if she was withholding sex after the seventh baby then 80 per cent was his fault,' says psychoanalytic psychotherapist and couples counsellor Brett Kahr. 'But having done this work for a long time now I can say hand on heart that it is usually fifty-fifty. When you start to unravel the story of the affair we find that each one has had a contribution to make in hurting the other. The aggrieved women are often quite biting and critical, which can then drive the man into the arms of a more understanding woman almost so that she can accuse him of the infidelity and discharge all her aggression. When it is the woman who has had an affair there is often passivity in the man, which seems to anger and propel them. There's a very complicated unconscious dance in couples which involves a lot of provocation and goading, with each taking up positions. It's far too facile to see blame as only the justifiable reaction of the aggrieved spouse. When you start to peel back the layers in couple therapy you find that it is not so black and white. You find that each has been needling the other, sometimes for years.'

Esther Perel, counsellor and author of *Mating in Captivity*, agrees. She describes on howdini.com a client who was emotionally devastated by his wife's affair even though they had barely enjoyed any sexual intimacy in the past eight years. 'At one point in the sessions I asked him why he was so interested in everything that she had done and so uninterested in everything that he had *not* done,' she says. 'Why was her betrayal so much bigger than his indifference, his neglect, his stonewalling of her? There are lots of ways that people let each other down. An affair needs to be put within the larger context of the relationship.'

It is much easier for the one who has been betrayed to blame the third party for trespassing and ruining everything or their spouse for the transgression, rather than face up to all the subtle and subconscious ways they might have pushed them so far away that an affair had more purchase. Far too many take refuge in the easier option of kicking out the perpetrator in a flurry of self-righteous indignation, often encouraged by friends and family, for we feel we devalue ourselves even more by not doing so. In this common scenario both spouses pour every ounce of energy into destroying each other rather than addressing the slow decay of the relationship which lies at the heart of the affair. 'I was the guilty party, according to the law,' says Tim, who was kicked out of the family home on the night that his wife was telephoned by the husband of the woman he was having an affair with. 'No one was particularly interested in whether there'd been a history to the breakdown. I'm sure that in the children's eyes, I'd been the one who broke the family up. It's not quite as black and white as that, as anyone who's been in a similar situation would understand.'

Recovery after the shock of the discovery of an affair is bound to be a gradual process. All of the research and anecdotal evidence from those who have lived through it suggests that it is only with time, and enough distance from the drama of the affair, that they can gain enough perspective on the relationship to be able to make the important decision as to whether or not to separate. 'His affair saved our relationship, although I was so devastated that I didn't know that when the whole thing came out into the open,' says Isabel. The months after she discovered her husband's affair were fraught with rage and uncertainty. It is only now, years after the event and following numerous conversations, that she feels able to say, 'I know now that we were both equally to blame. We had got very stuck. I wasn't really there for him, I was distracted by my parents dying and other horrible things happening and I didn't want anyone near me. I think she just came along and gave him what he wanted at the time and I can't feel cross with him for that. I don't think infidelity is necessarily about infidelity. It's like an earthquake and then you have to look closely at what has happened and count the costs. It is ridiculous to have a knee-jerk reaction to it with "How can you ever trust them again?" because you can. Eventually. People can fall off the wagon, can't they?'

Modern society has become so disapproving of all sexual infidelity that we find it hard to feel tolerance when a person strays. The monogamous ideal is upheld by a press that is largely sanctimonious about sexual betrayal. The new ethos is that affairs are always wrong. Pillars of the community feel they have no choice but to lie to protect their reputation rather than admit to common human frailty, for those who commit the sin of infidelity are considered not fit to serve. Privileged worlds have to become closed communities to preserve their privacy. What happens on set stays on set. The wives of rock stars, footballers, politicians and actors have little choice but to keep quiet about their husbands' dalliances. It is only once elements of the couple's private lives become public knowledge and the wife runs the risk of being humiliated or embarrassed by it personally that she has to take a stand. Friends and family prolong the deceit and the denial by turning a blind eye to any sexual transgressions. They do not want to cause trouble, get drawn into the drama, lose friends by being forced to take sides, or be the sanctimonious prig or the bearer of bad news. They have nothing to gain unless they want to use the information for their own ulterior motives.

We seem to be more understanding of other frailties, such as alcoholism or depression, than we are of infidelity. Blame isn't appropriate in these afflictions; pity and understanding are. Infidelity, however, is different. There are only 'villains' and 'victims'. It is simply considered weak. We could all be selfish and self-indulgent if we chose to be, the thinking goes, and so we reproach ourselves and others for failing to show restraint. As adults we have to face up to the fact that if we stray sexually, nobody forced us to leap into bed with somebody else. But nor is it reasonable to suggest that the adulterer bears all of the responsibility for the transgression, so that their spouse can maintain the illusion of total innocence.

The vast majority of affairs are not triggered by evil, uncaring villains, intent on gorging as much physical flesh as possible. People stray out of momentary weakness, as a form of breakdown and out of boredom and unhappiness, which are the norm in many marriages, fortified by the delusion that they can control this brief adventure. The trouble with blame is that it masks the truth of what has really been going on between two people, often for years, and it cranks up negative emotions, particularly acrimony, clouding possible solutions and improvements to the relationship in the immediate future as each tries to heave complete responsibility for their difficulties on to the other. 'The truth is that infidelity is not some monolithic thing. It happens for a million different reasons and means a million different things,' Julie Powell told me in an email exchange after the publication of her memoir of infidelity, *Cleaving*.

Nareen found herself isolated and ostracised when she came close to an affair after four years of celibacy with her husband. Before anything physical happened she tried to talk to one of her closest girlfriends, who refused to discuss it and said that she found it deeply unacceptable – 'I cannot know you if you continue with this.' So Nareen looked for support online, posting questions on threads, hopeful that someone would empathise and offer good counsel. 'It's really scary doing this without anyone to just say, "I understand" but almost everyone said all the usual stuff, like, "You should stay and make it work"; "You took a vow to stay together"; "You whore"; "You're a slut"; "You want to have your cake and eat it", even though I had told them the whole sorry story. What no one seems to gets is how undermining his sexual rejection of me is. There is very little empathy around affairs – people see them in very black and white terms. I Googled "affairs" and most of the articles were either critical, vilifying the one who is unfaithful, or they were about how you cope if you have been betrayed. Society says that affairs are always wrong and I get that, but what nobody seems to realise is that for the past four years I have lost all sense of self-worth in my marriage.'

Denial is integral to blame. The more hostile society becomes to any infidelity, the greater the need to lie about any transgression, both to oneself and to each other. In sexually non-exclusive relationships it is the violation of agreed boundaries which is considered to be the real betrayal of trust. If the rule is that you never take phone numbers or see the same person twice, these are the boundaries of intimacy which must not be crossed. In other parts of the world Pamela Druckerman found very different cultural attitudes, as she explains in her book *Lust in Translation*. When she put the maxim 'It's not about the sex, it's about the lying' to the French, they 'Just looked confused. How exactly could you have an affair without lying about it?' An American who tells his mistress that he is unhappy with his wife comes across as sensitive and in need of love rather than as a low-level two-timer. 'In China, however, I discovered that married men routinely praise their wives to their mistresses, to prove they respect women and to set boundaries for the affair.'

By contrast, in British and American culture lying has become crucial to every single aspect of infidelity because of the myth that any sexual transgression will inevitably destroy a relationship. Few believe or want to believe that their secret life will be discovered at the beginning of their exciting, escapist adventure. With such a sense of omnipotence at the beginning of an affair, most fool themselves that there won't be any consequences. 'If you were to stop and think about what you are doing, everything then becomes much too scary and dangerous,' says Isabel, who had a brief affair early on in her marriage which her husband never discovered. People delude themselves that they can manage the danger and conceal it from their partner because they want to justify something that they know in their hearts isn't right. And that's not a wise decision given how well their partner will have grown to know them and how easily they might spot that something subtle has shifted in the quality of their relationship.

It is easy to justify sexual straying with, 'What they don't know won't hurt them'; or 'It's just sex'; or the idea that your lover entered the arrangement voluntarily and consequently nobody suffers because of your actions. It is easy to explain away the affair by seeing only your partner's unreasonableness and all of the things they do not do for you. It is easy to use the romanticised ideal of passionate love to justify your betrayal of other values such as loyalty or trust. It is even easy for many to lie to themselves about whether they are actually being unfaithful, for blow jobs don't count. The majority of those who stray never realise that the longer the lying goes on, the further they also stray from addressing the difficulties that provoked the affair in the first place and the more likely they are to find fault with their spouse. Blame escalates, bringing in all sorts of other things – failing to get back in time for parents' evening, not showing enough interest in a work difficulty, failing to appreciate the other's efforts.

There is also a danger that the lying becomes a very powerful and insidious weapon in the blame game. Whenever the suspicious spouse questions their partner's behaviour or even dares to ask if they are having an affair, the lying response 'undermines the other person's confidence in his own emotional reactions and his own perception of reality', as the psychologist Harold Searles writes in his seminal paper 'The Effort to Drive the Other Person Crazy'. Defensive answers such as 'You're just paranoid, you would know if I was having an affair' and 'You don't trust me' may seem like mere efforts to protect the secret and the spouse from the emotional consequences of discovery of the betrayal, but these answers shift the blame back. When they are repeated over time they can seriously unsettle a person who senses instinctively that there has been a shift in the quality of attention they are getting but is reassured repeatedly that nothing is wrong. 'There are lies you tell to a person who's being given a surprise party, lies told in a spirit of fun,' writes Jonathan Franzen in his novel *Freedom*, 'and then there are lies you tell a person to make them look foolish for believing them.'

When the affair is with someone of the same sex, the taboos surrounding homosexuality are still so strong that the need to lie and push all blame back and forth is even greater. Philip knew there had been problems in his fifteen-year marriage. The couple's arguing was affecting the children and his wife drank heavily, but 'I could never understand what I was doing wrong. However, I was always the one who was some-how at fault,' Philip told me after they had separated. Then he began to suspect that his wife's friendship with another woman was so close they could be lovers. 'They spent more and more time together. If we went anywhere the girlfriend had to come too but whenever I asked, "Is there something going on – we can organise a separation," she would deny it vehemently. She told all our friends that I didn't appreciate her when she showed no interest at all in me or my life. Then she started doing these really odd things when we were on holiday. I started finding texts from this other woman on her phone saying things like, "I love you, you mean the world to me." Then she left a letter to me via this other woman lying around on the kitchen table saying, "I don't know how to tell Philip," but when I confronted her about it she just grabbed the letter and her phone and started deleting everything and denied that they had ever been there, when I had read all those words.'

Philip says that he knew then that Jane had probably been lying to him all along. 'You feel a bit sick in the pit of your stomach but I was more relieved than anything else. A lot of things started making sense, like how interested she had sud-denly become in what money we had, and I just thought, at last I can do something about this.' But Jane continued to deny that she was having an affair and fought Philip over every-thing through solicitors and then in court. He says she tried to secrete as many of their assets as possible and get him kicked out of the family home by accusing him of domestic violence. They have now reached a settlement but Philip still considers that his ex-wife bears most of the blame. 'Even though she was the one who had committed adultery, on more than one occasion she fought me about everything through the courts and tried to make out everything was my fault. They still deny they are lovers to this day even though they spend all of their time together. They tell everyone they are sisters but everyone knows they are not. But rather than admit that, they have tried to turn all of our friends against me by saying I have been the monster for forcing through the divorce and then giving her nothing for the children, which just isn't true. She was the one who had tried to brand me as the wife-beater and get me kicked out of my own house.'

Levels of denial can be even greater in the spouse who is not having the affair. A certain amount of faith – that s/he wouldn't be unfaithful – is essential for sanity. You can't spend your whole life searching for signals and clues. However, our investment in keeping everything together, particularly when there are children, can be so huge that we refuse to see the blindingly obvious. We assume we see more as a relationship becomes established, but all too often we get so seduced by the need for comfort and certainty in a relationship that we actually see less. 'I think I was so entranced with being a couple that I didn't even notice that the person I thought I was being a couple with thought he was a couple with someone else,' says Rachel in Nora Ephron's semi-autobiographical novel *Heartburn*.

The greater the sense of taboo and shame around the betrayal of infidelity, the greater the need to refuse to see the signs. Denial becomes an essential defence for the one who is being betrayed. 'I didn't see it even though people would make references to their affair obliquely,' says Naomi. 'I should have picked it up but I was too arrogant. I thought we had it made and nothing like that could ever happen to us.' People refuse to join up the dots because they are afraid of what they might see. Once the secret is out, they cannot avoid dealing with the consequences: confrontation, possible separation, public shame if the news gets out, for we were not sexy or loved enough for our partner to stay faithful, as well as loss.

Philip admits now with hindsight that there was a slow downward decay in their relationship which he was probably refusing to address at the time. 'I suggested counselling right up until the last minute but she refused. She told me all these stupid lies for nearly six years but I didn't want to leave because I was worried about whether she would be able to cope with the children and I didn't want to be a part-time dad. I think our relationship was dying long before the affair happened. We had sex a few times after the second child was born but it wasn't even mechanical sex, God knows what it was. I wonder now whether I could have done things differently. Maybe she needed more attention but I also gave her too much rope because there were definitely casual one-night stands with other men and I didn't say anything about them. And then when I knew that she was having this affair even though she continued to deny it, I deliberately went out of my way not to have sex with anyone else, when there are plenty of single women around when you go away to conferences. I just knew she would have spun that to make out she was the victim. She would have told the kids and I was not going to give her that chance. I wanted to make sure the blame rested on her shoulders so that when history judges the break-up of this family people will see it was all down to her and not me.'

The contortions of the deceiver and the denial of the person who is being betrayed together form a subtle dance. Such is our need to preserve reputation that the delusion that one cannot possibly be being betrayed sexually has increased now that fidelity is the main symbol of commitment. I met one woman who had been 'happily' married for twenty-eight years. She went for routine tests for an infection and then became indignant about the fact that she had received a letter from the doctor telling her that she had tested positive for chlamydia and needed to go back for more tests. 'Did you?' I asked. 'No of course not,' she replied angrily, 'they must have got it wrong. We have always been completely faithful to each other.' When I pressed her on this and said she should put her own health first, she told me that she didn't want to know and had no need to worry about her fertility now anyway. She had had just one conversation with her husband on the subject. She showed him the letter when it arrived and said, 'So what do you think of this then?' He took one look at it and replied 'You tell me, then?' The hospital could have made a mistake but this woman, who works in the 'relationship saving' industry, was not prepared to go back and find out whether indeed that was the case, which means there will always be a lurking doubt in her mind.

'There are couples where women want to know if there is a trust issue because they think their husband is using prostitutes but are not sure. If you think you can live with prostitutes, that's fine, but actually don't delude yourself, because then it's a health issue, not one of trust,' says Verity the infidelity detective. 'They ought then to have the guts to say, "I want you to go to the doctor to make sure that you haven't got any nasty diseases," because if they care enough about you they will.'

The social norms supporting monogamy are still so strong that many third parties also use denial to justify their behaviour and diminish their contribution. Women in particular still stand to lose so much more reputationally by having an affair with a married man. So, this is 'real' love; their lover's marriage is just a sham. The mistress dons the mantle of the socially acceptable 'other' wife – more attentive, more massaging of his ego, more seductive and therefore more faithful – to reassure herself that she is not being used just for sex. Many if not most women having affairs with married men endorse the morality of monogamy by buying into the myth that their lover only has sex with them, not his wife or partner. For such a woman, her fidelity in the relationship is proof of the fact that her conduct is honourable, but she overlooks the fact that his isn't and that she is helping him not to be faithful. The third party will buy into no amount of lying. 'Here, in no particular order, are some of the things Lenny told me,' recalls Dani Shapiro in *Slow Motion*, her memoir of being a mistress to a rich married man. 'That he and his wife didn't sleep in the same bed; that they hadn't had a "real marriage" in years; that she was undergoing electroshock treatment in a clinic outside Philadelphia; that he had cancer and had to fly to Houston three days a week for chemotherapy; that his youngest daughter, aged three, had a rare form of childhood leukaemia. That he could not get a divorce for all of the above reasons. That he was heart-broken that he could not leave his wife and marry me.' All were of course untrue. The wonder is how she could have believed him.

Many men pretend they are unattached and their lovers choose to believe them, never asking the all-important question. Many women justify their actions with the notion of romantic love and tell themselves that you have less control over who you fall in love with than the route you take to work. The power of love is greater than the power of morality. Then there is the argument that all marriages are flawed, so why restrict yourself? A woman need not necessarily be a 'sister' since the whole institution of marriage oppresses women anyway, the reasoning goes. Lovers avoid guilt by avoiding all discussion of his or her family life. Alternatively they can adopt the role of therapist so that they only hear about the bad bits. Lovers can be hypocritical, accepting that the wife or husband came first, but if s/he were to betray them for another, their affair is over. It takes a conscious and often humiliating leap to accept that you play your part too. 'I began to see, through the fog of my desire, that there were moral problems,' writes Susan Cheever in her essay 'In Praise of Married Men'. 'It wasn't enough of an excuse to say that "men do this all the time". It wasn't enough to think that since everyone said that married men never left their wives, I wasn't hurting a marriage; they did leave their wives. It wasn't enough to say that we were all adults or that I wasn't lying to anyone. By being part of a situation that was a lie – even if the man did all the lying – I was lying as surely as if I made the calls to say that I would be late at work or that I had been held up in traffic or that I had two days of business out of town.'

It isn't that hard to spot the signs that your partner could be having an affair. The straying spouse starts coming home later than usual or goes out at unusual times, says they have to stay overnight somewhere for business meetings, or becomes deeply interested in a new hobby which doesn't include you. They start spending an exceptional amount of time with a friend or work colleague. They start keeping their phone with them at all times, even in the shower, and delete all their text messages, except maybe one very precious one. Or they uncharacteristically leave their phone lying about, because they have bought another one for just their lover, which they keep with them at all times. They buy sexy underwear and don't bother to hide the receipts. There are sudden changes in grooming habits or clothing styles. They start spending hours on the internet and get exceptionally grumpy. They stop saying, 'I love you.' They become passionate in bed, deploying a new range of techniques, or there is a sudden decrease in the amount of marital sex. Countless spouses refuse to address these signs or see them as potentially significant enough to start having a conversation about the state of their relationship.

For those with a strong religious faith adultery is a sin, and so the sense of blame is greater, as is the need to deceive and deny. Laura and Tim are practising Christians who married young. Tim lied throughout their seven-year marriage but Laura never realised the extent of his deceit until after they had separated. He lied about his upbringing, about being bullied at school and about jobs he never had, and Laura believed him because she was an honest person and assumed he was too. 'I now think he must have had such a low sense of self-worth that he felt he had to make up all these stories because people wouldn't like him if he was just himself. He thought he could make friends and impress people if he made his life sound more interesting.'

Tim struck up a friendship with a younger woman when they were working on a summer holiday camp for children. In spite of the fact that they regularly exchanged texts, went to a festival together and the 'friend' came to stay with them once they had their first child, Laura believed Tim when he said there was nothing going on. Large phone bills began to arrive because of his use of premium-rate porn but he told Laura it was fraud. Again she believed him. 'He liked to tell stories but I never realised that he was a fantasist, a congenital liar. I also never thought he would have an affair because he spent years telling me how much he disapproved of infidelity.'

Tim began spending two or three nights a week away from home, claiming first that he was doing youth work and then that he was working on recording an album with a group. His excuses escalated. He told Laura that he had been arrested in possession of drugs as a student before they met but had not been charged. The police had offered him protection provided he did undercover drugs work for them on the street. He told her that they put him on teams with trained marksmen and that a solicitor friend had tried to get him out of this contract but had failed. 'He made it all sound so believable and that he really hated going. He would say, "I have to go away for three nights next week, I have no choice," and I would cry and make him his favourite cake for when he came back.'

This pattern of being away for several days at a time went on for months. Then Tim told Laura that he needed to go away for a week to a Christian retreat in the country and had bor-rowed the money from his parents. Both Tim and Laura were regular churchgoers. He was supposed to call her when he got there, but he didn't. Twenty-four hours later he phoned to say there was no reception at the retreat and not to call, but when she sent him a text about something to do with the children he answered straight away. When she then rang she got an inter-national dialling tone, but still he lied his way out of that pretty hefty clue by pretending that he had had his phone diverted to someone else.

At this point Laura decided to ring the retreat and discov-ered that her husband had never arrived. He was in Italy with his lover, 'Which I found particularly difficult because we had no money and I hadn't had a proper holiday in four years other than a few days in a static caravan.' When he told her the affair was over, she believed him, even though he continued to spend nights away from home. 'When you really love your husband and you have young children you want to believe him. I am very loyal and committed. I have only just accepted that the affair never ended because I think at the time I was trying so hard to save our marriage.'

As a single mother now, bringing up two very young children on social security benefits, Laura can be forgiven for her complete loathing of her husband for his pathological lying, and for her belief that he is entirely to blame. She understands now that his dysfunctional family history might have played a part in his habitual lying and inability to commit once they had children, but at the time she never considered that it could be a problem for their relationship. Tim's family moved every two or three years and he never put down roots. But it is also easy to blame everything on the family of origin and not see how as a spouse you can exacerbate those early attachment difficulties. Laura is five years older than Tim and quickly became a maternal figure to him. 'I always enjoyed taking care of him, ironing his shirts and making his favourite foods.' Once they had two small children she shifted her attention to them and he felt abandoned all over again. 'He admitted to me once, about six months before the affair, that he was jealous of them and of the attention they got, particularly after our second child was born, but I didn't really take any notice of that even though I can see now that he must have been very jealous of his younger brother. He said everything changed when his brother was born. His parents told him off all the time and made him save up for the things he wanted, while his brother just got given everything he asked for. He once said that he felt the same way the moment I got pregnant,' says Laura, 'that he was being pushed out of the marriage and those feelings must have deepened once our second child was born.'

Laura and Tim fought a great deal. She told me he would often shout things like, 'I hate you and I want to leave you,' 'which is easy to say when you have someone waiting for you in the wings, isn't it?', she added, reassuring herself by blaming the third party once again, as she did throughout the interview rather than accepting that she might have been negligent too in failing to see that there was something fundamentally wrong in her marriage. 'In my head I kept thinking, adultery, adultery adultery, but I didn't ask him directly, I just said, "What is going on?", so he carried on constructing this pack of lies and he made them sound so believable. I never knew about the extent of the lying until after we had separated and I talked to his father. It never occurred to me that someone could be like that. By the time I realised that our marriage was really bad and I was trying to sort it out the affair had been going on for months and it had been heating up for years. If you had said to me just a year ago that "By this time next year you will be living on your own with two small children and your husband will have left you for another woman" I would not have believed you. I just thought we were going through a bad patch.'

For Laura, marriage was something you committed to for life, and having grown up with both parents at home she assumed that the same was in store for her even though Tim's background was very different. While his behaviour was both selfish and cruel, Laura also contributed to the slow and highly acrimonious collapse of her marriage by refusing to see the danger signs and failing to challenge her husband more effectively before the conflict, and the distance between them grew so wide that separation was almost inevitable. 'I have read books on infidelity and I can see now that all the signs were there, he did all of them, but I was too scared to look too hard at it and admit that he might be having an affair. I just couldn't comprehend that he might do that when he also went out of his way to say how much he detested people for being unfaithful. I now think he had checked out of the marriage before the affair began.'

Sometimes the betrayed spouse perpetuates the distance between the partners because of their own personal history. Instead of noticing the signs of an affair and challenging odd behaviour, 'victims' with a childhood history of insecurity are more likely to retreat, to be the accepting doormat, just as they had to be when they were children. Instead of being able to say openly, 'I deserve better,' they have such a low sense of self-worth that they say, albeit unconsciously, 'Why wouldn't they do that to me and I am lucky to have had them for so long.' It isn't difficult to see how gendered attitudes allow women to respond in this way. Some will even go to great lengths to provoke it, proving the inevitable: that they will be betrayed. 'It's easy forensically – we can say it's all "John's" fault because we found lipstick on the collar,' says psychoanalyst Brett Kahr, 'but we don't know to what extent "Mary" unconsciously provoked the affair because she wanted to have a reason to hate "John" so that she could then justifiably discharge her lifelong history of rage towards her mother or father.'

Others resort to more gendered patterns of behaviour by making themselves so dependent on their spouse that they cannot leave. Andrew's wife became depressed, was diagnosed with chronic fatigue and then had a cancer scare after she discovered his affair. 'Somebody who is afraid that their husband will leave them may make themselves more dependent as a way of keeping them,' says couples counsellor Liza Glenn. 'The more dependent they are, the more guilty the man will feel and he can't possibly do it.'

Gendered stereotypes reinforce notions of denial and blame. The presumptions around what it is to be male or female create distance within a relationship because so many aspects of the relationship need never be discussed or negotiated. A man can excuse his infidelity through his wife's reluctance to have sex, rather than looking deeper into the reasons for her withdrawal. Women are socialised to be kind and nice. Anger is not very 'feminine' even though it is an entirely human emotion equally common in both sexes. Pushing a man into an affair is one way a woman can get *really* angry with him, and then forgive, putting herself in the more powerful and maternal role. 'I think women enjoy the notion that men are these testosterone urging animals because that idea allows women to protect themselves from the self-knowledge that they might have driven their man to an affair,' says Brett Kahr. 'It's all to do with his penis and his testosterone. I think we like to think that gendered differences are inbuilt so that we can explain away our own contribution.' My female divorce lawyer agrees. 'When I am acting for a woman, the anger about his affair will stop her from taking any responsibility for it. We see a lot of "shotgun" divorces where a man just disappears from a marriage and the woman is completely unaware that there was anything wrong, so he becomes the baddie, or the other woman.'

Whether male or female, the cheating partner cannot act on their own. They depend upon others to support and endorse their behaviour. Sharon's story illustrates the way that both spouses can allow an affair to happen. Sharon met her husband at university and they had been married for fourteen years. They earned good money, bought a family house in London and wanted to start a family. But when Sharon was pregnant with their first child, her husband confessed to an affair and left immediately, saying, 'You can't want me around.' Sharon feels in hindsight that, for him, the combination of the responsibilities of impending fatherhood and a big mortgage on the house they were about to move into, as well as being put on notice for redundancy (which didn't happen), was too stressful and destabilising. But in hindsight too, and one year after their separation, Sharon is only just beginning to wonder what part she might have played. 'I thought I had supported him well but in retrospect I think he had a real crisis of confidence whereas I was on top of it and kept pushing, saying, "We always wanted to have a baby and we are going to need a bigger house anyway." I knew something was wrong because he had been quite withdrawn and really didn't want to do anything, just sit around staring into space, but I had no idea that he was having an affair until he confessed. Whenever I asked him what was wrong he would say, "It's work," until he finally told me.'

Sharon acknowledges that their sex life was never very exciting and that they found it hard to share intimacies: 'I don't show vulnerability easily, I don't see it as a strength.' And she now recognises that there were earlier indications of extra-marital dalliances which she never challenged – sex-texting on their honeymoon and an 'emotional' affair with someone at work. 'These were shocking but I think now I was just too scared to confront him about what this all meant for us and I also didn't want to say, "That's it, its over." Maybe I never gave him enough validation but maybe he never grew up too, because his parents were quite indulgent with him as a child.

But maybe I was also complicit in allowing him to be like that. I never pushed him or confronted him to make him more responsible. I don't think I ever had the get up and go to say, "This is not good enough." Our lives were very intertwined, which has made the separation very difficult, and although we did talk, I don't think we ever talked enough about what we were feeling or the emotional depth of things.'

The notion that one person bears the blame for infidelity hampers the possibility of recovery. When relationships are smothered with high levels of lying and denial, higher levels of blame inevitably flow back and forth. It is then much harder for a couple to shelve the sexual betrayal temporarily so that they might be able to address some of the root causes. The wounds of blame and acrimony are so painful that neither is prepared to relinquish their main defence by seeing how they might have contributed to their own difficulties. Countless couples fail to move out of unhappiness to a richer future, either together or apart, because of their reluctance to talk honestly to each other about what has happened between them and why.

Adam has always been keen to do the right thing by his wife and sons, but has also had a series of extramarital sexual encounters throughout their thirty-year marriage. When he fell in love with a woman who tried to coerce him away from his family responsibilities, his wife found out and was distraught, so Adam ended the affair. He hadn't the strength to leave.

'We had a big row just recently because I get moody, I still miss my lover,' he told me. But rather than confiding that to his wife he said rather aggressively, 'It's OK for you, you got what you wanted, and I didn't.' Her reply to that was, 'Well, actually I didn't – you're scarred and irascible and that's not what I wanted. I want the man back that I married.' But you can't go

back. Adam's wife hasn't truly forgiven the affair by understanding why it happened and her part in that betrayal. She has
resigned herself to a limbo because she feels powerless to
pursue any other choice. But it's what's *not* being talked about
which really matters. That he resents the amount of weight she
has put on by not looking after herself, exercising or eating
properly. That she is clearly more depressed than he is but
refuses to do anything to help herself. That she has made herself so dependent on him that he cannot leave her because the
guilt would overwhelm him.

'We have a shared reservoir of memories and humour,'
Adam says. 'There is a lot of companionship there. She is very
loyal but that's not always a good thing. She says things like, "I
just want to grow old with you." She's happy to do whatever I
want to do. She loves being with me to the point where I am
overly dominant and I have tried to say that independence is
the attractive thing, not dependence, but she is not strong
enough for that. She just doesn't have any get up and go. I
really love her but I can't say any of these things to her. We
haven't really had that eyeball-to-eyeball conversation. I did say
to her once, "Where is your self-esteem? If you had done the
same thing, I'd be off."'

What's less clear in this gender-stereotypical scenario is how
the spouse often colludes through their passivity and how
much an affair by the more powerful of the pair, of either sex,
might be a statement that they want their partner to stand up
to them more. By prodding the overly acquiescent spouse, the
straying partner might be saying, 'Don't let me get away with
it. I do not like how I feel about myself if you let me walk all
over you.' 'There's a lot hidden in the unconscious contract
between two people,' says psychoanalytic psychotherapist
Jenny Riddell. 'A lot of provocation goes on in couples which

is actually a last act of loving, an act of desperation, a way of slapping someone out of their weakness, or a depression which they have been struggling with for years.'

The betrayed spouse can be co-dependent, mistaking the intensity of the chaos that ensues after the disclosure of an affair for intimacy. They can misinterpret as security the control they now exert over their partner as a result of the betrayal. And while Adam might find it easier to see how his wife has made things so difficult for him by not ending their marriage so that he could move in with his lover, he found it harder to see how his romanticised idealism about what a good relationship should be might also be contributing to the distance between them, even when I pressed him.

'The scorecard thing, yes ... I think I was so busy working hard when I was young that I met people I liked who I wasn't sexually attracted to and I never met anyone who ticked all the boxes, they were either one or the other, so when I did meet someone this late in life it kind of blew my mind.' Instead of recognising that he might have found it harder to choose between these two women because he had only invested a part of himself in each, Adam blamed both his wife and his mistress for failing either to be perfect and do what he wanted, or conform to his romantic script. When I asked him whether all his extramarital activity over the years might have stopped him from becoming more intimate with his wife he replied, 'That's a good question. I don't think so, because it was just sexual gratification. I think variety is so stimulating and if we hadn't fallen in love with each other she would have been the perfect mistress.' He then changed the subject.

When these sorts of power games determine the emotional currency of a relationship the equilibrium is being distorted in a profoundly unhealthy way. It is much easier to blame one's partner for not being perfect than it is to accept responsibility for the compromises we have had to make. It is much easier too for couples to separate after an affair has been revealed, and pour all of their energy into blaming the other litigiously, egged on by friends and family, than it is to accept that blame and punishment serve no purpose when it comes to building a lasting commitment based on greater honesty, forgiveness and tolerance of each other's frailties as well as our own.

When an affair has shattered the trust of an established relationship the answers have to lie in challenging and changing how we view and approach our partner rather than blaming them for everything that is not right. Both have to find ways to talk to each other about their dissatisfactions with life and the nature of their dependency on each other without making the other feel at fault for not making them entirely happy. Each has to feel able to talk honestly about how they have felt in the relationship, what has been bad as well as good. Each has to feel they have been heard by the other, which means setting aside the clichés of 'How could you do this to me?' or 'If it hadn't been for the baby . . . '

The conventional approach, where blame lies with the 'cheater' and all empathy is with the deeply wounded betrayed spouse, damages relationships far more than the act of sexual betrayal itself. It polarises couples rather than brings them together. It allows the 'victim' to hurl all of their resentments and rage with life generally at the drama of the affair and how they have suffered as a result. The 'victim' reconstructs the narrative of the affair to emphasise, both to themselves and the world, how wronged and wounded they feel, minimising their own contribution or guilt, and so gaining traction in the power politics of the couple.

But the assumption that the 'villain' who has strayed distorts the story more than their partner so as to mitigate their transgression isn't supported by the research, for both 'victims' and 'perpetrators' seem to twist the narrative to equal degrees to shore up their position. 'Victims' tend to exaggerate the severity of the transgression while 'perpetrators' tend to downplay it and divide blame by presenting their motives as understandable.[1] The gap between them then gets wider and neither can think constructively about what they might actually want from the relationship, because their positions have become so polarised. The longer we obsess over the details of the affair as the 'victim', the more likely we are to use it as ammunition in subsequent legal battles, fighting over every penny, every hour of contact with children, in the divorce courts. All our energy can be poured into gaining retribution for the betrayal and ensuring that our position is seen as the wronged one, rather than using it to rake through the embers for signs as to how we might live a better future, together or apart.

A large body of research shows that distressed couples are more likely to interpret marital events in a more negative fashion, and to make more negative predictions about their future, than happier couples. It isn't easy to cut through the wounds and the deep hurt of betrayal and it is often exhausting trying. However the costs of not doing so are particularly high for the 'victim'. In this role it is difficult not to feel diminished as the object of pity. The hard feelings of rage and sacrifice can have a corrosive effect on our sense of self. We continue to see weakness and passivity as a part of our identity which can undermine our ability to function in other spheres of life as well as damage future relationships.

If we can get the obsession under control we are halfway out of the abyss, for we can then see the betrayal as something which has happened to us as a couple rather than as an individual humiliation. It is only when each can acknowledge the pain of the other that they stand a chance as a couple of moving on. We can't take back the hurt, but we can spend a great deal of time talking about all of the more uncomfortable issues that we might have been avoiding, building trust by sharing all of our emotions (even the more ugly ones) and accepting the feelings of our partner as valid (even the more ugly ones).

'It is possible to come back from the brink, but I never thought that could ever be the case when it first happened,' says Clare, whose husband of over thirty years had an affair with a much younger woman. 'There were lots of big conversations and he is in therapy, which denotes someone who is at least prepared to look at changing. It was such an explosive event that it gave me permission to talk about things I had kept quiet about, or maybe was in denial about or just couldn't be bothered mentioning before.'

Clare's husband has a traumatic family background and has a tendency to be depressive and emotionally abusive, which has erupted occasionally in violence against doors and tables. She acknowledges now that she had played a part by pushing him away for years, unable to cope with his psychological baggage and controlling behaviour any longer, and she sees his affair as yet another example of abuse. But it was the way his sexual betrayal attacked her sense of identity and value as a sexual person as she was going through the menopause which provoked enough of a crisis for her to consider the marriage was over. 'The conversation then became about whether or not we were going to stay together and I don't think he ever wanted us to separate. We had some really deep conversations about what we were using our marriage for and I felt empowered and strengthened by that. I was able to say things like, "You have to allow me to be who I am and not bully me around." Knowing that we are trying to work this out together has made me much more aware of how I have hedged bits of my life to accommodate his disapproval and I don't do that any more.'

Is blame appropriate if we accept that most infidelity is caused by marital unhappiness, depression, a sense of powerlessness or feeling abandoned? These are common human frailties, the stuff of life in every potential relationship, not crimes which need to be punished by sending the 'villain' to purgatory to suffer for their sins. These are the core issues which have to be addressed, not the act of sexual betrayal or the drama of the affair.

When you scratch the surface of most affairs there are no obvious 'villains' and 'victims'. All suffer. It's often a quagmire of confusion where blame is a diversionary tactic prolonging the agony and limiting the possibility of recovery and a happier future together. Blaming a partner for all our unmet needs stems from the false expectation that anyone is capable of meeting them. An affair can highlight what's missing and satisfy that urge temporarily. Or it can confirm that there is a larger and more permanent need that isn't being addressed. In which case turn to your partner and tell them so. If the relationship is genuinely over for you, then there is no shame any more in that fact, for one of the great social benefits of our age is the right to separate from an unhappy marriage. But at least find the courage and the generosity to do so with kindness and a sense of decency.

If one of the pair really wants out, the relationship is over. The more mature response then is to accept your own contribution to the relationship's demise rather than dumping all of the blame on the 'villain' for straying. 'I wouldn't have wanted him to stay with me just because he felt a sense of obligation or habit or fear of what would happen if we parted,' says Isabel, who discovered three years ago that her husband had been having a six-month affair. 'I would rather be on my own and have my heart broken but feel that I had behaved with a certain amount of dignity. I don't mind the damage, the scars and the bruises but I would mind if I was so frightened and small that I had to make him stay with me otherwise my life would be meaningless. When you are angry with someone you want them to be as unhappy and crabby as you are, it's a kind of *schadenfreude* and I don't want to be that person, or the spy or the punisher. I want to feel dignified and tall even if I am heart-broken. If you love someone wholeheartedly you want them to be happy. That sounds noble. If he told me tomorrow that he was leaving me for someone else, I would of course yell and scream and break things and tell everyone what a complete bastard he was, but eventually I would like to remember what it was that I had loved.'

Sometimes the escape valve of a little romping is all that one of the pair needs to shake them back into the sanity of reality and what they could lose in the way of history, family, friends and financial well-being. Both then take stock and analyse what has been going on, in an attempt to change the future. That requires time for contemplation and dialogue, time that couples living through the aftermath of an affair rarely give themselves. Our interpretation of the gravity of infidelity fluctuates over time, depending on our sensitivity and our partner's subsequent behaviour towards us. 'Sometime after he said the word *Pause*, I went mad and landed in hospital. He did not say *I don't ever want to see you again* or *it's over*, but after thirty years of marriage *pause* was enough to turn me into a lunatic,' begins Siri Hustvedt's novel *The Summer Without Men*. Her narrator, Mia, discovers that her husband has been having an affair with a much younger French woman with 'significant breasts that were real'. She goes home to spend the summer with her mother. The affair comes to an end and over time Mia gains a little more perspective on her husband's mid-life crisis. 'Can I really blame Boris for his *Pause*, for his need to seize the day,' she concludes towards the end of the novel, 'while there was still time, still time for the old timer he was swiftly becoming? Don't we all deserve to romp and hump and carry on?'

Maybe. A lasting, committed relationship has to be built on an honest dialogue, an acceptance of human frailty and tolerance of the way we all change through circumstance and over a lifetime. Delving into our family of origin with a counsellor can illuminate some of the root causes, for we all bring assumptions and patterns of behaviour from our own family into the one that we create with another person. Honest conversation can highlight how we might be withholding the parts of ourselves that we least like in case these should disappoint our partner or even cause them to panic and leave. We try to be nice and avoid hurting our partner's feelings when commitment requires complete disclosure. That is a large part of its joy and point.

It is only once a couple can begin to address these issues that the one who has strayed can begin to take responsibility for their behaviour and apologise, without blaming their partner, in ways which the other person is really likely to accept. This then paves the way for a more genuine sense of forgiveness. If they decide to continue together that relationship is then more likely to last. If they decide to separate they are less likely to bring all of that baggage into their next relationship and may well improve its chances of survival because of what they have learned about themselves and their behaviour in their previous love.

The marital landscape after an affair is inevitably different from what it was before. Few things in life escape change. If we can learn new ways of relating to each other where the need to blame and lie both to our partner and to ourselves is replaced by honest talk and listening; if we can establish clearer, explicit boundaries between our togetherness as a couple and our need for autonomy as an individual; if we can give up the fantasy of perfection and accept that every person makes mistakes and every relationship has flaws; if we can take responsibility for our past behaviour and make a conscious choice to try to behave differently towards each other in the future, we lay solid foundations for happier family life. We also establish healthier models of relationship for our children. 'Perhaps the sexual life is the great test,' writes Graham Greene in *The Comedians*. 'If we can survive it with charity to those we love and with affection to those we have betrayed, we needn't worry so much about the good and bad in us. But jealousy, distrust, cruelty, revenge, recrimination ... then we fail. The wrong is in that failure even if we are the victims and not the executioners. Virtue is no excuse.'

# 8

# THE IMPACT ON THE CHILDREN

In the midst of all the lies which surround affairs parents easily lie to themselves about their children. They are too young to understand what is happening. They cannot see what is going on. It doesn't concern them. That is what people hope and want to believe when they are wrapped up in the trance of an affair. All of the evidence, however, points to the contrary.

Parental infidelity can have a profound impact on children. On the rare occasions when young people are able to voice their opinion they talk of feeling betrayed and confused by the way their loyalties have been split between two people they love equally and depended upon entirely. There is something badly wrong with a situation where someone places their own sexual entitlement, or their sense of personal injury at having been betrayed, above the needs of their children. As a society we seem to have become more concerned with the idea that regular sexual stimulation and release is essential, and that divorce or separation is an inevitable consequence of an

unhappy marriage or an infidelity, than we are with the fact
that children need a secure and stable base.

An affair is often buried deep within the debris of a divorce
or separation and it can be hard to unravel the effects of sexual
betrayal from the overall damage caused by family breakdown.
Infidelity can deal the final blow to a relationship which has
been riven with conflict and unhappiness for years. But a child
understands little about the sophisticated ups and downs of
adult love relationships. All they care about is having both parents close by. A child's way of thinking lacks adult complexity
too; it's more categorical, seeing everything as right or wrong,
with little room for ambivalence. Everything can be easily
blamed on the betrayal or on the person who stole their mother
or father away, particularly when that is stoked up by the
parent who is left behind, as it often is.

While we like to believe the modern truisms about separation – that children are resilient, that they recover quickly, that
many of their friends have separated parents – to justify our
own behaviour and ease the guilt, research shows that this can
only be the case when parents behave responsibly, putting their
child's interests first and giving as much age-appropriate information as that child needs. However, parents are usually
ill-equipped to do this during the emotional upheaval of sexual
betrayal. We know now that there can be long-term effects on
children, particularly when it comes to forming their own relationships as adults. Lesley's mother took her and her brother
back to her home town after she discovered that her husband
had been having an affair with a work colleague. Her mother
was the last person among the couple's circle of friends to
know. Lesley had to leave her home, her school and her friends,
'because of what my dad had done. I still find it hard to trust
that when my boyfriend is late or not with me and doesn't

answer his phone that he is doing what he says he is doing. It's as if disaster is always waiting in the wings, he is going to leave me, even though all this happened when I was eight and I am now twenty-eight.'

When a parent takes the monumental leap into the unknown by transgressing the social norm of monogamy, they are likely to behave irresponsibly in other ways. They can become so wrapped up in finding ways to meet their lover, waiting for the next text or email, that they not only abandon their partner, but abandon their children too by being unavailable to them. The emotional environment at home changes and children sense that, for this is their entire world. Children see every-thing, but they just can't necessarily understand or process what they see. Children are tuned in to every nuance of their parents' behaviour because they need them. They grow to know their parents intimately, their habits, sounds, what irri-tates and pleases them. They watch their body language, listen in to the subtext of what they might be saying and can sense far more than adults usually give them credit for. Children are primed to learn from adult behaviour and the slightest change in routine, tone of voice, preoccupation or absence can signal danger.

When an infidelity threatens the parental relationship, chil-dren often feel as if they have been abandoned by both of their prime sources of security. If a woman knows she is being betrayed, or simply senses that something profound is wrong with her relationship, she is likely to be less available to her chil-dren, preoccupied with what might be going on, forgetful and less able to put their needs centre stage. If their father is having an affair, he is likely to be home less often, 'working late' or away at 'conferences'. Pat told me that her daughter would be 'really upset if the call came and he said he had to work and wouldn't be home in time to read her a story because she adored him as a child and I believed him because I thought he could never do that to his daughter. I still feel bitter about the fact that he wasn't there enough for the children.'

If it is the mother who is being distracted by an extramarital sexual adventure, she likewise can be more absent, picking her children up less often from school or arranging for them to have more play dates or sleepovers with family friends. If the children are young she might involve her lover in family life or use the children as an excuse for an outing where the 'friend' comes along too. In her right mind a mother would never advise another woman to do this, but if she is desperate to spend time with someone she is much more likely to bend the rules to justify her own needs. She may delude herself that this is a happy family time, even though the adults are likely to be more concerned with finding ways to connect illicitly, sending the children off rather than playing with them, abandoning them there too in the delusion that they suspect nothing. 'My husband could have an affair without the children knowing, but the only way I could see my lover when the children were small was to hatch plans to go to the zoo or the seaside together,' one woman told me. 'So they knew him and they knew that he was important to me but it was a double betrayal of them in a way because I couldn't hide his existence from them and I still feel guilty about that.'

When either parent is absorbed by an affair, with finding time to meet, with the need to suppress deceit, no amount of pretence can disguise the fact that they will inevitably have less emotional energy for their children. 'In looking at affairs, we are dealing with the disruption of the deep structures of family life, where the physical or psychic incursion into the family of an "alien lover" represents the "betrayal" of one parent by the other,' write sociologists Jean Duncombe and Dennis Marsden, 'And children of whatever age come up against some of the deeper family secrets that parents feel impelled to keep from them.'[1]

If either parent has an affair while their child is under three years old, there can be emotional withdrawal at the stage when a very small child needs to feel a sense of total envelopment by the passionate adoration of both parents. The seeds of an anxiety with no name are sown which can resurface years later in moments of adult intimacy. Many men have affairs while their partner is pregnant or after the arrival of a baby and even the suspicion of this, let alone the discovery, alters a mother's chemistry, inevitably affecting her relationship with the baby inside her womb or in her arms.

Young children can be brought along to illicit encounters and while they may not entirely understand what they see, they can sense that their mother or father is happier, distracted and might be on the lookout for snatched kisses or fondles. They might also hear the other parent being discussed. The younger a child is, the more they experience family as their entire world and the more threatening any sense of being abandoned will be.

A child over the age of five is more likely to think that they might have caused thei m,r parents' difficulties. Their greatest fear when they hear them arguing is that they might separate. As a consequence, young children often have nightmares or powerful flashbacks before they go to sleep. Behavioural problems at school are common, as well as other regressive behaviours such as bed-wetting, thumb-sucking or being especially clingy with both parents, trying to bring them together in an instinctively self-protective way. The primary-school social network is such that many parents forge new friendships at the school gate and families spend weekends and holiday time together. The discovery of an affair between a child's father or mother and another parent in this close-knit world can cause profound disruption to that child's social world at school as well as at home. Imagine then what it must feel like to see their own father picking up other children from their school or giving presents to other people's children when they never did the same for them. I have heard examples of both.

With older children or during the first rumblings of adolescence things start to get considerably more complicated. Teenagers are more likely to discover an infidelity or to bear the weight of family secrets by being used as a confidant or go-between. Adolescents are developing their own sense of identity and the capacity for abstract thinking. They can be idealistic, highly moral and sensitive to hypocrisy. They are much more critical of their parents as they begin to see them as less than perfect human beings. If they then discover that one parent has betrayed the other, the parent they once placed on a pedestal is now a liar and a cheat. A young person's whole sense of themselves, their family history and their sense of what relationships should be is challenged at a time when they are likely to be fumbling their way towards first love, physical intimacy and boundaries around trust, lust and loyalty.

Adolescents need their parents to be role models, demonstrating the values of integrity, honesty and sensitivity towards those they care for, in order to help them grow up well. They need to feel that parents are the deeply stable roots of family from which they can pull away in order to forge their own more adult and separate lives. That can be difficult for a teenager living with a lone parent, disillusioned and depressed at having been left by their spouse. Children are then likely to be needed as a source of support for that parent, sometimes even for both parents as they struggle to make new lives on their own.

When parents delude themselves that their teenage children are old enough to understand or cope, they are often finding ways to justify their own promiscuity, unaware that they themselves might be feeling threatened by their children leaving home or envious of all that youthful sexual experience. When you are a teenager the idea that your parents have sex at all is pretty disturbing. The suspicion or the discovery that they are having sex with someone outside the marriage feels like a violation. It is almost as if, by choosing to display their sexuality through an infidelity at this point, parents are attacking their own child's emerging sexuality, shutting down space for the sexual exploration which is the essential work of adolescence.

Older children and teenagers are highly sensitive to the ways in which the humiliation of domestic trouble might play out in the wider world and at school. It's deeply shaming if the affair is known about by others in the community and they feel torn between their natural love and loyalty to family and the wider chorus which plays up the immorality and the selfishness of any infidelity. When the straying partner is their father the betrayal for some can be mitigated by the general consensus that it is more excusable in a man, particularly when so many celebrities and public figures, from President Clinton to footballers, get caught doing much the same thing. But if it is a child's mother who is having the affair, children are likely to hear others repeating the words of their own parents – that she's a 'slag', a 'whore' and 'he deserves better'.

Marital problems and infidelity can provoke some extreme reactions and reckless behaviour in the turbulent world of teenagers. They get angrier, usually with the parent they feel most secure with, who is also probably the one who is being betrayed and least able to cope. They might act out more at school, get into fights, start fires or play truant. They might get depressed, get sick or stop eating. Or they might just indulge more in all of the other more typical teenage behaviours such as drinking or taking drugs. A teenager's sexual behaviour can also be disrupted. The research seems to indicate that teenagers either become more promiscuous at an early age, or they shut down entirely sexually. What few parents realise is that by screaming their distress in these various ways, they may be, albeit unconsciously, trying to bring their parents back together again by making themselves even more vulnerable than they already are.

Given that many infidelities are the product of marital unhappiness, it is hard to assess whether these examples of 'acting out' result from the sense of abandonment brought on by the infidelity or whether the trigger is the general climate of conflict and insecurity which ensues, or might have preceded the affair. Decades of research show that an environment of entrenched and ongoing acrimony between parents can have a debilitating effect on a child's psychological development. Violence, heated argument full of blame and character assassination, as well as the 'cooler' conflict of silence or withdrawal from each other can manifest itself in children in a number of ways, including increased anxiety, depression, aggression, anti-social behaviour and poor academic attainment.[2] The two are, however, inextricably linked. If family life is unhappy, one or both of the parents is more likely to be pushed into or seek refuge in an affair, which can then damage the children.

Affairs and repeated infidelities are more common in people with childhood difficulties themselves. When that is the case there are likely to be other manifestations of their own child-hood insecurity in the way that they parent, such as depression, sudden and extreme rages, being over-controlling or narcis-sistic and unable to see things from their child's perspective. Attachment problems can make parents less resilient to change. That means it can be less easy for them to tolerate a child's changing needs as they grow up. When you then add into the mix an affair by a parent which causes them to be distracted and nurture grandiose delusions, the unstable foundations of insecure attachment are much more likely to be passed down to the next generation, usually unknowingly.

Another aspect to consider is that the young are now much more likely to discover a parental affair because of the way they can whizz round mobiles and computers. They know of others involving parents who have separated and worry that the same could happen to their own. When they suspect something they often don't know who to turn to. Deidre Sanders, Agony Aunt on the *Sun* newspaper, tells me that she gets more and more letters from teenagers in particular, asking her what to do. 'I tell them that they cannot take responsibility for their parents' rela-tionship and that they should not tell the parent who has been betrayed. Instead try to tell the parent they have caught them out and how unhappy that makes them feel.'

Even if you are a young adult, the discovery of your parent's infidelity always puts you in an intolerable position. Freddie is in his early twenties and told me how distraught his girlfriend was when she discovered that her mother was having an affair. The mother was in the kitchen and a text arrived on her phone which the daughter opened. It talked about how great sex had been the night before and when she scrolled through the his-tory she saw that the affair had been going on for months. She couldn't talk to her mother because she knew she shouldn't have been looking at her phone. Freddie added, 'It's been really upsetting for her because she doesn't know what to do with this knowledge. She has always believed that her parents were happy, that they loved each other and as a Christian is deeply disapproving of adultery. She has also been quite judgemental at times about how my parents divorced and hers would never separate. So in some ways she has over time had no choice but to forget about it to confirm this idealised notion of who her parents are. I daren't mention it now – it's as if it never happened.'

Infidelity, poor family relations and childhood difficulties are closely intertwined. And the consequences often extend into young adulthood. Jean Duncombe taught Family Studies for many years. 'I am amazed by what students bring up. I am not looking for (parental) affairs but what surprises me is how common they are. As every year goes by more and more students come from divorced backgrounds. Some parents seem to think that once their children have gone to university it doesn't matter any more because they are adults now, but they are still children within that context, so they are absolutely devastated. It's the lies, I think, which cause the deepest damage.'

Couples psychotherapist Liza Glenn agrees. 'I hear grown-ups remembering how they found Mummy on the floor with another man, or worse, in the bedroom, and then the child is drawn into the secret, which I think is probably about the most destructive situation because whatever they do it's a betrayal – either they collude with Mummy and betray their father or they betray her. There is no other option.' Oliver remembers finding his father with another woman when he was sixteen and the damage that did to his relationship with his father. 'We owned pubs as a family and my father was a bit of a player and he must have been caught a few times but I only really understood what was going on when I found him in bed with someone else and I went and told my mum. She was very upset and that turned into a huge row between me and my father, which was unusual for us because up until that point we had been very close.' As an unhappily married man with two daughters Oliver now feels tortured about the fact that he has been having an affair, betraying his dead mother as well as his wife and children, for she begged him never to turn into his father.

When an affair is uncovered, the emotional explosion ripples through the house. Both parents are likely to be preoccupied, anxious, angry, even traumatised, and have limited resources for dealing with yet more stress from their children, who are likely to be more demanding than usual. The grown-ups row, vicious things are said and there are tears. Sensing their parents' withdrawal and their own vulnerability to abandonment, babies and small children will cry in a desperate plea for more eye contact, more attention, to feel held. Children will demand more from their parents to soothe their own anxieties because they are feeling so threatened. Their parents, however, are likely to be so wrapped up in their own immediate emotions and anxieties that they find it difficult to respond effectively.

Julia can still remember vividly the time when her father came home unexpectedly early and found her mother with someone else. She was six years old. There were rows for several days. Then her father announced that he felt so betrayed that he was going to kill himself and left the house for weeks. Neither parent realised that Julia was sitting at the top of the stairs, listening to every word. 'It was only when my dad was really ill and I was grown up with a family of my own that I was able to say to him, "You never thought about me, did you?", and he had no idea what I was talking about. Dad always maintained that it was Mum who had broken up the marriage by having affairs. So I asked him if he knew where I was when he left and he didn't. So I told him that I was sitting on the stairs and that the last thing I heard him say was that he was going to kill himself and then he didn't come back. I was heartbroken, so upset, I thought he really would do it and there was nothing I could do to stop him. That has stayed with me more than anything else. He never knew I was sitting there listening to every word because he was so upset.'

In some families the offending parent, usually the father, just disappears from the home, leaving the other parent upset, angry, distracted and depressed, giving the children little more by way of explanation than 'Mummy and Daddy aren't getting on very well at the moment.' In other families the children cannot help but be sucked into the emotional upheaval that occurs as soon as an affair is revealed. Their parents are so shocked, outraged, hurt and humiliated that they cannot think or behave responsibly. Lily only discovered that her husband was having an affair when her twelve-year-old son, in true *Parent Trap* fashion, showed her a photograph of her husband with another woman. The couple's son and daughter had been spying on him for weeks. They even used to entrap their father by asking him to explain something they knew the answer to and then watching him lie. 'The first I knew about any of this was when my son came to me with all this evidence. My husband had set this woman up in another flat so this was a serious affair and after we divorced he married her. I am not proud of any of this but I was so angry with him I called him all sorts of names in front of them. I was horrified and left, which in retrospect wasn't the right thing to do for the children either.'

Lily decided that her marriage was over and embroiled her children still further by asking them who they would like to live with. 'I didn't handle it at all well. I simply asked them if they wanted to come with me, dividing their loyalties even more. My daughter left with me but I think in retrospect that my son felt so guilty that he had caused the break-up that he felt he had to stay with his dad. My husband then moved his mistress into our home and pretended that she was a lodger when my son knew all along that wasn't true. When my son eventually challenged them there was this huge row and my husband denied everything and lied again. My son then said he wanted to live with me. I believed they were all right because I was,' said Lily. 'It was only when I asked them as adults what they thought the impact of their father's infidelity and the divorce had been that all sorts of dark stuff came out. I asked them why they had never told me before and one of them said, "Because you never asked us, Mum."'

Susan Berger, an American psychotherapist, posted a blog on aboutaffairs.com in 2008 on the impact of affairs on children. All of the children, now young adults, who posted comments on her article (and there were many) were without exception vehement about the damage caused. Reactions were full of unexpressed rage and therefore unforgiving. 'My father had an affair when I was thirteen. The effect it had on me was so profound that now at twenty years old I still don't regard him as my dad,' commented one young woman. 'I am thirty-seven years old and my father's repeated affairs have ripped our family apart. He refuses to accept any responsibility for any pain he has caused me. Even though we are adults we are still their children,' comments another. 'I just want my family back and feel like no one understands what I am feeling,' comments a twenty-two-year-old still living at home in the full knowledge that both parents are conducting affairs. 'I was eight years old when I found out my mum was having an affair. This man was suddenly around and my dad seemed oblivious,' comments another. 'As a teen I started taking drugs, starting fires and running wild. I felt like nothing mattered any more as "everything was all a big lie". I'm forty-five now, I've suffered repeated bouts of depression and I have never had a success-ful long-term relationship – my self esteem is so low.' One of the saddest, shortest comments merely says, 'My dad died the day I found out he had been cheating on my mum for the past ten years. He was my hero but now he is my zero. That hurts.'

Separation and divorce are a common consequence of the discovery of an affair and while the infidelity might not be the prime cause of the breakdown of the relationship, it is often used as an easy focus for blame and acrimony because, as the previous chapter has explored, people are reluctant to delve deep into their matrimonial difficulties and the part each person might have played. We have substantial research now on both the short- and the long-term effects of divorce on children if the break-up is not handled impeccably well: low self-esteem, a sense of being abandoned, poor performance at school, anti-social behaviour, as well as the heartbreak of simply missing the absent parent. Approximately half of all fathers lose contact with their children within two years of the separation.[3] Families are usually less well off after a divorce and they may have to move away from friends and their social support network and change schools. A child's whole world focuses on their home, their parents and their school. If the parental break-up threatens all three of these fundamental sources of security, a child can be profoundly destabilised in ways which adults often find hard to understand. For the parents divorce can be deeply painful but it represents the end of something that didn't work, a remedy for an unhappy relationship. For children separation often makes no sense at all, mainly because they cannot fully appreciate the depth of their parents' suffering. Divorce can be just the start of their difficulties as their entire world is thrown into chaos without a clear understanding as to why.

Separations provoked by an affair tend to be the most acrimonious and the children are easily drawn into their parents' battles. Each parent regresses, shoving the blame for the split on to the other, refusing to acknowledge their own contribution, and forcing the children to take sides by supporting their version of events so as to justify their own position. By tearing their children's loyalty in two in this way, parents can inflict lasting damage, forgetting that the children have a right to a relationship with each of their parents. 'In our research we heard some really sad tales,' continues Jean Duncombe. 'Mothers who tell their children that they have to hate their father because what he has done is so unforgivable but then they take him back, leaving the children in a state of utter confusion. Young people want to understand why their parents would do these sorts of things because they believe that if you marry someone or if you have a child there has to be commitment and that even if you are tempted you should just say "no". In the research we tried to get the students to see things from their parents' perspectives. Some said they understood but didn't forgive it. They had this soft script about what we have done to them and to the world and to relationships by being so flighty in the 1960s and that's why the divorce rate is so high, and they are adamant that it is not going to be the same for them.'

The romanticised narrative of True Love, Soul Mate and Happily Ever After is so strong culturally that young people have little other than the over-dramatisation of television soaps to go by when it comes to looking for a realistic portrayal of loving relationships. Children and young people inevitably have a limited understanding of the way that people and relationships change through life because they have yet to experience it themselves. Their idealistic minds have little or no room for the ambivalence which is the stuff of human life and so they search for the truth, easily manipulated by their parents and heavily conflicted by being given two such contrasting versions of events. Sometimes a child will even hear two very different interpretations of the other parent in the same day. Their father cannot love them if he can betray them as a family in this way, but later on, in a more conciliatory mood, that same mother will comment on how kind he can be, and the child will not know what to believe, or where they should place their loyalty or trust. They have little choice but to settle on one story which will suffice, until such time as another piece of information triggers new questions which then remain unanswered.

The secrets and lies can percolate through the wider family and extended network of friends and neighbours. The idea that blame lies solely with the one who is sexually unfaithful is so widespread that people feel justified in taking sides to support the betrayed, which usually isn't in the best interests of the children, for they cannot help but hear a parent they love being attacked by other members of the family. One woman with a six-year-old son told me how her former in-laws just shut her out completely when she had an affair which broke up her relationship. Her son says things like, 'I hate Grandma. It's like you're dead when I go there.' It is hard for any child to understand that their relationship to a grandparent is entirely separate from the one his parent has with that generation. It isn't easy either for a family to remain impartial when they see people they love either badly hurt or behaving badly. Another woman, a grandmother, talked about how difficult it was for her to hold the family together when her son had an affair with his wife's best friend, breaking up not just one family but two. 'It's hard for the kids and it's hard for us. We have to be so careful not to make alliances even though we feel strongly about the fact that what our son did was wrong.'

Men often move swiftly on to another relationship and the children are just expected to accept this, as well as other stepchildren, possibly even half siblings, without enough explanation to ease their anxieties. The new woman then becomes the 'bitch' who broke up the family in their mind's eye unless the situation is handled sensitively. Sarah says that her children know where they come in the pecking order of their father's new life. 'First there is Shaznay, then there's the dogs because they don't have any children, then there's the business and the kids come after all of that, whereas I have steered clear of any relationship which might compromise my life with them.'

Sarah and her husband divorced over a decade ago and her children are now at university but she still feels that her daughter has been badly affected by her father's emotional withdrawal. 'She always got less attention from him and he teased her a lot, patronised her and made out she was not really capable of much. She does have very low self-esteem around her father and I am afraid that will be affecting her relationships with men. I told her she ought to write a letter to him to tell him how she felt and not send it and that helped a bit. Her dad also took her away with him on a business trip to South America when she was on her gap year and that helped too. I think he realised that this might be his last chance with her.'

Sarah's daughter will also have seen how devastated her

mother was by their divorce and inevitably bore witness to
how hard she had to fight her husband for years in the courts
to get child support. A child cannot help but absorb some of
that hostility and feel a sense of divided loyalty at having been
betrayed too. But Sarah's daughter will also have absorbed
a one-sided version of the events which led to her parents'
break-up because of her distant relationship with her father
and the fact that her parents have been unable to resolve their
differences and move on as effective co-parents. Consequently
Sarah cannot help but use her children's father's behaviour
by way of example. 'I have always felt that I didn't want to
harbour a grudge or become embittered because that affects
the rest of your life, but that is difficult to do. I didn't want
the divorce to damage my children more than it had to and
instead they have been able to use it as an important life exercise. They know the whole story and I have said to them,
never use this as an excuse but as an example to live the best
life that you can, and I hope they won't think it will be OK
to be unfaithful. You have to try and avoid overstepping the
mark because once you are unfaithful it is very difficult to
step back.'

Lily says that her adult children still find it hard to trust and
respect their father because he lied to them as children and
continues to lie about that past to them to this day. He still
denies that the affair with the woman to whom he is now married began before the divorce and is ignorant of the fact that
they have concrete evidence that this is not true. Lily goes on,
'My son went through a very bad period as a teenager, drinking too much and he ran away and said things like, "My dad
is living with a whore" and my ex never appreciated how angry
he was because he couldn't see it from our son's perspective.
They all mind to this day that he has never come clean about

what really happened. The odd comment will come from my ex's new wife at family events about what they were like as children, which indicates she was around for a long time, but their dad always denies it, even though at one point my son even challenged it and said, "Look, I have the photographic evidence with the date on the back!", but he still can't admit to it because he doesn't want to be seen as the bad person, he wants to retain the image of being a good family man largely because that matters for his job. My daughter hasn't settled down with anyone yet – she doesn't trust that it could last – and my son has got married but not without a real heart-to-heart conversation where he asked me if I thought infidelity might be in his genes because of the fact that his father was a serial shagger. He seriously considered not getting married at all because he didn't want to put himself in the position of hurting his girlfriend in the way that he had been hurt.'

People do not just betray their partners when they shatter family life with a serious affair, they can also betray their children. Many grow up believing that their parents have been unfaithful to them too. Loving parents have to fathom deep emotional resources, placing their own hurt, humiliation and guilt to one side so that they can continue to put the interests of their children first. We are so conscious of all of the other things that the young need, such as enough sleep, good, additive-free food, age-appropriate stimulation through the best teaching, educational toys, sports, music and after-school activities. Yet when it comes to the most important foundation of all and finding ways to nurture a constructive and loving relationship between the only two parents that child will ever have, either together or apart, we turn a blind eye and delude ourselves that children are resilient.

When a parent has had an affair which hasn't been adequately addressed and talked about so that it can be absorbed
into the narrative of that child's family history, the effects can
cascade down to the next generation and damage a young
person's ability to form their own lasting intimate relationships.
We grow up internalising images and interpretations of our
parents as individuals, but we also absorb the minutiae of their
interactions as a couple. It is the only human relationship we
see daily in thousands of different ways and from that template
we learn a huge amount about how to be with someone else.
Family is not just where we learn about ourselves: it is also
where we learn how to relate to others. Our parents' relationship acts as the primary role model for our own.

Rising numbers of young people are reacting to the poor
example of fidelity set by their own parents with rigid condemnation of any sexual betrayal, without any understanding
of the way that loving relationships can be battered by circumstance because that essential family template has been
broken. Most young people consider infidelity to be always
wrong, whatever the circumstances. 'Cheating' is the worst
possible crime in a relationship. Young lovers will separate
when they go to different universities in order to free each
other up to the possibility of sleeping with others, whereas in
my day we just did it anyway. Sexual fidelity cements young
lovers as couples. Young men and women are more socially
integrated than ever before. They become friends at school,
work together, share interests and flats, spend time with each
other, even love each other. Everything *but* make love to each
other. So it is the exclusivity of their sex lives which has
assumed more meaning as a marker of their commitment. 'My
daughter knows all about her father's infidelities and says that
she is grateful because the moment her boyfriend were to even

look at another woman she would ditch him,' says Pat. 'She says she just wouldn't put up with it like I did.' This certainty about the complete immorality of an infidelity then sets an impossibly high standard for lasting relationships.

For others, the disruption to their sense of childhood security, because of either a messy divorce or dramatic and repeated infidelities, has been acute enough to prevent them sustaining relationships at all. Two separate and substantial research studies conducted in the US over twenty-five years on the same people by eminent psychologists Judith Wallerstein and Edith Mavis Hetherington have found that 'Contrary to what we have long thought, the major impact of divorce does not occur during childhood or adolescence. Rather, it rises in adulthood as serious romantic relationships move centre stage,' writes Wallerstein in *The Unexpected Legacy of Divorce*. 'From the viewpoint of the children and counter to what happens to their parents, divorce is a cumulative experience. Its impact increases over time and rises to a crescendo in adulthood. At each developmental stage divorce is experienced anew in a different way. In adulthood it affects personality, the ability to trust, expectations about relationship and the ability to cope with change.'

Some find it hard to trust that someone will not betray or leave them enough to commit and show a deepening love. The failed template of their parents' relationship means theirs could fail too and that fear overwhelms them when it comes to settling down. This sense of 'failure' doesn't appear to be handed down to people who have lost a parent in death. Many adult children of divorce exhibit classic symptoms of attachment insecurities by being very promiscuous, more accepting of short-term or multiple relationships, more able to separate sexual pleasure from emotional depth or to engage in coercive sex, which in turn leads to the rejection they expect. They are also more likely to have affairs.

'Anxiously attached' adolescent girls are more likely to use sex to bolster their self-esteem because being sexually desirable is a crucial affirmation of self for young women. Conversely, adolescent boys who are similarly insecure are less likely to use sex to cope with their negative emotions because sexual initiation is still considered to be a man's responsibility and they feel reluctant to place themselves voluntarily in the path of yet more rejection.[4] It is hard sometimes to unravel sexual motives and early attachment difficulties from power and gender. 'Whereas an anxious woman's intense desire for love, affection and approval may cause her to acquiesce to male sexual partners' demands, including ones that are not ideal from her standpoint,' write Mikulincer and Shaver in *Attachment in Adulthood*, 'men's attachment anxiety is incompatible with a male gender role stressing assertiveness, confidence and dominance.'

As we saw in Chapter 5, early attachment insecurities can inhibit sexual expression and exploration within a relationship, making it harder for people to reach orgasm and to feel confident about their own sexual attractiveness or their ability to satisfy their partner. This can in turn lead to a sense of marital failure now that sex is considered so much more important to the long-term health of a committed relationship. The greater the attachment problems in children, the harder it is likely to be for them as adults to be able to commit to one person and to merge continued sexual desire and growing intimacy in their relationship with that person.[5]

Liza Glenn tells me that she automatically asks a client who has had an affair whether one of their parents did too, 'and it usually is the case'. Research conducted by Jan Havlíček and his colleagues at Charles University in Prague found that men were more likely to stray if their fathers had been unfaithful when they were growing up, whereas they did not find a similar link between girls and their mothers' infidelities.[6] 'Often a boy has almost no choice if his father has been a serial philanderer,' says psychoanalyst and couples psychotherapist Brett Kahr. 'It is going to be very hard for him in terms of his internal working model of what it means to be a man to not be seriously tempted in that direction, both out of identification with the father and also as a wish to compete with him – you have three mistresses; I've got six.'

If a child witnesses a great deal of argument or violence in the family home, but little in the way of compromise, negotiation, apology and resolution, conflict in their own adult intimate relationship will inevitably become more difficult to deal with. Research shows that those with more insecure backgrounds are more likely to experience greater extremes of despair and anger during difficult relationship moments and either bottle these up in case it pushes their partner away, or explode with rage at the slightest provocation.[7] Many find it harder to discuss marital problems or express dissatisfaction in case this leads to rows which will inevitably trigger visceral and unhappy memories. And so the resentments build. And the deeper the resentments, the more likely they are to see an affair as a solution or a means of revenge. 'When a parent's affair is never addressed, the child's burden extends into adulthood,' writes Emily Brown in *Patterns of Infidelity and Their Treatment*. 'Marital problems and affairs are a common result. Many adult clients, whatever their agenda for therapy, have unresolved feelings about a parent's affair that occurred in childhood.'

*

The art of mothering is learned from having been mothered; the art of loving from having been well loved. It isn't perfection that a child requires from their parents: it is the parents' ability to think about the effects of their actions and behaviour on others. The more capable parents are of seeing how life might be from their children's perspective, the more likely they are to be able to explain marital difficulties in ways that allow those children to continue to feel loved and secure.

All young people need appropriate boundaries around them to help them feel safe whatever their circumstances. When parents are together the healthiest families maintain enough space between them for their children to be children, learning through play and the exploration of their imagination, trusting all the while that the adults have their best interests at heart. Parents draw closer together in order to present a united front, and refuse to allow the young to drive a wedge between them. The family shape is strong enough to take the load because there is enough space between the two points of the parents and the apex of the child to create the strongest triangle – an equilateral one.

When affairs, conflict, separation and divorce upset that shape, the interests of our children are best protected by maintaining those boundaries between them and our behaviour so that we help them to go on feeling safe. All couples fight. It is the manner in which we do so which impacts upon a child. It can be extremely distressing for a child to witness and hear aggression and argument full of character assassination between their parents. But if that child witnesses more constructive conflict, where their parents listen to each other, argue their corner, talk about the impact of the other's behaviour on them, respect the right of the other to have a different opinion and resolve to work on those differences, that child grows up with a much stronger internal model of relationship.

The same is true of separation and divorce. The statistics suggest that approximately 20 per cent of parents who divorce will have high levels of conflict subsequently and a further 24 per cent will be tense and uncooperative.[8] That means children in nearly half of all separated families live with one parent absent, the other parent in all likelihood needing more support from them, and all this in a climate of acrimony. However, all of the research shows that when parents, even if they are really upset or angry, set appropriate boundaries around their behaviour so that the children's interests always come first, those children will fare better throughout the ructions of divorce.

That means presenting a united front and cooperating with each other around the children. That means day-to-day involvement by both parents in their children's school activities, as well as phone calls or texts to them. That means finding ways to unload stress and rage far away from the children and refusing ever to argue near them or bad-mouth the other parent in front of them. That means seeking support from other adults and not from their own children. That means sharing with the children as much information as they need to understand that while their relationship with each other may be over, their relationship as co-parents to them never ends. Those who continue to present this common front continue to make their children feel secure and establish healthier foundations for adult intimacy. They also establish a more constructive role model for ending a relationship which has gone badly wrong.

Affairs happen. As this book has shown, infidelity is common and likely to happen in many long-term committed relationships. It is what we learn about ourselves and each other as a result which can help to build a stronger partnership for the future. The way we handle an affair and establish effective boundaries between our personal flirtations and the needs of our children can limit the negative impact of parental infidelity upon them. It might feel like a natural reaction to rage and scream abuse, to storm out or kick the one who has strayed out of the house, but that is the last thing a child needs to see. It will leave them feeling bewildered, threatened and concerned about whether the parent they no longer see daily is all right. However hard it may be to contain feelings of rage and hurt, the problem is between the parents. It isn't and should never be the child's.

It takes Herculean strength to put deep wounds to one side when the feelings of anger, betrayal and humiliation are so overwhelming. More often than not, it is women who are left with small children. Laura is now on jobseekers' allowance and has two under the age of three. She feels her husband chose his 'happiness over that of his children when I think we could have worked on it. I don't want to punish the children because he is an arsehole but I do struggle over what to tell them. I say, "Daddy doesn't live here any more but he loves you very much," when clearly it isn't that true otherwise he would be here, but I want to reassure them. You want to protect them and be this perfect mother to make up for their useless father.'

Children need age-appropriate information about their parents' relationship difficulties and it must always indicate that the adults are in charge. When a child knows there has been an affair, either because they have heard their parents arguing about it or they have heard gossip, and then asks a direct question about it or knows the lover, the parents exacerbate the damage to the child's trust in them if they do not sit down with them and talk it over. Older children will understand something about affairs but usually this will be from their over-dramatic and stereotypical portrayal on television and in films. Rather than this, what they need is to have their exaggerated fears dispelled by being told the truth. This will reassure them that the affair is not their fault and that the door is always open for them to ask questions about what is going on when they are worried. Family secrets are rarely healthy. Without the truth, children tend to suspect the worst. They need to feel included in family difficulties without being made to feel responsible for holding the family together.

It's always about hearing the voice of the child. Jean Duncombe believes that the attitudes and taboos surrounding infidelity are similar in some ways to those around domestic violence, 'in that we think of children almost as objects, even if they see they won't understand and they won't tell because they are not articulate enough. I am quite puritanical when someone tells me they are having an affair now because of work we have done on the impact of divorce on the children. If people say to me that the kids don't know I say things like, "Are you sure? Perhaps you should explore that a bit more," or "Think about what you are doing to the children," and I never would have done that twenty years ago.'

Subscribing to the myth that infidelity does not concern children, that they do not notice or understand what they see, can be far more damaging to a young person's emerging sense of self and their sense of safety within the family than the affair itself. For in a child's mind the seed of betrayal takes hold and can grow, distorting its significance in all sorts of fantastical ways. Take this story on Susan Berger's blog from a young man who found out that his father was having an affair when he was a teenager and never told anybody except his girlfriend. He thinks the affair ended and his parents are still together and seem 'very happy. I love my mother beyond words and I didn't say anything because I couldn't bear to see her alone. I wish I had, there was an opportunity when I could have told her, selfish as it might seem, at least then I could pass the problem on. It's my sister's wedding in a few weeks and all I think of is the moment my dad gets up to say his speech and I'll have to sit there with a smile plastered on my face when I really want to scream at him for effectively ending my life and creating this huge rollercoaster. My choice is simple. Tell my Dad or Mum I know what happened and ruin a family or don't say anything and at least save some happiness that I haven't caused the same pain to everyone else that I feel every day.'

This young man has absorbed all of the family guilt and the shame of an affair because it has not been talked about. It could even be that he has been carrying this burden pointlessly because his mother knew all along about her husband's infidelity. Perhaps they even discussed it and she forgave him. Perhaps it was caused by a minor nervous breakdown, or by flattery from a younger woman which his father now regrets foolishly responding to. How can the son possibly understand anything about the significance of affairs, their causes and their solutions without an example from the only other relationship that he knows intimately?

If the revelation of an infidelity is accompanied by high levels of blame, shame and righteous indignation, that is the message about the betrayal of trust that a young person will carry into their own future relationships. If instead they see their parents working together in an effort to rise above their differences before they decide whether or not they have a future together, young people grow up with a healthier and more tolerant internal model of how a committed relationship should be, where difficulties are worked at, mistakes are forgiven rather than avoided and acceptance of human frailty and imperfection is the norm. They absorb the message that their parents care enough about them to at least try to put their interests first. Who knows how many children could be spared the added trauma of divorce if their warring parents could find sufficient maturity to make sure that the boundaries around their needs as children remained intact? For they might then also find enough of a sanctuary to be able to work on their relationship problems in peace.

The wider taboos and ignorance around affairs do not help children and their parents either. The social humiliation and subsequent shame isolate families in a time of need. Clearly people find it easier to reach out to friends and family for support when they can be sure that they will not be judged harshly. It takes a village to raise a child. This means that as a society we could do a great deal more to help the young by being less sanctimonious about the morality of infidelity and more generous about the fact that it happens, that it hurts badly and devastates relationship but that it also isn't the end of the world and can be recovered from.

What strongly resonated for me while writing this book was the emotional fallout on the young and the terrible example many parents set through their sexual betrayals and their refusal to behave responsibly either as polygamous or separating couples. The young need stability and honesty about sexual relationships if they are to go on to form fulfilling and lasting partnerships of their own. We like to think of childhood as innocent, a time of purity which needs to be protected. But perhaps that is just because it suits us to think this way. And perhaps we overstep the mark when we deny them important knowledge about how to sustain a loving relationship through the bad times which are likely to occur. If we are grown-up enough to form relationships and have children, we owe it to them to be grown-up enough to find a way through the emotional devastation left by infidelity, to either continue life together or separate in a way which will limit the effects on our young.

We can break the cycle of insecurity and heal the widespread lack of trust in the possibility of a long-term loving relationship by building up more realistic models of relationship. For we owe it to the younger generation to avoid handing down the mistakes of the past to their future, so that their children, and indeed society, will reap the benefit.

# 9

# COMMITMENT

There is a common perception that a loving relationship should be easy. It should feel right, like sliding into a warm bath. Compatibility, it is presumed, is born of true love, the matching of like-minded souls. 'I'll know when my love comes along.' In truth it is the ability to stand squarely in the face of the inevitable numerous differences between us – different backgrounds, characters, obsessions, expectations of a relationship, different attitudes to sex, money and how to spend it, different opinions on children or how to raise them well, differences over politics or how we like to spend our spare time – through a life of change which determines whether a relationship falls at the first hurdle or builds to a lasting commitment.

We expect life to be challenging, yet our relationship as a couple has to be a sanctuary of peace and harmony. If it isn't, there must be something wrong. An excuse to leave it and find someone else. But the reality is that loving and living with another person through time is one of the hardest things we ever have to do. Love requires work, a reaching for something beyond the ease of sliding into that warm bath, which is why we value it so highly. It has the potential to offer us oceanic rewards – companionship, a lasting sense of place and purpose, a sense of narrative to our lives with a shared history leading to what will hopefully be a shared future. Good relationship is good for us, physically in the care that we can give to one another and emotionally as a source of continued support. It is also essential psychologically, for no other person can offer us such a mirror into the deepest recesses of our behaviour so that we come to understand ourselves better.

The person we fall in love with will change as they grow older, buffeted by life. As indeed will we. Commitment lies in being flexible enough to change in roughly the same direction. Love is not effortless. It is effortful. It means striving to know and support someone in the places where they are weak as well as strong, so that we are also supported and fully known. To be truly loved means to be seen as unique, exceptional, irre-placeable as well as accepted as flawed by someone we also value in those terms. There is an inherent exclusivity to such a bond. If that exclusivity is broken by an infidelity, as it often is, commitment to the relationship hasn't necessarily vanished, it has just been buried for a while beneath the detritus of per-sonal unhappiness – unfulfilled expectations, failed ambitions of love, loneliness, depression, boredom and resentment – that is the stuff of modern life.

Marriage may have its down sides – monotony, routine and boredom at times – but affairs have their problems too. They are not usually the carefree utopia we might imagine when things get tough. They can be troubled and tortured. They can cause a great deal of suffering, as well as confusion over choice. It's hard work concealing an ongoing infidelity and finding times to meet. Lying takes its toll on us emotionally and psychologically. We don't like who we become. We do not like inflicting such cruelty on a partner we still care for. Affairs may seem glamorous and enviable to those who feel they lack the courage for such bravado but they can leave a tsunami of desperation in their wake.

Most of us aspire to be monogamous and choose fidelity as a symbol of our commitment. It requires sacrifice, renunciation and tolerance of disillusionment. And that's no bad thing. We need boundaries to our desires. Fidelity is a symbol of honour and integrity. It is noble and respectful of others, kind to those we care about, raising them on to a pedestal as special. We may kid ourselves that an extramarital dalliance doesn't mean anything, or that s/he would never find out. But you would know. We may play with the idea, craving the drama and excitement as an antidote to the safety and monotony of a stable relationship, but think of all the down sides.

Think about all that lying and deception, the codenames for some seedy hotel, the new mobile phone you will have to keep concealed at all times, finding times and places to meet. Think about the expense and all those unknowns about this new lover and their past which could jump out and bite you. Think about all of those insecurities about your body and your sexual performance as you shed your clothing, or worse, they shed theirs. You could get pregnant or pick up some ghastly disease. And then there is the guilt, the covering of your tracks, the anxiety about the hurt and damage it could cause to your relationship if this 'meaningless' sexual encounter was ever discovered. All this effort and danger, in the short term, may electrify a life that has been dulled by monotony, but in the long term it might be less complicated, emotionally draining and cheaper just to turn to the person you now know so well and say, 'Let's go to bed and find new ways to play with each other,' or to take a sabbatical from each other completely. It might be less hard work to change the fabric of your relationship rather than assuming that new sex with a new body will do the job, in this acquisitive consumer society, like acquiring a new pair of shoes. Even the third party, the mistress or the lover, risks more. 'Why jeopardise a marriage, passionless and quarrelsome as it may have been,' writes Lynn Freed in *Running the Smalls Through*, 'for an affair that, at best, provided only cheap hope?'[1]

There is no easy, clear-cut answer to the essential conundrum of relationship, which is that, with commitment and stability in a long relationship, some sexual boredom is inevitable. We seem to want everything. We ask for stability and then complain when we get it that things are always the same. Infidelity and affairs are deceptively seductive as the instant solution. It is easier to get your rocks off by making love with another than it is to find a deeper intimacy with your partner. They know you too well. The longer you are together the more important it is to find ways to differentiate yourselves as individuals within that couple. Only then will you be able to understand that they are allowed to have thoughts or sexual feelings about other people which do not include you. Only then will you continue to see them as someone who is potentially attractive to others, and therefore someone you might want. Only then will you be able to replace aspects of certainty, which can be so erotically numbing, with a sense of erotic danger where your inner desires can be exposed and played with.

The intensity of passionate sex may feel fleeting but that is largely because we are overwhelmed by very narrow cultural interpretations of what passionate sex should be. 'Even though sexual and attachment behaviours are governed by functionally different systems,' write psychologists Maria Mikulincer and Philip Shaver, 'the systems still influence each other and contribute jointly to relationship quality and stability.'[2] Good sex fosters a closer emotional connection between two people and the greater sense of trust and security which results can enhance sexual life. It is sensitive and responsive care towards each other and not sexual attraction which is the most accurate predictor of a lasting relationship. They are, however, not mutually exclusive needs. The key challenge for couples today is to find the means to have both by overturning the ever stronger myths around how a good sexual relationship should be.

Blame lies at the heart of many relationship difficulties but never more so than when one has been sexually unfaithful. We accept that it takes two to make a relationship, but when it comes to infidelity there are only villains and victims. The person who strayed shoulders all of the responsibility for having transgressed. They should have said, 'No thank you' or showed self-restraint. What's interesting and overlooked is why they didn't.

Perhaps it was because they were not brave enough to leave the stability of their relationship without someone else to run to. Perhaps it was not a means to leave but a means for them to stay. Perhaps it was a cruel form of revenge for other 'crimes' in the relationship, such as withholding or withdrawing entirely from sex, for refusing to listen or engage with their partner's life or to take their resentments seriously. Perhaps it was a form of depression management, or a desperate attempt to inject a sense of danger and the drama of secrecy into the deadness of monotony. Perhaps it was an act of rebellion against the confines of marriage. Many of us resort to sex as a form of empowerment when we feel disempowered in other areas of our lives. We have affairs not necessarily because we are looking for another person, but because we are looking for another version of ourselves, to escape the responsibilities of parenthood, the encroaching mortality of mid-life or the vacuum left behind in family life once the children have left home. Sex is often the least important aspect of an affair.

The work of relationship is hard. Inevitably couples drift apart at certain times, hurled around by the volatility of life. Infidelity is both the result of those emotional strains and a catalyst for sorting them out. That is the great paradox. 'Our relationship was saved by his affair because it would have capsized with all of the things that were not being talked about,' Isabel told me. 'People get so busy, so involved in their own little traumas, that they forget about each other. We can laugh about it now because there were some very funny aspects to his affair, but I also think that one of the most important things was that I understood why it had happened. I never had a moment where I was confused or amazed by it. It took me a long time to recover, yes, but how long is a long time when you have a lifetime together?'

A small number of people are simply selfish, sexual users. Others have disturbed, dysfunctional family backgrounds which can lead to repeated infidelities as they seek out sexual sustenance to fill a void within, like a baby needing constant soothing. If you can say with all honesty that the problems in your relationship fall into either of these categories, then you need the help of counselling, for people can be addicted to sex and sexual conquest in the same way that others have problems with drink, drugs or food. Many of us, however, simply slide into something sexually illicit because we were flattered and seduced. We deluded ourselves that it didn't matter and believed we could keep it secret. We could control it. Only to find ourselves sucked deeper into the quicksand of a deceit where the only way out was to send out more and more obvious signs. This does not excuse bad behaviour, merely begin to explain it. And knowledge rather than blind ignorance lies at the heart of committed love.

Commitment cannot be imposed any longer by the institution of marriage, religious sanctions against adultery as a sin, or social taboos against the absolute immorality of infidelity. The new sanctimony which has mushroomed around the paramount need for fidelity since the 1950s, just as sexual freedoms and women's emancipation began to erupt and change our world, is a last-ditch attempt to cement couples together with some sense of permanency. The costs have been great. The notion that affairs are always wrong has exacerbated our sense of hurt, humiliation, guilt and betrayal. It has cranked up the need to lie, cheat or become blind to the signs of our partner's infidelity, or the implications of our own behaviour sexually because of what that might mean. And it has pushed a great many couples into separating when perhaps, with a little more tolerance, conversation and understanding, they could have worked things out for the better.

If our relationships are to last we need a new ethos, a new morality where blame is replaced by greater understanding and a sense of personal responsibility; where secrecy and shame are replaced by far greater honesty about the truth of the matter, which is that we all share the same human need for constancy and support in a loving relationship but that to presume that love will be enough to prevent our partner from finding others attractive is a delusion. True love is complete acceptance of each other's difference: not the romanticised mythology of the 'One', the 'perfect fit'. True intimacy is only possible when we accept the other as they really are rather than who we would like them to be. And in doing so we in turn are also accepted in our entirety.

Affairs do not have to be serious. Most are not. Plenty of people manage to contain minor sexual dalliances or flirtations because they are mature enough to know that these will never be strong enough to provoke separation and the consequent damage to family life. They take responsibility for their actions. They do not need to confess their 'sins' in order to be forgiven. It is when people find themselves seduced by the delusional possibility of a utopia where sexual pleasure can be enjoyed without emotional consequences that there is true danger. When you find yourself lying to cover your tracks and then contradicting your first alibi because you have forgotten what it was, deeper consequences lurk for both you and your family. When you find yourself devoting hours of each day to thinking about how you might meet your lover, you do not control the affair; it controls you. It is time to take stock and think about how the excitement of this new other hidden life is masking deeper emotional needs or feeding unrealistic expectations as to what any committed partner can or should offer.

In his essay on adultery Tim Parks, who lives in Italy, talks about the fact that the divorce rate there is lower than in much of the Anglo-Saxon world. 'It's a place where people expect a little less of each other, and of marriage. Above all they don't expect the privilege of unmixed feelings.' He describes a friend's passionate affair and how the obsession began to highlight the disappointments in his friend's mar- riage, affecting his ability to sleep, think clearly, work or make a decision as to whether to leave his wife or stay. Finally Parks persuaded him to see a therapist, whose advice reflected a cultural understanding of affairs very different from what we might expect to hear in Britain. The therapist told his friend that only the wildest optimist would 'divorce in order to remarry, presuming that things would be better next time round'. He told him to leave his lover and have another affair at the earliest opportunity, but to 'Keep it brief. Meantime he might remember that he had an ongoing project with his wife. They had been through a lot together.'

The old presumptions of marriage no longer apply, so we have to set new boundaries and limits to our togetherness. While the vast majority of us value monogamy as an ideal and reject the idea of an 'open' relationship, we can look at the practices of non-monogamous couples to see how they try to make them work – usually by sticking to negotiated rules on what is and what is not allowed. These partnerships have to be based honestly on what they are prepared to tolerate. The partners have to be consciously creative, rejecting the accepted norms of how relationship should be as they try to find loyalty, fidelity and commitment on their own personal and bespoke terms. Their exclusivity is based on the holistic uniqueness of their connection and not just on sexual fidelity. They search for a balance between meeting each other's needs and their own in a new form of emotional democracy.

We cannot cleave each other to fidelity by doing everything together, following each other's every move, monitoring each other's every conversation. Suffocating a person's sense of autonomy within the modern ethos of Total Togetherness is in all likelihood causing more infidelity than it prevents, as people reach for an affair just to be able to distinguish themselves as an individual. In any committed relationship genuine trust has to embrace the ability to let our partner out into a world full of more and more sexual enticement. It lies in the spaces between us and in all the unknown details of each other's lives. It lies in the understanding that we cannot be all things to each other and that each is bound to find an attractive affinity with others outside the relationship – that may be sexual, but it can also be emotional, intellectual or just a shared love of tennis.

Rather than turning a blind eye to the sea of pornography, or opportunities for blossoming friendships at work or the school gate, we need to find new, more constructive ways to talk about these threats openly. If the internet now offers a plethora of sexual opportunities to those who before might never have strayed sexually, we have to be honest about that and find new ways to set limits to our behaviour if we feel we need them. If one of the pair has a proclivity for porn which is ruining their sex life, look into software which can block access to porn sites or link your internet use to the browser of your partner. Talk about it and find new boundaries to the problem, just as you would with an alcoholic and their drinking.

Greater honesty with each other about the darker depths of our erotic fantasies would make it easier to resist the welter of unrealistic, male-dominated representations of sex which surround us. The more honest we can be with our partner about our sexual likes and dislikes, or the real reasons for not wanting sex when we don't, the greater our understanding will be of each other's pleasure. Where do the boundaries of our tolerance lie? Is flirting or seeing members of the opposite sex socially on one's own allowed? Is watching porn, masturbating alone or using chatrooms acceptable? If you do not regularly share the most basic honest intimacies about how you feel, how can you possibly build strong enough foundations for a lasting love? And if we can find room in our hearts to forgive our partner dozens of other damaging betrayals, why can't we do the same when the marital crime is infidelity? All betrayals happen

for a reason, even though that reason may remain unacknowledged. Often a major contributory factor is the unique alchemy
of denial in each couple which builds over time.

There is huge social pressure to build the right kind of marriage in which to bring up a family. A marriage needs to
provide a stable, loving base for healthy children. It needs to be
solvent, sexy and loving, with all of the material trappings of
the good life, from a white picket fence around your front
garden to happy family holidays. In marriages where the need
to be seen as the perfect family matters most, conflict and dis-
appointment tend to be suppressed, for these could be seen as
a failure. Energy is poured into doing the 'right thing' for the
family, rather than into nourishing the emotional intimacy
between the two protagonists, or understanding the ways in
which this intimacy might be being avoided.

Monogamy, or at least its semblance, is crucial to maintaining this public face. Yet ironically it renders a relationship more
vulnerable to infidelity, for each partner is more likely to seek
emotional sustenance elsewhere as they grow tired of being
nice, of creating a model family and putting their own needs
last, leaving a void as the children grow older and move away
from home. It is also that much harder for the woman who has
been left by her partner, usually for a younger woman, to cut
through her obsession with the betrayal because she has
invested so much in the family project, believing, as she has
been led to believe, that was the 'right' thing to do. She was
only putting her children first. Revenge is therefore more justified, or so we believe.

The myth that most other marriages manage to sustain
monogamy at all times means that we are not prepared for the
emotional devastation when it happens to us. It means we rush

to the conclusion that it is only our relationship which has failed because s/he has betrayed and behaved so badly. 'I have just been unlucky.' It means too that those who stray are more likely to underestimate the impact of their behaviour on their partner and children because they have no close personal experience to inform them. If the mildest dalliance cannot be talked about, it cannot be nipped in the bud because of the notion that such a revelation would almost certainly destroy a relationship irretrievably. The longer an affair is kept secret, the more complicated it becomes, the stronger the sense of shame about the betrayal and the greater the need to be seen to get even.

Society is very unforgiving of infidelity. So it isn't easy for us as individuals to find ways to forgive our partner. But perhaps forgiveness has become the ultimate test of commitment because of the new sanctimony surrounding absolute monogamy. 'If you really loved me you would forgive even this.' We voluntarily render ourselves vulnerable by loving another. We trust them with our welfare. It is then doubly difficult when the person who fulfils so many of our most basic needs is also the source of our deepest pain. Yet in every committed relationship some pain is inevitable. And when that happens we are faced with only three choices: harbour resentment in the tit-for-tat of married life, seek the solitude of separation, or seek solutions through honest dialogue and acceptance of each other's human frailty. 'Forgiveness offers an alternative,' writes clinical psychologist Roy Baumeister. 'If the victim can forgive the transgressor, the relationship may be repaired and possibly even saved from ending.'[3]

The concept of forgiveness is woven into the fabric of our lives and is tested daily by the man who pushes past us to grab the last seat on the bus to work in the morning or the friend who forgets to keep a promise and call you that evening. Forgiveness is a central tenet of religions and moral systems all over the world, yet few of us understand how to apply it to our most important relationships. If society's view of infidelity were a little more sophisticated, it would be much easier for couples to find the support they need to get through such a crisis in a more positive way. Given that few of us are likely to escape being badly hurt at some point, finding ways to maintain that essential loving link with honesty and acceptance of each other's frailties is crucial now that the external social constraints such as lifelong marriage and hindrances to divorce no longer keep us together.

So here is the theory on how we might develop these essential new relationship tools, gathered both from academics studying the new 'science' of forgiveness and from those I have interviewed who have survived an affair and gone on to live a happier life together. First the transgression has to be confronted with conversations about what has actually taken place. Never assume. Be more curious. Ask more questions. Then emotions have to be managed and there has to be a 'cooling off' period while each partner tries to make sense of what has happened. Each needs to talk about how such a violation has affected them emotionally and really hear the other rather than presume to know. The transgressor has to express a genuine apology in order for the other to grant forgiveness. Only then can the couple move on to renegotiate the new terms of their relationship. This cycle applies to all relationship difficulties, from minor differences as to who does what at home to major betrayals over money or infidelity.

We forgive each other for a reason, and that means considering what that reason or reasons might be. Forgiveness will condone abusive behaviour and endorse new acts of betrayal and infidelity if it isn't supported by a rational weighing up of every other aspect of the relationship and the establishment of new boundaries. We are conditioned from childhood to say 'I'm sorry,' so it is as easy for the transgressor to rush to apologise as it is for the one who feels betrayed to sweep the whole thing under the carpet by forgiving without addressing what the transgression means for each of them. Recall occasions when you were forgiven by a parent, teacher or friend and the relief and gratitude you felt when you were released from your guilt. Think about all those better times that you have spent together as a couple and the characteristics you have loved, respected and admired in the other person. What explicit changes in your relationship would make amends? Spell them out. Set new boundaries and forge new contracts about how you might now live together. And how appropriate is an apology if an affair has filled some gaping hole in a person's life? 'He had an adventure but I am not sure that I need him to be sorry for that,' says Isabel. 'I am not sorry about having had an affair with a terribly handsome man when I was younger, because it was so exotic. What was hard was the fact that he carried on with the affair when I had asked him to stop it. But that was difficult for him because he was enjoying it and I understood that even though it hurt. He was having fun smoking behind the bike sheds, as it were, and that's what the bike sheds are for.'

We should apologise profoundly and atone for hurting others intentionally, but if it was unintentional, if it was something we slid into and soon lost control over, might that fact not be enough to begin mitigating the hurt? Or what if it was something we enjoyed and do not regret? Isn't it still better to talk about that in a grown-up manner? How has such an interlude shed new light on your relationship? How do you want things to be different in the future, or has the experience been so life-changing that you do not want a future together at all? If things have been bad between you for a while, what were the things that prevented you from leaving? Your partner has a right to know the whole story. Only then will you both be able to discover enough forgiveness to move on.

Patrick and Naomi are among the most courageous and consequently forgiving couples I have ever known. Both were virgins when they met and each has had the odd undiscovered extramarital sexual encounter over the forty years of their marriage. Then in mid-life, when Naomi was depressed and preoccupied with her difficult mother, Patrick fell in love with another woman. Naomi was devastated. 'I stayed with Charlotte for nine months and we got on fantastically well but I never ever felt at home and comfortable there, no matter how generous or kind she was,' Patrick told me. 'I remember sitting round the dinner table with some of her friends and thinking, I have nothing in common with them, and that's very isolating. I wanted to go back to a world with more breadth and interest in it.'

Meanwhile Naomi lost four stone because of the shock and was determined to win her husband back. 'I knew why he had left and I also knew that our story wasn't over.' She waited patiently. Her friends told her that she had to let Patrick go and her children were deeply hostile to him for what he had done. Naomi, however, began to take charge of her own life, and found a new and invigorated sense of self by travelling alone, making new friends and finding a new job. 'Our lives were too enmeshed before the affair,' she told me. 'My daughter doesn't take her husband whenever she goes to see a girlfriend but we had always done that. I was never on my own and it wasn't that I hated that, I loved it, but there is another way of being as a couple which I now know is much stronger.'

Patrick had never fallen out of love with his wife. He adored her. They had simply lost each other for a while. He took a piece of paper and wrote down on one side all of the good things about his marriage, and on the other side all of the more negative things. 'I concluded I was crazy. I knew why I had gone but that didn't add up to a relationship. I was swapping something complete for something reduced, for the gratification of affection. I will never do that again because it was such a waste of time, time I could have been spending with Naomi. Forget sex for a moment and just think of a loving commitment as admiration, respect, a desire to be with one another, and none of those things have changed. I think you can measure the success of a relationship by how much you laugh together and we do, a lot, about the silliest things. Some of the best times we have are alone together and that's what love is. You can have sex with anybody but you can't love just anybody.'

Naomi took Patrick back and forgave him because she knew why he had left and acknowledged her part in their estrangement. At times before the affair she had been so depressed that she hadn't wanted to speak or move for days. 'It was easier for me to run away and hide in a depression or sulk than it was to face up to my own unhappiness by talking about it. I must have been quite difficult to live with. But I also know that I became more of a mother to him than a lover and men don't want that. They already have a mother and often she wasn't that easy to live with. We are both much more honest with each other now. I had to make a conscious decision not to bring up the affair the whole time and castigate him but to let it go, because that was the only way we were ever going to move on, and life is damn good now, better than it was before,' says Naomi. 'Lots of people take umbrage when they should be thinking there is more to be pitied than scorned. Yes, he has hurt your pride but he is still the person you married and probably going through hell underneath.'

Patrick too feels that their marriage is stronger than ever and he relishes each day they spend together now that they are retired and in the later years of their lives. 'In the end it's a shared experience because it's so painful. The amazing thing is that she would want me back at all. How many people would do that? Perhaps that is why our marriage is better than it has ever been, because one of you has been fantastic and prepared to forgive? We have a stronger relationship because we have learned and experienced so much together, whether that's through the people we have met or the places we have been or the difficulties we have lived through together.'

Acceptance is equally important for the person who has dabbled extramaritally as it is for the one who feels betrayed. Genevieve had an affair early on in her marriage and wanted to leave. But her husband John wouldn't let her go. They have had counselling and some deep conversations and Genevieve now understands how important it is to accept that neither of them can be perfect. Her words seem to echo Naomi's even though she is technically the 'betrayer' rather than the 'betrayed'. 'I am more tolerant now. I don't expect so much from him and I am not going to break up my marriage just because he doesn't tick all the boxes. I am learning to accept him for the way he is, appreciating all of the things that he does, and he sees that and that makes him happier. He is very loving, kind and generous and every single reason why I married him is still there and I tell him that.'

John talks too about the transformative silver lining to her affair, even though it was extremely painful for him. 'I love my wife and I love our children and I don't want to do anything to endanger them. I could see the affair falling apart and I made the decision to stay and do everything I could to make our marriage work, and that's what I have tried to do.' He moved Genevieve and the family back home to London from the Middle East so that she was less bored and isolated. He also sidelined his own personal feelings of hurt so that they could work on deconstructing the affair together. 'We sort of became partners, talking and sharing the whole drama,' he told me. 'I would say things like, "I know he is never going to leave his wife so let's find a way to prove that to you." Genevieve tracked down his wife's number and called and they had a long chat. The wife then said she wanted to talk to me so we agreed that we would do whatever we could to keep our spouses apart for both of our sakes and for our children.'

John and Genevieve lived through an emotional hell for more than a year, but they had the courage to talk about it, to go to the heart of their difficulties both individually and as a couple. Consequently John feels that, 'We get to the nub of emotional problems quicker, I think, because we have been through so much and plumbed those depths. I understand now that she feels I failed her, that I betrayed her in a way by not standing up for her in front of my mother. I was probably just a typical man who failed to see the signs and never took it all that seriously. But for her it was serious. And through the whole thing, even though it was such an agonising time, I came to know my wife much better and how deep her feelings of abandonment are because of her own family background. She is constantly on the lookout for men letting her down and will even find ways to provoke that, to test me out. I fell into that trap by not being there for her when she needed me in her mind. I never realised she had such depths to her character before we had some counselling. I love my wife and I always will.'

With hindsight John can see that there were plenty of warning signs, times when Genevieve would say that the relationship was over and she wanted a divorce, but he never took them seriously, or even asked her why. And he says that through their conversations she has come to accept how much she has hurt him in the past. 'When I relay some of the things she said to me, she has no memory of it and cannot believe she could have said those things, and she has apologised. The only time I ever get really angry with her now is if she says, "You weren't strong: I would have respected you more if you had left me or kicked me out." My answer to that is that I think I should be worthy of far more respect because I didn't do that. That would have been the easy option. Have a massive row and end up in the divorce courts. That's a well-trodden path. Instead I took a step back and saw how our marriage was worth saving and that is where we are now. That was and continues to be a much harder road to travel. We are all faced with choices but at the end of the day it is not what happens to you but how you react to what happens to you which defines you and how your life goes.'

Forgiveness and being prepared to accept each other as a frail and imperfect human being are powerful positive forces when it comes to building a long and contented committed relationship. While there is no clear definition of what forgiveness is, it helps perhaps to consider what it is not. It is *not* the saintly, selfless, 'turn the other cheek' religious idea which so many of us have been brought up to believe in. It is *not* unconditional. You cannot forgive someone without a sincere enough apology or the expectation of a better future. Forgiveness is not a sign of weakness which in turn condones bad behaviour. It is a sign of strength if we remove the barrier to a better kind of communication and assert our right to better treatment. The maxim 'forgive and forget' is misleading too, for forgiveness is only possible in the face of a remembered wrong. We never really forget the wounds of the past and nor should we if we are to learn from them. 'Forgetting,' as Lawrence Smedes writes in his book *Forgive and Forget*, 'may be a dangerous way to escape the inner surgery of the heart we call forgiving.'

Forgiveness requires thought and a sophisticated understanding of the ambivalence and tortured schisms of the human mind, even if the behaviour that these can lead to causes us a great deal of pain. It isn't easy to relinquish the moral high ground and release the transgressor from their 'debt'. Yet we invest a huge amount of emotional energy into being unforgiving and who nowadays has enough spare energy, or the time, for that? Forgiveness can be transformative, as you free the psyche from the burdens of the past to improve relations for the future, if you are also willing to put your own weaknesses on the line. 'I think the infidelity on both our parts came, eventually, to be seen by us as a rough patch that luckily illuminated the insecurities and unhappiness we were unable to express to each other,' Julie Powell told me. 'We are much better at talking to each other now. An argument is not a disaster, the expression of dissatisfaction is not a deal-breaker and we are much clearer on why we like being and remaining married, but I will confess that recovering from that period in our lives was a pretty long haul.'

Forgiveness is good for our mental and physical health. It appears to reduce stress hormones in the bloodstream and triggers a different brain chemistry which could affect the immune system. Forgiveness reduces blood pressure and chronic anger, which has been linked to cardiovascular troubles.[4] Forgiveness is also associated with less depression and anxiety, for there is less introspection, obsession and rumination as people choose to sidestep the sense of hurt and betrayal and look out towards others. Forgiveness seems to foster greater altruism generally and a willingness to see others who have nothing to do with the original offence in a better light.[5] Forgivers are also more likely to see things collectively, recognising that they are part of a wider humanity which is flawed.

Couples say that the capacity to forgive and be forgiven is one of the most important factors in a long and happy relationship.[6] The sooner we start practising the art of forgiveness in a relationship, the more likely we are to iron out difficulties early on, lowering the chances of an infidelity happening at all. Forgiveness may be driven by our overriding sense of commitment to another, but there is also evidence to suggest that greater forgiveness fosters a stronger sense of commitment and closeness in a relationship.[7] The closer the couple, the easier it is to forgive, or to see the motives or the offence in a less negative light. When the person who has violated the relationship contract feels the glimmer of forgiveness, they exhibit less anger, sadness, guilt and shame and are therefore more able to reach out to their partner.[8] It really is in our interests to talk from the very beginning about all of the smaller issues that seem to divide us, before resentments become entrenched, to learn how to explain our actions as we apologise, to practise talking honestly about who we are and how we feel about things. The longer the relationship continues, the more each learns how to forgive the other in smaller ways. It is also easier for most people to move on after a single transgression than a series of accumulated hurts over time.[9]

Forgiveness is the process by which we build and re-establish love and trust. We learn that most essential skill through practice, not because some of us are more forgiving than others.

The great power of a long, loving relationship is what we learn from it as individuals: a greater acceptance and tolerance of each other's flaws and shortcomings, which means that we too are accepted. Perhaps, in an imperfect world full of troubled people, the greatest gift we can offer is to forgive each other for being unhappy at times, and ourselves for not being able to wave the magic wand of eternal joy over our beloved.

Forgiveness is the art we have to practise and master if we want to make love last. John recognises that he stands to lose even more by taking his wife's affair too personally. 'I could get up on my high horse and say, "You have cuckolded me, you have offended my pride and there is no way back from this," and tear the whole house down, which would have been a perfectly valid and socially acceptable thing to do. Or I can try and understand why this happened and accept that there might be a degree of blame attached to me.'

The wider world is unforgiving enough. Relationship is perhaps the only place where we can and should expect to be forgiven, if we are also allowed to be our true, imperfect selves. A more nuanced understanding of the numerous reasons why people slide into sexual straying forms the foundations for forgiveness and contributes to better relationship health. While there is no research on how forgiveness at group level, culturally or racially helps to foster greater personal forgiveness at an individual level, common sense dictates that there must be a link, for we are social beings, heavily influenced by social norms and dependent on social acceptance. We know how important support from others is at times of ill-health, stress or bereavement. It is therefore likely that a lack of such support for the couple going through the crisis of infidelity, largely in private, prolongs the pain and complicates the outcome.

In a committed relationship each has unparalleled knowledge of the other. When one has had an affair, the other often holds key insights as to why they might have strayed, provided they can push the need for revenge or separation out of their mind. Perhaps each of us is so ignorant of what really lurks deep in another's heart that we can never have the proper moral right to judge them. Yet rare is the person who has never felt wronged, betrayed or hurt by someone they care for and trust, so we make those judgements. But the question we have to ask ourselves is not whether they will let us down in some way, but when and how? And then, how will we deal with it? True forgiveness has to be based on rational thoughts rather than emotions, on the weighing up of all the pros and cons in a relationship. In this way we can honestly assess our commitment and, hopefully, move on from a troubled present to a happier future.

Forgiveness doesn't mean that you don't still feel hurt by what has happened or fearful that it could happen again. It takes a conscious leap of faith to truly believe that there is enough good in the rest of the relationship to make it worth saving. And even then there are bound to be times when that faith fluctuates as we are reminded of the offence, moments of high suspicion and anxiety that we might be hurt again. The scars are still sore. 'You rebuild trust because you want to but it takes a long time and even now, years later, I have wobbles,' says Isabel. 'Pure brute insecurity in that I think it is happening again. A letter will come and I won't recognise the handwriting so I will steam it open and then feel sordid and think, this is beneath me. I should have trusted. But it's like malaria, you get attacks of lack of trust, because it's so much more tumultuous than you ever think it is going to be.'

Clare has been back with her husband for over a year and

talks about feeling a seesaw effect where suddenly she feels all her confidence draining away as she picks up patterns of behaviour which lead her to think that he could be having an affair. 'We went shopping together in a department store the other day and he went to the men's section and I went somewhere else and then I saw him talking to this tall, attractive blonde woman and I recognised her but couldn't think who she was. I started imagining all sorts of horrors but decided not to say anything, luckily. Later that night over dinner he said, "Oh I bumped into Annabel today when we were in John Lewis," and I didn't say, "Yes, I saw you and that sent my heart rate up," because it turned out she is the estate agent who sold us our house.'

There is no template, no right way, to be together as a couple. It is no longer enough to simply slip into the social constructs of the nuclear family, the old-style gendered roles of wife and mother, husband and father. We are the pioneers. And while countless people feel that juggling demanding jobs and children as well as their relationship is difficult, all of the evidence suggests that those with a more egalitarian partnership stand a better chance of making it through the long haul, for they have to find ways to negotiate and therefore communicate and one of the pair is less likely to be too controlling of the other. Good relationship is not about passing some external test and adhering to rules imposed by the wider society. It is having the courage to seize responsibility for making it work from the inside. Only then can we build a partnership which will open doors to new ways of loving and living which will in turn offer healthier models of commitment to our children.

Sexual puritanism feeds sexual prurience and ignorance, setting a terrible example for our young growing up in a world so dominated by pornography's take on intimate relationships. And social disapproval of infidelity as always wrong, together with the new heightened levels of deceit and denial within individual families where an affair has taken place, is placing an intolerable burden on them. 'It's the children who have to hold it all – the secrecy, the shame, as well as the pain and humiliation of the parent who has been betrayed – when it is not being talked about culturally or privately,' says psychotherapist Jenny Riddell.

We have to find new ways to talk about sex, relationship, loyalty and commitment if we are to break the growing trend of separation, divorce and heartache affecting our young people and enable them to find happiness and a greater sense of safety in their own love lives. 'Every affair needs to be talked about,' continues Jenny Riddell, 'weaved into the narrative of that family, just as other stories are, to take the stigma out of it.'

Most of us have experienced the hurt of unrequited love. In a committed relationship the extramarital 'goings on' hurt a great deal too, but at least there is hope that you can salvage something stronger for the future because you also share a past. Nursing resentment or exacting revenge can never be entirely satisfactory responses because we continue to pay such a high price personally. Rediscovering the humanity of the person who has hurt us and surrendering the right to get even brings greater peace of mind. That is of fundamental importance to our integrity as individuals, whether or not we stay together as a couple.

It is unreasonable to expect any clear-cut solutions to the vortex of emotional difficulties that is human relationships. Yet the best partnerships provide us with enough space and privacy to chew over life's pressures in a non-judgemental way. Where better to do this than with someone we have shared so many other intimacies with? If we choose to think of an infidelity as an adult form of 'acting out', even a nervous breakdown, rather than a rejection of our entire sense of self-worth, we are much more likely to move on to a more fulfilling future together. The affair may have been a hurtful and immature thing to do, but we all regress at times of stress or acute anxiety.

Rather than trying to control the behaviour of our partner, which signals dependency, we would do better to attempt to control our own. We have no right to engage in destructive or violent behaviour just because we feel hurt, humiliated or abandoned. We can, however, step up to a higher level by being kinder, more attentive and more affectionate. We can do a great deal for each other by showing more love. It is men who fail in this challenge who tend to lose their lovers, permanently. Rather than monitor our partner's every move for signs of continued deceit, it is wiser to nurture our own assets by paying attention to our own health and welfare. In that way we grow stronger inside, rather than being diminished by guilt-inducing emotional manipulation.

Letting a person go, with enough slack for them to feel free enough to return willingly, means that we have been chosen. With true commitment each partner has to be brave enough to invest everything in the intimacy between them as a couple even as they face squarely up to the truth that the relationship could always end for some reason, whether foreseen or not. The knowledge that our partner is capable, independent and attractive to others means that we are more likely to find them continually attractive too. 'I often talk to couples about how healthy flirting is. It's a way of saying to yourself and to other people, "I am still desirable,"' says Jenny Riddell. '"But I will only go so far and come back to you revitalised because I know that I choose to do that, not because I feel I am stuck with you."

I see a lot of stuck people in therapy. The fact that they have to stay together for whatever reason, usually financial, becomes an excuse for not doing the work of learning how to be together in a more nourishing way, and that feels very tragic.'

We see dozens of attractive people each day that we could easily have a delicious time with in bed, but we don't jump at those chances because part of being a mature adult means being able to appreciate, enjoy and tolerate the constancy of seduction and eroticism all around us – from advertising hoardings and chatrooms to flirtatious behaviour at work. Self-control is good for us, and we know that in our hearts. It keeps us in check and holds us responsible to those we care for. 'It is all about, in short, our relation to obstacles; our distinguishing the intractable from the changeable,' writes psychoanalyst Adam Phillips, 'what we have to acknowledge from what we can influence; whether our desire is forbidden or not – whether we want a cream cake or another man's wife.'[10]

While the presumption is that infidelity inevitably destroys a relationship, this is not supported by some of the evidence. Approximately 60 per cent of people in one major study threatened to leave as soon as an affair had been uncovered, but only 23 per cent of that 60 per cent did so.[11] Because of the history. Because of the children. Because it would bankrupt them to split the assets. Because they actually still quite like each other. Because they are terrified of being on their own. Some give their partner another chance without revealing the infidelity to anyone. Others find the courage to bear even more pain by reaching into the more uncomfortable, emotional nether regions of their relationship, not to excuse bad behaviour but to understand it, and therefore each other, better. Differences have to be faced, sexual desires and emotional

problems discussed, dark truths about fears of being abandoned, about our pasts and what we do not like about each
other or the relationship need to be revealed. Only then, with
sounder and more truthful foundations, can a more rewarding
and loving intimacy be revived which has trust and exclusivity
at its heart.

By focusing solely on the symbolic significance of sexual
betrayal, we distort and devalue all of the other, much more
important, less tangible qualities of commitment within a relationship which keep us whole. We imagine that happiness must
exist somewhere beyond all of the obstacles which stop us from
having everything we want – enough money, more time, better
loving. But maybe all we would have then is another set of
problems. We delude ourselves badly by thinking that there can
be heaven on earth for more than a few moments in our love
lives. True heaven lies in sharing the ordinary, the conundrums
and the humour of life and the eternal struggle for a sense of
contented peace with someone else by our side. There is a
special poetry to the tiny detail of daily life, to the discovery of
new small sources of amazement and in the way we triumph
over difficulty together. That's what keeps the passion of a long
relationship alive.

Therapists and counsellors say that rising numbers of
couples are now coming to them for help after an affair. While
there are countless 'how to' books on surviving infidelity,
'We have no empirical data addressing the process of disclosure of the affair, the emotional reaction to disclosure, the
interaction process of the couple dealing with the affair and
the healing process among those couples that survived the
affair,' conclude the authors of one study.[12] There are no
hard-and-fast rules. Which means that you can make them
up. Every affair in every relationship is different. It is up to

the two people concerned to navigate their way towards an understanding of at least some of the possible causes before they can even begin to take responsibility for the consequences of that affair.

Some find that the revelation of an affair clears the air in a radical way. 'It was the best and worst day of my life,' one woman commented. 'It was the first time his words of love and his actions were congruent,' said another. 'I felt respected, relieved, outraged, sick. It gave me hope for our relationship.' Many talk of a sudden heightened appreciation of their spouse once they could lose them. 'It was odd because his affair made me feel so intense about everything, it set me alive.' Some couples find that their relationship is invigorated by the explosion of an affair, for it is stitched back together in an entirely new way. They forge a deeper intimacy by seeing the infidelity as something that they are both responsible for. They come to see the affair not as the definitive event but merely as an episode in their shared history. 'We can't return to how we were together before it happened, because nothing in life is that constant or fixed.' And yet somehow we expect that from a relationship between two people even though they cannot help but change as they grow older. You can, however, move on to a future with a deeper commitment than ever before, for as Ernest Hemingway writes in *A Farewell to Arms*, 'The world breaks everyone and afterward many are strong at the broken places.'

The intense emotions which surround sexual fidelity – particularly fear of loss or being replaced by someone better – are healthy reminders of what it is to be alive, with all its uncertainties. The ubiquitous possibility of seduction keeps us on our toes. We have to look after each other. The knowledge that commitment is no longer held together by the impossibility of divorce means we have to work at relationship continually, feeling intuitively around the contours of each other's sense of autonomy, resisting the temptation to control or be controlled, respecting each other's right to be different. Only then can we build enough mutual trust and respect to surrender to the possibility that this could indeed be a love that lasts.

John may be perceived by many as weak because he did not kick his wife out when she confessed to having an affair, but he feels he has done the strong thing by forgiving Genevieve, however painful those times were. I asked him what he felt he had learned through such a tortuous experience, and I would like him to have the last word as he speaks for so many couples who have survived an affair. 'That life is more complicated than you might want it to be. That however much you might want people to think and act in a certain way, they have their own separate lives with their own separate history which you cannot possibly know all about. I must have thought a million times, why did I marry her, why did I pick her when there were so many other lovely girls who might have adored me for the rest of my life? But when I look back I know I chose her because she was challenging. She has a strong personality and was extremely good at her job. I knew she would always keep me on my toes and we joke about that now.

'I used to say to her that if she was ever unfaithful, I would kill the bloke first and then I would kill her, but what has really surprised me about this whole ghastly thing is that even though it has actually happened, I now feel that there is no reason why our marriage can't be good again and it is good. I think what you should get from our story is that there are no rules to marriage and that once trust is broken [don't think] the whole thing is ruined because that's not true. It's what you make of it, and the rules change from day to day. Where we are today may not be where we are tomorrow and it certainly isn't where we were yesterday. And yes, I suppose faith in the security of marriage has been undermined but it has shown me that such a construct is as fragile as you choose to make it. Sure there is a bond of trust that has been broken, but I think that is one of those clichés that marriage has to be this unbreakable perfect vessel and that once it is shattered it can never be repaired. There are a million different issues of trust and annoyance that can come up every day in a marriage. You can never be really safe, you are only safe from one day to the next, and a good marriage depends much more on your day-to-day behaviour than some overarching vessel of trust that has got a crack in it.

'I think we are stronger now than a lot of other marriages that haven't been tested in this way because at least we know what we are capable of getting through together. You could say that we have a stronger vessel of trust which is harder to break now because it is made of better material than the old one.' As if to prove that point, the diamond in Genevieve's engagement ring cracked in half when they were on holiday with the children. 'So I got her a new one – a four-carat instead of a two-carat, a stronger one with not so many rough edges. It's symbolic because hopefully we too have something new and better than what we had before.'

# NOTES

## Chapter 1: Is Monogamy Possible?

1 Shirley P. Glass with Jean Coppock Staeheli, *Not 'Just Friends': Rebuilding Trust and Recovering Your Sanity After Infidelity*, Free Press, 2004; Peggy Vaughan, *The Monogamy Myth*, Newmarket Press, 2003

2 David P. Schmitt, 'Patterns and Universals of Mate Poaching Across 53 Nations: The Effects of Sex, Culture, and Personality on Romantically Attracting Another Person's Partner', *Journal of Personality and Social Psychology*, vol. 88, no. 4, 2004

3 Dani Shapiro, *Slow Motion*, Bloomsbury, 1999

4 Christopher Clulow (ed.), *Rethinking Marriage: Public and Private Perspectives*, Karnac Books, 1993

## Chapter 2: The Anatomy of Modern Love

1 Jean Duncombe, Kaeren Harrison, Graham Allan and Dennis Marsden (eds), *The State of Affairs: Explorations in Infidelity and Commitment*, Lawrence Erlbaum Associates, 2004; Pamela Druckerman, *Lust in Translation*, Penguin, 2007; Osmo Kontula, 'Sustaining Successful Marriages and Relationships – Dream or Reality?', International Commission on Couple and Family Relations, Helsinki Conference, 10–13 June 2008

2 Gunter Schmidt, 'Sexuality and Late Modernity', *Annual Review of Sex Research*, 1998

3 Ellen J. Helsper and Monica Whitty, 'Netiquette Within Married Couples: Agreement about Acceptable Online Behaviour and Surveillance Between Partners', *Computers in Human Behaviour*, vol. 26, no. 5, 2010

4 Schmidt, 'Sexuality and Late Modernity'

5 Duncombe, Harrison, Allan and Marsden (eds), *The State of Affairs*

6 BBC website, 16 December 2008

7  Tara Parker-Pope, *New York Times*, 27 January 2008

8  Beatriz Lia Avila Mileham, 'Online Infidelity in Chat Rooms: An Ethnographic Exploration', *Science Direct*, 2004

9  M. M. Olson, C. S. Russell, M. Higgins-Kessler and R. B. Miller, 'Emotional Processes Following Disclosure of an Extramarital Affair', *Journal of Marital and Family Therapy*, vol. 28, no. 4, October 2002; Douglas L. Kelley, *Marital Communication*, Polity, 2012

10 Victoria Zackheim (ed.), *The Other Woman*, Warner Books, 2007

**Chapter 3: Heirs and Spares**

1  Keith Thomas, 'The Double Standard', *Journal of the History of Ideas*, vol. 20, no. 2, 1959

2  Stephen Brook (ed.), *The Penguin Book of Infidelities*, Penguin, 1994

3  Thomas, 'The Double Standard'

4  Lawrence Stone, *Road to Divorce: England 1530–1987*, OUP, 1995

5  Claire Langhamer, 'Adultery in Post-War England', *History Workshop Journal*, vol. 62, no. 1, 2006

6  Ibid.; Joanna Klein, 'Irregular Marriages: Unorthodox Working-Class Domestic Life in Liverpool, Birmingham and Manchester, 1900–1939', *Journal of Family History*, vol. 30, no. 2, April 2005

7  Cate Haste, *Rules of Desire: Sex in Britain: World War I to the Present*, Vintage, 2002

8  Langhamer, 'Adultery in Post-War England'

9  Ibid.

10 Thomas, 'The Double Standard'

11 Quoted in ibid.

12 Victoria Griffin, *The Mistress: Myths, Histories and Interpretations of the Other Woman*, Bloomsbury, 1999

13 Quoted in Thomas, 'The Double Standard'

14 Ibid.; Stone, *Road to Divorce*

15 Faramerz Dabhoiwala, *The Origins of Sex: A History of the First Sexual Revolution*, Allen Lane, 2012

16 *You* magazine, 9 January 2011

17 David Clark (ed.), *Marriage, Domestic Life and Social Change: Writings for Jacqueline Burgoyne (1944–1988)*, Routledge, 1991

18 Ibid.

19 Geoffrey Gorer, *Sex and Marriage in England Today*, Panther, 1973

20 Druckerman, *Lust in Translation*

21 Kontula, 'Sustaining Successful Marriages and Relationships – Dream or Reality?'

22 Duncombe, Harrison, Allan and Marsden (eds), *The State of Affairs*

23 Schmitt, 'Patterns and Universals of Mate Poaching Across 53 Nations'

24 Emily M. Brown, *Patterns of Infidelity and Their Treatment*, Brunner-Routledge, 2007

25   Schmitt, 'Patterns and Universals of Mate Poaching Across 53 Nations'
26   Warren Coleman, 'Understanding Affairs', One Plus One Conference, 11
      May 1995
27   Clulow (ed.), *Rethinking Marriage*

## Chapter 4: Sexual Desire

1   *Newsweek*, 23 June 2003
 2   Sandra R. Leiblum (ed.), *Treating Sexual Desire Disorders: A Clinical Casebook*,
      Guilford Press, 2010
 3   Steve Humphries, *A Secret World of Sex*, Sidgwick and Jackson, 1998
 4   Marcus Collins, *Modern Love*, Atlantic Books, 2003
 5   Simon Szreter and Kate Fisher, *Sex Before the Sexual Revolution: Intimate Life
      in England 1918–1963*, Cambridge University Press, 2010
 6   Susan Cebulko, *The Impact of Internet Pornography on Married Women: A
      Psychodynamic Perspective*, Cambria Press, 2007
 7   Douglas T. Kenrick, Sara E. Gutierres and Laurie L. Goldberg, 'Influence of
      Popular Erotica on Judgements of Strangers and Mates', *Journal of
      Experimental Social Psychology*, vol. 25, no. 2, March 1989
 8   D. Zillman and J. Bryant, 'Pornography's Impact on Sexual Satisfaction',
      *Journal of Applied Social Psychology*, vol. 18, no. 5, 1988
 9   Dolf Zillman and Jennings Bryant (eds), *Effects of Prolonged Consumption of
      Pornography: Research Advances in Pornography and Policy Considerations*,
      Routledge, 1989
10   Pamela Paul, *Pornified*, Holt Paperbacks, 2005
11   Christopher Clulow (ed.), *Sex, Attachment, and Couple Psychotherapy*, Karnac
      Books, 2009
12   Peggy J. Kleinplatz *et al.*, 'The Components of Optimal Sexuality: A Portrait
      of "Great Sex"', *Canadian Journal of Human Sexuality*, vol. 28, no. 5, 2009
13   Diana Diamond, Sydney J. Blatt and Joseph D. Lichtenberg (eds), *Attachment
      and Sexuality*, Analytic Press, 2007
14   Erica Jong (ed.), *Sugar in My Bowl: Real Women Write about Real Sex*,
      HarperCollins, 2011
15   Leiblum (ed.), *Treating Sexual Desire Disorders*
16   Daniel Bergner, 'What Do Women Want?', *New York Times*, 25 January 2009
17   Marta Meana, 'Elucidating Women's (Hetero)sexual Desire: Definitional
      Challenges and Content Expansion', *Journal of Sex Research*, vol. 47, no. 2–3,
      2010
18   Leiblum (ed.), *Treating Sexual Desire Disorders*
19   *Daily Telegraph*, 4 June 2011
20   L. M. Carpenter, C. A. Nathanson and Y. J. Kim, 'Physical Women,
      Emotional Men: Gender and Sexual Satisfaction in Midlife', *Archives of Sexual
      Behaviour*, vol. 38, no. 1, 2009
21   Leiblum (ed.), *Treating Sexual Desire Disorders*
22   Janet Reibstein and Martin Richards, *Sexual Arrangements*, Heinemann, 1992

## Chapter 5: What Does an Affair Signify?

1 Diamond, Blatt and Lichtenberg (eds), *Attachment and Sexuality*
2 Ibid.; Judith A. Feeney, 'Adult Attachment, Emotional Control, and Marital Satisfaction', *Personal Relationships*, vol. 6, no. 2, June 1999; Mario Mikulincer and Gail S. Goodman (eds), *Dynamics of Romantic Love: Attachment, Caregiving, and Sex*, Guilford Press, 2006; Christopher Clulow (ed.), *Adult Attachment and Couple Psychotherapy*, Routledge, 2007; Clulow, *Sex, Attachment, and Couple Psychotherapy*
3 Diamond, Blatt and Lichtenberg (eds), *Attachment and Sexuality*; Mario Mikulincer and Phillip R. Shaver, *Attachment in Adulthood: Structure, Dynamics, and Change*, Guilford Press, 2007
4 Mikulincer and Shaver, *Attachment in Adulthood*
5 Ibid.
6 D. Schachner and P. Shaver, 'Attachment Style and Human Mate Poaching', *New Review of Social Psychology*, 1, 2002
7 Diamond, Blatt and Lichtenberg (eds), *Attachment and Sexuality*
8 Brown, *Patterns of Infidelity and Their Treatment*
9 *The Times*, 5 July 2010
10 Omri Gillath, Emre Selcuk and Phillip R. Shaver, 'Moving Towards a Secure Attachment Style: Can Repeated Security Priming Help?', *Social and Personality Psychology Compass*, 2 April 2008
11 Ibid.; Mario Mikulincer and Phillip R. Shaver, 'Boosting Attachment Security to Promote Mental Health, Prosocial Values and Intergroup Tolerance', *Psychological Inquiry*, vol. 18, no. 3, 2007

## Chapter 6: Betrayal

1 Olson, Russell, Higgins-Kessler and Miller, 'Emotional Processes Following Disclosure of an Extramarital Affair'; Kelley, *Marital Communication*
2 Frank D. Fincham, 'Forgiveness: Integral to Close Relationships and Inimical to Justice?', *Virginia Journal of Social Policy and the Law*, vol. 16, no. 2, 2009
3 Brown, *Patterns of Infidelity and Their Treatment*
4 Rosemary Lloyd, *Closer and Closer Apart: Jealousy in Literature*, Cornell University Press, 1995
5 Esther Perel, 'After the Storm', www.pschotherapynetworker.org/magazine

## Chapter 7: Who is to Blame?

1 Everett L. Worthington (ed.), *Dimensions of Forgiveness: Psychological Research and Theological Perspectives*, Templeton Foundation Press, 1998

## Chapter 8: The Impact on the Children

1 Duncombe, Harrison, Allan and Marsden (eds), *The State of Affairs*
2 Andrew Balfour, Mary Morgan and Christopher Vincent (eds), *How Couple Relationships Shape our World*, Karnac Books, 2012
3 Duncombe, Harrison, Allan and Marsden (eds), *The State of Affairs*

262    OUR CHEATING HEARTS

Diamond, Blatt and Lichtenberg (eds), *Attachment and Sexuality*; Mikulincer and Shaver, *Attachment in Adulthood*
5 Diamond, Blatt and Lichtenberg (eds), *Attachment and Sexuality*
6 *Observer*, 26 June 2011
7 Feeney, 'Adult Attachment, Emotional Control, and Marital Satisfaction'
8 E. Mavis Hetherington and John Kelly, *For Better or For Worse: Divorce Reconsidered*, Norton, 2002

**Chapter 9: Commitment**

1 Zackheim, *The Other Woman*
2 Diamond, Blatt and Lichtenberg (eds), *Attachment and Sexuality*
3 Worthington (ed.), *Dimensions of Forgiveness*
4 Ibid.; John C. Karremans and Paul A. M. Van Lange, 'The Malleability of Forgiveness', http://portal.idc.ac.il/en/Symposium/HerzliyaSymposium/Documents/dcKarremans.pdf
5 Ibid.
6 Jill N. Kearns and Frank Fincham, 'Victim and Perpetrator Accounts of Interpersonal Transgressions: Self Serving or Relationship Serving Biases?', *Personality and Social Psychology Bulletin*, http://fincham.info/papers/pspb-pervict.pdf; Fincham, 'Forgiveness: Integral to Close Relationships and Inimical to Justice?'
7 Jo Ann Tsang, Michael E. McCullough and Frank D. Fincham, 'The Longitudinal Association between Forgiveness and Relationship Closeness and Commitment', *Journal of Social and Clinical Psychology*, vol. 25, no. 4, April 2006
8 Fincham, 'Forgiveness: Integral to Close Relationships and Inimical to Justice?'
9 Ibid.; Karremans and Van Lange, 'The Malleability of Forgiveness'; Frank D. Fincham, 'Kiss of the Porcupines: From Attributing Responsibility to Forgiveness', *Personal Relationships*, vol. 7, no. 1, 2000
10 *Guardian*, 4 September 2010
11 Jennifer P. Schneider, Richard R. Irons and Deborah Corley, 'Disclosure of Extramarital Activities by Sexually Exploitative Professionals and Other Persons with Addictive or Compulsive Sexual Disorders', *Journal of Sex Education and Therapy*, vol. 24, no. 4, 1999
12 Olson, Russell, Higgins-Kessler and Miller, 'Emotional Processes Following Disclosure of an Extramarital Affair'